'Few people in the financial services industry understand the challenger bank battlefield better than Devie Mohan. In this book she provides a platform to discuss why challenger banks exist and the different business models being used by fintech firms and big tech organizations to compete with legacy banks. This is the essential guide for those new or tenured in the banking space.'
Jim Marous, co-publisher of The Financial Brand, owner of Digital Banking Report and host of podcast Banking Transformed

'There is a definite lack of comprehensive guides to our industry and even fewer examples of unbiased, research-driven perspectives, while the sector continues to grow with new professionals who need a shortcut to make sense of an intensive last 20 years arriving every day. What Devie Mohan accomplishes here, both as an insider who has lives it and as an astute scholar and exceptional analyst, is a one-of-a-kind must-read for anyone who has true interest in anything to do with either fintech or financial services in general.'
Duena Blomstrom, author of *Emotional Banking* and co-founder and CEO of PeopleNotTech

'Devie Mohan combines a deep understanding of the evolution of fintech with a comprehensive view of its impact on financial ecosystems globally. This is essential reading for anyone in the financial services space.'
Jay Palter, Chief Engagement Officer, Jay Palter Social Advisory

'This book is a valuable resource for both sides of the equation: traditional financial services firms and their potential fintech partners. Devie Mohan provides a step-by-step practical approach for creating the best partnerships and producing winning outcomes for firms, fintechs and end customers. Anyone who reads this can benefit from her broad experience and subject matter expertise.'

April Rudin, CEO, The Rudin Group

The Financial Services Guide to Fintech

Driving banking innovation through effective partnerships

Devie Mohan

KoganPage

First published in Great Britain and the United States in 2020 by Kogan Page Limited

2nd Floor, 45 Gee Street	122 W 27th St, 10th Floor	4737/23 Ansari Road
London	New York, NY 10001	Daryaganj
EC1V 3RS	USA	New Delhi 110002
United Kingdom		India

www.koganpage.com

ISBNs

Hardback   978 1 78966 106 4
Paperback   978 0 7494 8637 2
Ebook   978 0 7494 8638 9

British Library Cataloguing-in-Publication Data

A CIP record for this book is available from the British Library.

Library of Congress Cataloging-in-Publication Number

2019044214

Typeset by Integra Software Services, Pondicherry
Print production managed by Jellyfish
Printed and bound by CPI Group (UK) Ltd, Croydon, CR0 4YY

CONTENTS

01

Banks versus fintechs during the economic crisis

Disruption can be a scary phenomenon.

However, disruption can also present significant opportunities in times of change and has single-handedly given us fintech, a fascinating industry whose sole purpose is innovation.

The financial services industry had been immune to severe disruption until the early 2010s, well after several other industries like energy, utility, transportation, entertainment, hospitality and retail all went through significant change processes, structures and systems in the 1980s through to the 2000s. One of the fundamental drivers for disruption in these industries was the need to have more control over customer ownership. Uber, Airbnb, Skype, Alibaba, Netflix, etc were major disruptors in their industries by focusing on one common aspect – the transfer of control to the customer by shifting the business models from asset ownership to customer ownership. Netflix thrived while Blockbuster, with vast amounts of physical resources, died; Amazon disrupted several major physical bookstores and Airbnb emerged as the 'hotel' without rooms.

Well before this round of disruption, the energy and utility industries saw major disruption in the 1980s through the process of vertical disintegration due to sudden deregulation. Instead of owning all the infrastructure and processes from generation to transmission to distribution to retail marketing, energy players decided to focus on core competencies and key strengths while engaging collaboratively with other players vertically above or below them in the energy value chain. The highly expensive, difficult-to-maintain transmission infrastructure was owned and controlled by one company, whereas the business model shifted towards a better focus on creating new offerings, pricing structures and marketing messages for the consumer. The energy industry thus became a marketing game.

When transformation hit the financial services industry, it was due to a variety of factors including the economic crisis, loss of consumer trust in banks, and deregulation driven by these changes. This disruption manifested primarily in the form of disintermediation in the financial services industry. The focus by start-ups was to cut the middleman – to remove the intermediary so as to offer cheaper, better products in a faster and more transparent way than the traditional banks and investment firms.

This worked so well that these start-ups, the key part of the fintech ecosystem, have successfully disrupted processes, systems, service channels, marketing channels, products, services and pricing in the financial services industry with significant long-term impact. And with much more to come.

The crisis

The effects of the economic crisis that affected almost the whole of the global banking system – especially in the US and the UK – during 2008–2012 continued for a long time. The financial shockwave that was set in motion by this global economic crisis impacted devastatingly on many of the world's most venerable financial institutions, creating headlines that would have been quite hard to imagine just a few years earlier. Perhaps the most profound impact was on the public perception of the financial system and the organizations that they had trusted with their money and well-being.

In retrospect, the seeds of the financial crisis were thoroughly sown before it occurred. While sub-prime mortgages and a laxity towards consumer credit in general certainly contributed to the creation of this dangerous financial climate, the overall system was already teetering on the brink of disaster. The level of both public and private debt accumulated, coupled with what could reasonably be described as irresponsible and greedy conduct, almost inevitably caused massive structural problems.

This shouldn't have come as a massive surprise. It was already extensively reported in 2008 that the behaviour of investment banks with regard to credit default swaps (CDS) – a form of derivative – was endangering the liquidity of US bonds. A *Market Oracle* article (Engdahl, 2008) placed the value of the CDS market at $62 trillion. By way of comparison, in 2009, the GDP of the United States was just over $14 trillion.

Even the British *Daily Telegraph* – the most fiscally conservative of publications – described the CDS system as a 'casino', pointing out that the then Conservative Party Treasury spokesman, Philip Hammond, called for a public inquiry into the Financial Service Authority's oversight of AIG Financial Products in Mayfair (Koeing, 2008). Meanwhile, Bloomberg reported that the UK government had acknowledged that CDS had reached a record level in the UK, after the Treasury announced plans to see a record amount of debt.

Indeed, numerous commentators warned well ahead of the banking and financial crisis that there could be massive problems on a systemic level. For example, Erate.com (Osborne, 2008) noted that 'it was somehow lost on regulators and Wall Street that these very products could threaten the global financial system and that their misuse could spark a massive credit crisis of unforeseen proportions impacting all of us.' *Credit Writedowns*, *The Age*, and the *Economati* blog all also spoke out on this matter.

The *New York Times* (Story and Kanter, 2011) reported that the European Union was investigating banks over their derivatives policies, examining whether banks, including Barclays and Goldman Sachs, 'harmed rival organizations that could compete in markets for providing information and clearing a form of transaction that had become critical to the smooth functioning of the entire economy'.

CDS is just one aspect of a derivatives market that has been estimated at somewhere between $700 trillion and $1.5 quadrillion (Lendman, 2015). This is not a fanciful number when one considers that the forex market is worth \$2–3 quadrillion annually. Market-watch (2008) warned that derivatives is a 'ticking timebomb' that that behaves like a black market and could create a massive bubble that could implode.

In this climate, the additional stress of the sub-prime mortgage issue, the global banking meltdown, the European debt crisis and the worldwide financial malaise only added fuel to the fire, and the overall seismic activity was thoroughly predictable for those paying attention. What is perhaps more chilling is that the situation has not necessarily improved since then, even though measures such as the Dodd-Frank Wall Street Reform and Consumer Protection Act and Basel III have been put in place to mitigate against risks emanating from debt.

In the ensuing imbroglio that followed this breakdown in financial operation, many decisions were taken that were to prove controversial. Many European and US banks were bailed out. Meanwhile, governments often enacted swingeing austerity measures that impacted directly on the people. The crisis particularly hit Eurozone countries, with Ireland, France, Italy, Portugal, Spain, Slovenia, Slovakia, Belgium and the Netherlands impacted, as well as the UK. Unemployment spiralled out of control, national assets were sold off, and public services were decimated. But this was perhaps most strongly and notoriously felt in Greece.

Akin to the Argentinean riots of 2001, the streets of Athens burned during the global financial crisis. The Greek population faced deep wage cuts, rising taxes and the elimination of public services. The International Monetary Fund (IMF, 2010) demanded a series of extensive public spending cuts, and other conditions, including raising property taxes, reducing general tax exemption, and slashing public sector employment. Under these circumstances, it was perhaps not surprising that Greece experienced extensive rioting in December 2008, and further riots throughout 2009 and 2010.

A *Guardian* article (Christofer, 2008) described the riots as 'symptomatic of a society deeply disillusioned with the failures and dishonesty of its political class'. But it was perhaps the banking class whose public profile was placed under the greatest scrutiny. Greece was not the only nation to suffer at the hands of the global financial system. Ireland had to go cap in hand to the IMF, as did Portugal, Iceland was forced to bail out its three major commercial banks, and Spain rapidly descended from being in a precarious position to deny that it would seek a bailout from any such entity as the IMF, to eventually seeking €100 billion.

The economic ineptitude and requirement for financial support were not limited to governments; banks got in on the act as well. Big time. Between 2007 and 2012, the word 'bailout' became part of the common cultural lexicon. Here are a few examples.

One of the UK's largest mortgage lenders, Northern Rock, was bailed out in September 2007. In October 2008, three of the most prominent British high-street banks, Lloyds, Royal Bank of Scotland and the HBOS group, which owned the Halifax brand, were bailed out to the tune of £37 billion. In a rare example of a BBC journalist saying something remotely useful, Robert Peston described this as 'perhaps the most extraordinary day in British banking history' (BBC, 2008).

In Ireland, Anglo Irish Bank was bailed out with over £29 billion of public money, and Ireland eventually had to be bailed out by the IMF. The *Wall Street Journal* (Shah and Fottrell, 2010) reported that Ireland's national debt had nearly quadrupled between 2007 and 2010. Iceland had already been the recipient of a $4.6 billion IMF bailout in 2008 when its three biggest commercial banks collapsed. Portugal has also just received a €78 billion IMF bailout, or as it has been described, the end of its sovereignty.

Elsewhere, in August 2011, HSBC, the world's second-biggest corporation according to *Forbes*, announced that it was to cut in the region of 30,000 jobs over the next two years, despite making over £7 billion in profits in the previous fiscal year (Werdigier, 2011). However, even though banks were happy to grasp huge profits with one hand and hold the other out for public money, their inclination to do the latter showed no signs of diminishing. In July 2011, the European Banking Authority published a report detailing the stress test conducted on 91 banks across Europe to understand the probability of further bailouts (Acharya, Drechsler and Schnabl, 2011).

The biggest bailouts, however, were reserved for the United States. The insurance firm, and then sponsor of Manchester United Football Club, AIG, received $150 billion. In September 2008, the two biggest mortgage lenders in the United States, Fannie Mae and Freddie Mac, received $200 billion of public money. Although the *Guardian* (Pallister, 2008) described this as the 'world's biggest bailout', the *Daily Reckoning* calculated that the real cost of bailing out these entities, due to their outstanding liabilities, was more likely to be in the region of $2.5 trillion. Even this could be considered a conservative estimate, with CNN asserting that if you doubled this figure to $5 trillion, you would get closer to the real cost to the American taxpayer (Isidore, 2009).

Furthermore, 15 'counterparties', which constituted banks of various types, also received money during the bailing out of the insurer, AIG. These included, Société Générale (France), Merrill Lynch International, Deutsche Bank (Germany), Calyon, Crédit Agricole (France), UBS (Switzerland), Barclays, Coral Purchasing, DZ Bank (Germany), Bank of Montreal (Canada), Rabobank (the Netherlands), Royal Bank of Scotland (that had already received one bailout courtesy of the UK taxpayer), Bank of America, Wachovia (United States), the English arm of HSBC and Barclays Global Investors. And Goldman Sachs, notably considered to have an extremely close relationship with the Obama administration of the time, was the 15th 'counterparty', and received $12.9 billion.

Considering all that had occurred, considering some of the world's wealthiest and most powerful institutions having received barely conceivable amounts of public money, and considering that the public had been told, once more, that they needed to tighten their belts as a consequence... is it any wonder that by the end of this particular financial crisis, the general public wasn't overly enamoured with banks and the financial system?

And from this, the sprouting of an idea formed. People were ready to try something new.

Emergence of the sharing economy

The dawning and subsequent growth of the sharing economy can be traced back to a shifting sentiment among the general population, and also perhaps a post-austerity mood. Everyday people were ready to share what they had, and focus on life experiences and maximizing their potential, rather than greedily grasping every possible cent or penny for themselves, even if big business is still making big money out of the concept.

By now, the big players in this field have long since become household names. Most people have ordered an Uber, many of us stay in Airbnb places regularly, while there are a wide variety of other sharing services available, offering everything from house and pet sitting, to borrowing a neighbour's car. For a small fee, of course...

And there is also a raft of emerging societal trends that have helped to drive the rise of sharing economy organizations and businesses. In particular, the closely associated development of digital systems and social media has gone mainstream, meaning that people and organizations can more readily communicate and transact with one another. This also helps ensure that businesses in the sharing economy are significantly more scalable; always a key aspect of growing businesses.

Thus, it is now a broadly accepted notion that commerce is facilitated by social networking. Consumers are more likely to purchase products due to the social influence exerted by peers on purchasing decisions, not to mention the fashion-oriented impact of so-called social influencers. Many companies have taken advantage of this trend and focused on delivering group deals. This, then, becomes a significant factor in the growth of the sharing economy.

The continuing flight of people from rural to urban areas has also had a beneficial impact on organizations involved in the sharing economy. Not only does this mean that people are congregated in a relatively confined space, but it also leads to a series of problems and desires that can be addressed by new sharing businesses and organizations. Uber is a glaring example of a business that relies on a critical mass of providers and consumers, agglomerated within a particular geographical area, to make its platform work effectively.

Another noticeable impact on the rise of the sharing economy has been the combination of rising prices and dwindling resources. The cost of living has never been higher, while it is becoming increasingly obvious that human beings are consuming an excess of resources, which is leading to potential environmental catastrophes. In this context, there is a gradual but steady shift away from ownership, as people begin to understand the environmental degradation being caused by consumerism, and also the financial cost associated with owning goods that can ultimately be considered trinkets.

These push factors for the sharing economy are also accompanied by a variety of pull factors, which underline the benefits that people derive from this new industrial mindset. There are apparent benefits of this new mode of consumerism, which particularly appeal to media and technology-savvy millennials – undoubtedly the largest and most enthusiastic consumers in the sharing economy market space.

The sharing economy has a massive potential to reduce fraud and lifestyle stress particularly by working together to develop open source detection techniques. It also has the potential to redefine the way we think about employment interfaces and contracts, making many aspects of the working world automated, and even more flexible.

Further potential exists for the sharing economy to improve the way assets are managed and maintained. By using software, sensors, and cryptographic technology, businesses will be able to deliver a new level of transparency, enabling users to track and examine everything involved in transactions in real time.

And the sharing economy can also have a positive impact on the environment, by simply enabling fewer resources to be used. The spirit of working together can also result in businesses cultivating strategies to reduce packaging, materials, and carbon emissions. This will become increasingly important and valuable as the push to be more environmentally friendly accelerates in the coming years.

Fintech firms emerge

In this context, there was, and is, suddenly a market space opening up for agile, innovative new companies and operators. There is a public desire for new ideas in the finance market, and fresh thinking and new brands, names and faces seem to be the best way to achieve this. So it's perhaps not surprising that a large number of agile and imaginative firms have emerged that are doing exciting things in the tech space.

San Francisco-based SizeUp is one such example. This upstart company works with banks in order to empower small businesses to be able to make smarter decisions by utilizing big data. Banking can often be a challenging aspect of running a small business, with less available access to finance and credit than established companies and corporations. SizeUp is, in fact, an excellent example of a new fintech firm working with the existing financial aristocracy, as its customers include Wells Fargo, Deutsche Bank, Bloomberg BusinessWeek, the US Small Business Administration, and the White House. SizeUp delivers data-driven insights, becoming a valued partner in the success of its business customers. The product is designed to enable banks to acquire and retain customers, particularly by introducing products at key decision points in the business lifecycle, and increasing engagement with existing customers.

Cashflower is a Silicon Valley sibling of SizeUp that provides a wealth of useful cash management and credit access tools. These help small businesses control their cash flow while providing a simple, user-friendly and intuitive interface as well.

Statistics indicate that around 45 per cent of small businesses run out of cash in their very first quarter of operation, with the majority of these choosing a non-bank lender. Cashflower has thus provided a solution for SMEs, offering them bank access and introducing smaller companies to preferable lines of credit. Cashflower provides cashflow tools that help banks attract and retain SME customers, while also working for SMEs as well.

SnapCard is another interesting product that particularly taps into the digital currency revolution. The mission of this tech solution is to enable both consumers and businesses to understand the value of accepting digital currencies alongside more traditional forms of payment. To achieve this, SnapCard makes it easy for consumers to access digital and cryptocurrency, including bitcoin, in a card format that makes them a viable form of payment. SnapCard is an excellent resource for businesses and everyday consumers alike.

Plaid is another example of a Silicon Valley company that is working in the digital fintech space. Plaid is based on a scalable API, making interacting with money both intuitive and straightforward, and changing the way that consumers, banks, businesses, and developers interact with finance. This solution streamlines and brings together the integration of new technologies that can often be troublesome for the existing financial architecture, and makes them accessible for people of all levels of financial means. Plaid is having a democratizing effect on the technical infrastructure APIs that are used to connect consumers, traditional financial institutions, and developers.

And, to give one final example, SigFig is a highly intelligent mobile solution which enables users to build robust investment portfolios affordably. SigFig uses existing research, science, and data to assist with investment decisions, and again has something of a democratizing effect on what can be a remote and inaccessible aspect of the financial system. SigFig is already guiding around 750,000 investors and expects to expand significantly in the foreseeable future (Mercadante, 2019).

In essence, these five examples merely scratch the surface of the digital fintech innovation that has emanated from Silicon Valley in particular. The new climate which encompasses digital finance solutions, new currencies such as Bitcoin, and diversified market access for businesses of all sizes, coupled with consumer and business appetite for these products, means that fintech's market prominence has escalated rapidly in a brief period.

The rapid growth of fintechs

Indeed, the growth of financial technology is underlined by some of the statistics associated with the fintech revolution. A recent report from Accenture – the global management consulting and professional services firm – which assessed 20,000 banking and payments institutions across seven markets, discovered that new entrants to the banking market had captured one-third of new revenue.

Accenture also gave an insight into some of the regional variations in the fintech market, with the UK and the United States actually lagging behind some other countries and geographical areas. The British government has been particularly keen to open up the fintech industry, as currently, the UK is still some way behind its European neighbours. Indeed, Accenture research (2018) shows that fintech new entrants are only responsible for 14% of total banking and payment revenues in the country.

However, this is a towering figure compared to the United States, where fintech and banking start-ups are responsible for just 3.5 per cent of the total $1.04 trillion in revenue (Bambrough, 2018). It is probable that the established nature of the financial system and institutions in the UK and the United States has provided obstacles for the establishment of new fintech entrants.

However, research also showed that Canada is one of the least disrupted banking markets, indicating that there is some way to go for fintechs in North America. Meanwhile, pluralized banking laws in the Eurozone have forced markets to open up access for fintech innovators.

Statistics also show that fintech companies raised $60 billion in funding in the third quarter of 2017 alone. The insurance field has been noted as a growth area for fintech in this figure, with 84 per cent of insurers expected to increase fintech partnerships over the next three to five years. And 42 per cent of payment companies had already partnered with fintechs by the end of 2017, a figure that is set to escalate further still in the coming years (KPMG, 2017).

In January 2018, the once decried cryptocurrency market had already achieved a market capitalization of $700 billion (Martin, 2018). And this was just one area in which fintechs had created massive market disruption. Consumer banking has been particularly impacted by the fintech revolution as well, but bankingtech.com lists even commercial banking as a significant area of disruption by new fintech providers.

The fintech alternatives

This disruption is illustrated by the emergence of fintech terms as alternatives to existing banks. There are many examples of this trend in the financial world, but I wanted here to look at four in particular. Firstly, TransferWise has made it possible for people to access bank accounts across the globe. Making payment easier for consumers, TransferWise will pay the recipient from its account in their own country, using the actual exchange rate. TransferWise thus boasts of being 800 per cent more affordable than traditional banking alternatives (TransferWise, 2018). This is why this fintech firm is already responsible for $3 billion of transfers every month (Browne, 2018).

Nutmeg is another fintech firm making waves. The company makes it possible for investors to gain access to an intelligent and diversified portfolio, making the firm a market leader in the digital wealth management field. Indeed, Nutmeg has already built up a six-year performance track record in the UK attracting 60,000 customers that collectively invested over £1 billion (Thurston, 2018).

Square is another familiar fintech name that is disrupting the commercial space. Square makes it easier for patrons to take card payments without requiring any complicated documentation. Simply downloading the Square app will enable you to receive card payments within a matter of minutes, and money will be available the next business day. This point-of-sale software has become hugely successful, and this is one field in which fintech has already been tremendously disruptive.

And Stripe is noted as one of the most robust software platforms for running any internet business. The company is already handling billions of dollars' worth of business on an annual basis and has connected with forward-thinking companies all over the world by providing powerful and flexible tools for internet commerce. Stripe particularly specializes in scalability, and, as discussed previously, this is particularly valuable for start-ups in the technology industry. This has attracted millions of companies to the Stripe solution, and Stripe has undoubtedly established itself as a viable part of the commerce marketplace.

Each of these four examples has achieved big things within the financial sphere, but something else also unites each of these young upstarts. The branding used by these fintech companies is considerably less stuffy than traditional banking architecture. These brands are very much marketed as mobile apps, in a way that will appeal to young people and millennials. This suggests that these new fintech competitors will expand still more in influence in the coming years, as more young people get on board with their fresh and vibrant message.

Three essential factors

There have arguably been three essential factors which have effectively converged to ensure that the wheels of the fintech revolution have been set in motion. The first of these was the general mistrust of the banking industry, which meant that many consumers were sceptical about traditional financial providers.

The second key factor was the rapid evolution of technology, which reduced the barriers to entry for many aspiring companies in the fintech space. Notably, the first iPhone from Apple was launched around 12 months before the beginning of the global financial crisis, and this conveniently corresponded with a time when a change was also needed in the financial industry.

And a general shift in consumer behaviour also had a significant influence on the financial sector. Banks had completely monopolized the industry for several decades since they simply had virtually no competition. This was extremely unhealthy for the financial services industry, as it meant that traditional providers were able to charge inflated commissions and introduce fees into products that were often extremely unfair. Yet consumers usually had no choice, other than to shop around within the existing banking industry, often to little avail.

Aside from the problems that the global financial crisis created for traditional financial services providers, it was also a time when the skilled people working within the industry grasped the opportunity to deliver something new and innovative. This was a bold step in many ways, considering that the financial services sector hadn't been disrupted for many decades. But a raft of highly qualified, ambitious, and entrepreneurial individuals all saw the potential to reimagine and rebuild the entire financial sector.

This quickly resulted in a slew of innovators, who began building the companies that would soon become big enough to compete with the institutions in which they had often worked. Revolut is one prominent example of this, having been founded by former traders from Lehman Brothers. After launching in 2015, Revolut claimed to be opening 7,000 new accounts each day, with over 2.5 million customers across Europe, and has cemented its success since then (Insights Success, 2018).

Companies such as Revolut were able to catch the customer zeitgeist by particularly focusing on technology. This is a central plank in the vision of the revolutionaries that broke away from the banking industry in order to deliver a new type of financial services company. There was an obsession within this new fintech field with developing better technologies, which ensured that products and services could be delivered in superior fashion, and, crucially, in a way that suited customers.

The banking sector was actually pretty slow to respond to the threat of fintech, which is perhaps, to some degree, understandable. When nothing has challenged your hegemony for many years, it is only natural for complacency to set in, and we can imagine why hugely established banks with a vast amount of capital and resources viewed some mere Silicon Valley upstarts with a reasonable degree of disdain. While the global financial crisis was in swing, banks were far more likely to focus attention on reviewing financial models and banking operations, to prevent future meltdowns, rather than seeking innovation and new ways of doing business.

But this turned out to be a missed opportunity, as the emergence of fintechs exposed the tunnel vision of the banking establishment. From day one, the most successful fintechs came to market with a technology-focused approach, which was intrinsic not only to their working methods, but also to the way in which the companies promoted themselves to consumers. There was a particular emphasis on connecting with younger banking customers, who could more readily relate to the way that fintechs did business, and who are also often discriminated against by traditional banking products.

The rise of the smartphone should also be acknowledged as a major factor in the new popularity of fintech services. In fact, it is hard to imagine a world without smartphones and fintechs going hand in hand, such is the ubiquity of the technology by now. With Wi-Fi and internet connectivity for mobile devices becoming ever more impressive, the financial sector will continue to be disrupted by mobile technology in the years to come.

While we may associate this specifically with the Western market-place, it is also important to emphasize that the popularity of smartphones has had a huge impact on emerging economies. The African continent, in particular, has almost bypassed landline tele-phone technology to go straight to mobile, and this has made what is a rapidly developing industrial landscape into a hugely fertile market for emerging fintechs. This same story is mirrored in other emerging markets in Asia and Latin America in particular.

In this context and climate, it became harder for consumers to accept the idea that larger financial institutions were 'too big to fail', and thus must receive unstinting support. This was already a contro-versial concept anyway, but since fintechs began to deliver exactly the sort of financial products that banks had been involved with previ-ously, the rationale behind this argument simply fell apart. It was, therefore, possible for fintechs to make up a significant amount of ground in a relatively short period, experiencing considerably less market scepticism than would probably have been the case at any time during the 20th century.

The recession that followed the global financial crisis also played its part in the success of fintechs. On the one hand, indebtedness increased significantly for both businesses and individuals, and, conversely, credit was suddenly harder to come by. This created the perfect environment for a new generation of lenders to come along, and it is it no coincidence that personal finance and credit has been a major boom area for fintech pioneers.

Above all else, the early fintech innovators recognized the need for a new breed of financial business, which rebranded the way that banking operates. The entrepreneurs that launched the most successful fintech companies realized that banking and financial services should no longer exclude people and demographics, and should refrain from being confusing, hostile and even predatory. There was a definite tone of transparency in the fintech revolution from its first steps, and this ethos has no doubt played a significant role in its ultimate success.

Payment – the early disruption

There is no better example of the rise of fintech in our daily lives than mobile payment systems, which established themselves as one of the earliest disruption segments in the market. It would also be fair to say that the traditional banking system indeed views the rise of these businesses as a disruptive influence, and there has been something of a stand-off between the two in the early days of fintech adoption. The current period in fintech is definitely about competition, disintermediation and disruption. There is still extremely minimal collaboration between banks and fintechs, and it could be argued that the two rivals are yet to really understand one another.

However, this is likely to change in the foreseeable future, as no matter how much traditional banks may see fintechs as unwelcome competitors, they will have to accept them as part of the economic landscape as the legislative environment opens up and becomes more diversified. Regulators are increasingly accepting applications from the financial technology start-ups for national bank charters. While this may be bad news for the traditional banking aristocracy, it will ultimately be a good thing for consumers who want the better services and lower costs that result.

Indeed, there is already an influx of bank fintechs emerging, with competitors such as Chime, Varo and Moven offering checking accounts, overdraft protection, savings accounts, and direct deposit.

Other financial technology companies are also interested in moving into this field, and even a massively successful provider such as PayPal has been closely monitoring the industry.

Forbes (Knutson, 2019) also predicts that one of the world's most influential companies may also get involved with fintech banking. Amazon has been dipping its not inconsiderable toes into numerous pools in recent years, and the retail giant certainly has the financial power to enter this lucrative new market. The *Wall Street Journal* (Glazer, Hoffman and Stevens, 2018) has already reported that Amazon has entered into talks to create a bank account product for its customers, with the particular aim of targeting younger people who may not have traditional accounts. While this is currently a part-nership scheme for Amazon, rather than an attempt to take over the industry, the potential for expansion is certainly there, and if there is one thing Amazon has been it is a disruptor.

There is little evidence that the existing paradigm is beginning to shift about the way that the established banks view fintech. Jamie Dimon, Chairman and CEO of JP Morgan Chase, had something complimentary to say about the fintech revolution, stating that 'hundreds of start-ups with a lot of brains and money are working on various alternatives to traditional banking' (Villante, 2019). However, the emphasis should perhaps be on 'alternative'; clearly, Dimon and JP Morgan still view fintech as a threat rather than a partner.

This perspective was echoed by Visa CEO Charlie Scharf, who threatened in 2016 to go after PayPal 'in ways that people have never seen before'. And that wasn't the end of his barbed comments. 'Because you've never seen us go target PayPal in the marketplace in any meaningful way', Scharf noted, ominously (Del Rey, 2016).

So there is quite some way to go before traditional banks view fintech firms as partners. But with fintech still in its infancy, there is still considerable potential for innovative firms in this sphere to form bonds with the big beasts of international finance. There have been many disruptive developments that were both welcomed and demonized in a wide range of industries. Yet, more often than not the established actors in any space can evolve to meet what they initially consider a threat, and eventually the two co-exist in peace, harmony and prosperity.

This has yet to occur with fintech. But the industry is still absolutely rife with growth opportunities and potential for more innovation. Convergence and cooperation between fintechs and traditional banks will inevitably expand, as the new arrivals to the financial marketplace continue to disrupt it. Banks will even become benefactors of fintech technology, both by investing in it financially and also by offering some of the infrastructure required for fintechs to grow and reach their potential.

Banks may not have quite accepted this yet, but there is an exciting and commingled future ahead for them and the fintech firms of which they are currently so wary.

References

Accenture (2018) Banks' revenue growth at risk due to unprecedented competitive pressure resulting from digital disruption, Accenture study finds, 17 October [online] https://newsroom.accenture.com/news/banks-revenue-growth-at-risk-due-to-unprecedented-competitive-pressure-resulting-from-digital-disruption-accenture-study-finds.htm (archived at https://perma.cc/R6LG-4F9M)

Acharya, V, Drechsler, I and Schnabl, P (2011) A pyrrhic victory? bank bailouts and sovereign credit risk NYU Working Paper No. 2451/31331 [online] https://papers.ssrn.com/sol3/papers.cfm?abstract_id=2284650 (archived at https://perma.cc/3CNT-2DQ9)

Bambrough, B (2018) Global fintech warning to traditional banks – the threat is 'real and growing', *Forbes*, 17 October [online] https://www.forbes.com/sites/billybambrough/2018/10/17/global-fintech-warning-to-tradional-banks-the-threat-is-real-and-growing/#1ffdb9662c71 (archived at https://perma.cc/Y868-UJTM)

BBC News (2008) 'UK banks receive £37bn bail-out [online] http://news.bbc.co.uk/1/hi/business/7666570.stm (archived at https://perma.cc/7DHY-VJ7Q)

Browne, R (2018) Fintech start-up TransferWise reports second year of profit, revenue almost doubles, *CNBC* [online] https://www.cnbc.com/2018/09/10/transferwise-earnings-second-year-of-profit-revenue-surges.html (archived at https://perma.cc/5SF9-2A6R)

Christofer, K (2008) Athenian democracy in ruins, *Guardian*, 8 December [online] https://www.theguardian.com/commentisfree/2008/dec/08/greece (archived at https://perma.cc/CC4L-HUTL)

Del Rey, J (2016) Visa's CEO just threatened to go after PayPal 'in ways that people have never seen before', *Vox*, 25 May [online] https://www.vox.com/2016/5/25/11768854/visa-ceo-paypal-threat (archived at https://perma.cc/GW3C-ZEN9)

Engdahl, F W (2008) Next phase of the credit crisis to hit credit default swaps $62 trillion market, *Market Oracle*, 7 June [online] https://www.marketoracle.co.uk/Article4984.html (archived at https://perma.cc/3KHN-GJ3L)

Glazer, E, Hoffman, L and Stevens, L (2018) Next up for Amazon: checking accounts, *Wall Street Journal*, 5 March [online] https://www.wsj.com/articles/are-you-ready-for-an-amazon-branded-checking-account-1520251200 (archived at https://perma.cc/JLM6-U799)

IMF (2010) Press Release: IMF executive board approves €30 billion stand-by arrangement for Greece [online] https://www.imf.org/en/News/Articles/2015/09/14/01/49/pr10187 (archived at https://perma.cc/ERK9-2SK3)

Insights Success (2018) Revolut increased revenue by almost 5x and trebled users in 2017 [online] https://www.insightssuccess.com/in-12-months-revolut-increased-revenue-by-almost-5x-and-trebled-users-in-2017/ (archived at https://perma.cc/DD6P-DTHE)

Isidore, C (2009) Fannie & Freddie: The most expensive bailout, *CNN*, 27 July [online] https://money.cnn.com/2009/07/22/news/companies/fannie_freddie_bailout/ (archived at https://perma.cc/Z8W6-R9DR)

Knutson, T (2019) Amazon, other bigtechs have the edge in fintech, say global financial regulators, *Forbes*, 14 February [online] https://www.forbes.com/sites/tedknutson/2019/02/14/amazon-other-large-techs-have-the-edge-in-fintech-says-global-financial-regulators/#2d4b72997fd0 (archived at https://perma.cc/VAF2-ZDK4)

Koeing, P (2008) AIG trail leads to London 'casino', *Telegraph*, 18 October [online] https://www.telegraph.co.uk/finance/financialcrisis/3225213/AIG-trail-leads-to-London-casino.html (archived at https://perma.cc/67SK-JV35)

KPMG (2017) The Pulse of Fintech Q3 2017 [online] https://assets.kpmg/content/dam/kpmg/xx/pdf/2017/11/pulse-of-fintech-q3-17.pdf (archived at https://perma.cc/QAA7-2UQS)

Lendman, S (2015) Global derivatives: $1.5 quadrillion time bomb, *Global Research*, 24 August [online] https://www.globalresearch.ca/global-derivatives-1-5-quadrillion-time-bomb/5464666 (archived at https://perma.cc/65Z4-FWUV)

Marketwatch (2008) Derivatives the new 'ticking bomb' [online] https://www.marketwatch.com/story/derivatives-are-the-new-ticking-time-bomb

Martin, W (2018) The global cryptocurrency market hit a new record high above $700 billion, *Business Insider*, 3 January [online] https://markets.businessinsider.com/currencies/news/bitcoin-price-global-cryptocurrency-market-capitalisation-january-3-2018-1-1012430198 (archived at https://perma.cc/FRY3-7PZ3)

Mercadante, K (2019) The 5 best investment tracking apps, *Consumerism Commentary* [online] https://www.consumerismcommentary.com/the-5-best-investment-tracking-apps/

Osborne, N (2008) The ABCs of collateralized debt obligations (CDO) & credit-default swaps (CDS), *Erate* [online] https://www.erate.com/collateralized-debt-obligations-and-credit-default-swaps#.XWOmz-NKjIU (archived at https://perma.cc/KU5Y-WULQ)

Pallister, D (2008) Fannie Mae and Freddie Mac: The world's biggest bailout, *Guardian*, 8 September [online] https://www.theguardian.com/news/blog/2008/sep/08/mortgages.useconomy (archived at https://perma.cc/Y37R-CC72)

Shah, N and Fottrell, Q (2010) Irish GDP drops unexpectedly, *Wall Street Journal*, 24 September [online] https://www.wsj.com/articles/SB1000142405274870338 4204575509363426865000 (archived at https://perma.cc/NS2U-HEWK)

Story, L and Kanter, J (2011) Europe Investigating Banks Over Derivatives, *New York Times*, 29 April [online] https://dealbook.nytimes.com/2011/04/29/european-regulators-investigating-banks-over-cds/ (archived at https://perma.cc/TT7U-YG93)

Thurston, J (2018) The story behind Nutmeg's rise to £1 billion, *CityWire,* 9 January [online] https://citywire.co.uk/wealth-manager/news/the-story-behind-nutmegs-rise-to-1-billion/a1078621 (archived at https://perma.cc/9LN8-XLF2)

TransferWise (2018) How is TransferWise 8x cheaper than a bank? [online] https://transferwise.com/help/11/getting-started/2974130/how-is-transferwise-cheaper-than-banks (archived at https://perma.cc/PM3M-X6BS)

Villante, T (2019) Fintech and traditional banks: the beginning of a beautiful friendship, *Yapstone*, July [online] https://www.yapstone.com/blog/fintech-and-traditional-banks-the-beginning-of-a-beautiful-friendship/ (archived at https://perma.cc/T88N-GRVU)

Werdigier, J (2011) HSBC to trim 30,000 jobs in cost-cutting move, *NY Times*, 1 August [online] https://dealbook.nytimes.com/2011/08/01/hsbc-to-cut-25000-more-jobs/ (archived at https://perma.cc/UD95-G3VV)

02

Fintech for customer experience

Perhaps the key area where fintechs can deliver something not on offer from the traditional big banks is customer service. The established players in the financial sector have a certain tendency to trade on an image of trust and respectability, allied with years of experience. The emphasis is all on transmitting just how safe your money will be with these venerable institutions, and this has been communicated above all else when building bank branding.

However, while this remains a cornerstone of strategy in the financial industry, there are two problems with this approach when dealing with modern customers. Firstly, the financial crash of which we spoke in the previous chapter has significantly undermined trust in financial institutions. While not all banks ran into difficulties during the credit crunch, it is now much harder for retail banks to present themselves as watertight and utterly dependable, as consumers have witnessed numerous very significant financial institutions getting into massive financial difficulties and being bailed out with inordinate amounts of money. And people tend to remember stuff like that!

Changing customer expectations

Secondly, the traditionally powerful banks are now perhaps failing to deliver on customers' expectations of how they should be treated, and even on their whole conception of what banks should be and what customer service represents. This is particularly true of younger people and millennials, who have formed their ideal of customer service and branding from exciting new companies in the tech space that they often deal with daily.

Conversely, unlike the unwieldy big beasts who have been operating a certain way for a very long time and have got rather wealthy doing it, fintechs are ideally placed to meet these rapidly evolving needs of customers. They can be branded appropriately from day one, and learn lessons from some of the world's most successful internet companies, such as Google, Facebook, Uber, Spotify and Amazon, and then put them into action.

Each of these companies is a household name by now, but they all bring different qualities to the table, and this has been instrumental in their success stories. Google was able to attract users over other search engines due to its beautiful simplicity and efficiency. Facebook and Spotify go to great lengths to ensure that users can tailor their experience to their personal preferences. Amazon has played a major role in creating a new consumer and retail culture, in which people expect to receive things at their convenience. And Uber has placed customer service and transparency at the heart of its taxi-hailing app.

There is also significant overlap between these companies, as each has learned lessons from the others' approaches, and built on the positive and negative customer feedback. Together they have helped forge a new approach to customer service, which has become the new normal. Customers expect to receive their purchases when they want them and be kept in the loop from the warehouse to the letterbox. They want to be able to access services 24/7, wherever in the world they are. And they demand everything companies do to be transparent and above board, particularly when dealing with them.

It would be neither fair nor accurate to state that traditional financial sector companies have ignored these trends, or singularly failed to respond to them. There has undoubtedly been some effort to embrace this new consumer culture. However, it would also be reasonable to state that the big banks still suffer from a stuffy image, and even view this whole new conception of how they should operate – along with the fintech companies themselves – with a good deal of suspicion.

And perhaps they are not best placed to change the way that they operate, and move gracefully, after many years of doing things differently. Indeed, it is a challenging prospect for the established financial aristocracy to brand themselves and appear cool and hip and new suddenly, which is where fintechs come in.

Fintechs have a monumental head start in terms of delivering the new customer service model for two reasons. Firstly, they can brand themselves in an entirely new way, and in a fashion that is consistent with the services and products that they're delivering. And secondly, fintechs are by their very nature intimately involved with the sort of technology that has been successfully utilized by the most famous technology companies. This means that fintechs can deliver the sort of agile and fresh products and services that modern consumers have come to expect.

Improving quality

One initiative that has influenced the development of customer service in the banking industry is the determination of traditional banks to improve their quality of customer service. This has been somewhat influenced by the fintech start-ups themselves, creating what has been a virtuous circle in the financial services industry.

Banks have undoubtedly become influenced by the approaches of fintech firms, particularly in the realm of customer service. With so much of fintech relying on mobile communication, banks are increasingly seeking more options for customers to communicate outside of the four walls of the traditional branch. This began before the fintech revolution emerged, but has definitely accelerated since a raft of fintech start-ups became extremely popular and successful.

Interestingly, a study conducted by Blumberg Capital (2016) noted that nearly 90 per cent of banking transactions are expected to be mobile based by the year 2022. There could hardly be a more illustrative indication of the impact of fintech on the financial sector, and it is this climate that has forced banks to rapidly evolve the way that they communicate and interact with customers.

While banks and fintechs may have disagreements, the shared goal of building relationships with customers through a strong foundation of communication means that they also have a great deal in common. With fintechs having made a customer-focused experience central to their operations from day one, this has meant that banks have needed to play catch-up and place the customer in a far more prominent position in their overall operations.

For example, banks are beginning to embrace the artificial intelligence technologies that have emanated from the fintech revolution. This innovation has the power to transform customer communication and help drive the self-service trend that is beginning to define customer demands and experiences. Chatbots and predictive analysis can assist with this process and transform the way that banks interact with consumers.

And the rise of artificial intelligence in this field has actually been rather rapid, increasingly transforming the customer experience for banking consumers all over the world. This is strongly illustrated by the Global Artificial Intelligence (AI) in BFSI Market Research Report 2019–2026, which suggested that artificial intelligence in the banking, financial services and insurance industry will achieve a 26 per cent compound annual growth rate over the next seven years. More and more organizations are getting on board with AI, recognizing that it can play a big role in improving the customer service standards of the financial sector.

Thus, routine banking tasks, such as resetting passwords, checking account balances, transferring funds between accounts, or paying monthly bills, are increasingly being automated. This offers additional convenience for customers but has also helped strengthen the ties between the banking and fintech sectors. And it has been fintechs that have been the foremost creators and communicators of this technology, and this has necessitated the beginning of a collaboration between the traditional financial industry and ambitious upstarts in the fintech sphere.

The importance of the millennial generation in influencing the expectations of customers cannot be overstated, with this demographic already representing 80 million people in the United States alone. Younger banking customers are noted to exhibit significantly different behaviours to established clients, with Burnmark research indicating that 64 per cent of high-net-worth clients under 40 years old expect to access their accounts via a website, and 54 per cent expect to use digital channels such as mobile applications, social media or video (Burnmark, 2017).

Mobile accessibility is thus one of the most essential features in modern banking environments, particularly as mobile devices have become the standard bearer for communication. This has had a massive impact on the desire for banking customers to access self-service options, with all manner of possibilities now available that would have been unimaginable until recently.

For example, just 10 years ago, it was still largely necessary for customers to visit branch locations in order to deposit cheques. This already seems a little old fashioned, as now virtually all banks deliver mobile applications equipped with remote deposit capabilities. The sorts of activities that once upon a time almost demanded a visit to a local branch can now be completed via a mobile device, and this has probably revolutionized the banking industry and customer service more than any other factor. And, of course, the syntax of being a fundamental driving force in this revolution.

In fact, customer data indicates that the desire to access physical branches is rapidly dwindling, and this trend is only likely to become more pronounced as the younger generation becomes a more prominent segment of the overall customer base. This is consistent with the policy of banks themselves, with the steady decline in the number of branches worldwide reflecting the understanding by financial institutions that the way they interact with customers needs to evolve.

Early fintech start-ups and business models

From day one, fintechs have adopted innovative new business models in order to set themselves aside from traditional banks. Fintechs have particularly concentrated on optimizing costs in order to deliver a superior financial ecosystem. This has run parallel very much with other technology niches, as innovations in other industries have driven expectations in the financial space. Customers now demand higher-quality and more personalized services, with seamless integration and access, and fintech has the capabilities to deliver this.

Recent research from Omidyar Network indicates that around 140 million Americans struggle with some aspect of their financial lives, whether paying bills or saving for emergencies, while also paying out $175 billion annually in fees and interest for financial products and services. Thus, it is highly relevant to everyday consumers that Omidyar's study (Morgenstern and Williams, 2018) discovered that fintech products could yield around $2,000 in annual savings for the average household.

In order to achieve this, fintechs have built revenue models that are both economically sustainable and that have built trust with customers. This latter point is particularly key, as it is arguably some of the trust that has been surrendered by the banking sector, which represents a key opportunity for fintechs. Indeed, a consumer survey by Edelman in 2012 found that the banking industry was now less trusted than estate agents (Pilcher, 2012), with Edelman noting a need for 'fundamental change' in banking culture and practice.

Returning to the Omidyar research, the self-styled 'philanthropic investment firm' found that fintechs are willing and able to charge customers directly. Indeed, 75 per cent of fintechs rely on one material source of revenue for their primary business model, and this is often charging customers directly. 'The key difference, though,' Sarah Morgenstern, investments principal at Omidyar Network, explained, 'is that they go above and beyond the established mindset around fee transparency to hit home to consumers what the real value-add is for them – a bolder way to build consumer trust.'

Meanwhile, successful fintechs are already grafting additional services to their core products. Stripe and Square are perhaps the best examples of this, and we're going to look at their operations in more depth later in this chapter. But both companies have been looking to diversify their revenue streams, as the increasing commoditization of payments is compromising their core business. Stripe and Square are thus already looking to leverage these to build new products and services, and then license these to their existing customer base.

Fintechs are certainly considered a threat to the existing business models of European financial institutions, according to Statista (Szmigiera, 2017). The online statistics, market research and business intelligence portal surveyed the financial sector and found that fintech firms are perceived as being the largest threat to banking revenues, with 61 per cent of respondents offering this perspective. However, there clearly is a potential for collaboration between fintechs and existing banks in the future, and this is something that the existing financial hierarchy is beginning to recognize. This is reflected in the 39 per cent of Statista respondents who deemed fintech firms as an opportunity to increase revenues for commercial banking.

And one key area where fintechs can really make a difference, and also carve out a paradigm-shifting niche for themselves, is in developing markets and the new superpowers. This has even been recognized by one of the world's wealthiest people. Microsoft co-founder and former CEO Bill Gates commented that 'digital technology provides a low-cost way for people in developing countries to send money to each other, buy and sell goods, borrow and save as long as the financial regulation environment is supportive' (Amberber, 2015).

If we take India as an example, this rapidly industrializing country represents an ideal setting for fintechs to gain market penetration. The need for technological disruption in the banking sector in such locations is particularly acute, especially as nearly 20 per cent of the Indian population has no access to banking services (Sanghera, 2018). With India being very much a country in thrall to technology, fintechs are presented with a fantastic opportunity to become particularly economically prevalent in such nations. This obviously has massive economic implications, considering that the population of India alone is an excess of 1 billion people.

India has seen the rapid rise of fintech start-ups in the past few years. There are some exciting Indian fintech start-ups to look out for, such as Faircent, a peer-to-peer lending company that offers a wide variety of innovative tools and instant credit access, and Kissht, another instant-credit provider intended to provide customers with swift access to funds at digital points of sale. These start-ups are not only helping to change the technology landscape but are also making a transformative difference to the lives of the population in a country in which poverty remains all too prevalent, even as the economy develops rapidly.

It is in emerging economies where the most radical revolution in customer service will continue to take place. If a portion of the population has been shunned by the banking establishment in the Western world, then this phenomenon has been far worse in developing countries. Vast swathes of the population in countries in Africa, in particular, are 'unbanked', ie they have no access to banking services or even basic bank accounts.

Fintech is already changing this, and with the enthusiastic uptake of mobile technology in many emerging nations, this means that consumers in these parts of the world can access an entirely new level of customer service; indeed, in many cases accessing banking services for the first time! Many fintechs have enthusiastically embraced these emerging markets, and this can be cited as another way that these vibrant innovators are changing the customer service experience in all four corners of the world.

With the volume of mobile app-based payments having increased at a rate of around 40 per cent annually in the United States in recent years, it is clear that the way customers are demanding banking services is changing at a rapid rate. Delivering what customers want and need is no longer a choice for banks in this climate, largely thanks to the efforts of fintechs. It has, instead, become a necessity.

Fintechs trying to attract customers away from traditional firms

Aside from the fledgling start-up firms that have tended to dominate the fintech industry, some of the world's most significant companies are also beginning to eye the potential of this niche, even if they're not traditional financial providers. For example, many market analysts are talking about the possibility of a banking service from the world's largest retailer Amazon, which Bain and Co estimates could swell to over 70 million US customers within five years (du Toit and Cheris, 2018). This would then make Amazon the third largest bank in America, equalling the size of Wells Fargo.

And Amazon is already talking to the likes of JPMorgan Chase and Capital One about the possibility of creating a checking account for its customers, which would accompany existing Amazon services (American Banker, 2018). Undoubtedly, this Amazon venture would represent a threat to existing retail banks.

Other innovators are also challenging the status quo. Another example of a start-up making a significant impact is N26, which is based in Berlin. N26 is nothing like the banks that most of us grew up with, having no branches or ATMs of its own. Instead, customers can obtain cash from N26 via other ATMs, or via 7,000 affiliated retailers. In common with many fintechs, N26 has particularly targeted millennials, who are often disadvantaged when it comes to traditional financial products, as well as finding banks and financial providers to be stuffy, unattractive, and even intimidating. Indeed, the 2017 Millennial Disruption Index discovered that 71 per cent of respondents would rather visit the dentist than their local bank (BBVA, 2015).

This tendency isn't limited to just millennials, though. How many of us really want to spend time on financial transactions in this day and age? There just isn't the time, never mind the will! We want things now, not in 15 minutes! So the onus with fintechs is on quick wins – easy transactions via mobile devices. This is such an attractive proposition to customers, as it makes banking possible in a matter of a few clicks (similar to the system that Amazon has cemented with its retail website). Any provider able to offer convenience and speed, lower the barrier of financial literacy required to use their products, build trust in their system and deliver a full range of banking products will undoubtedly fare very well in the current climate.

And this reality is strongly reflected in market research. In its lengthy 'Fintech Trends' report, digital analyst CB Insights discovered that 60 per cent of US bank customers are ready to try a financial product from a tech firm with which they're already familiar, and this rises to 73 per cent for those aged between 18 and 34 (CB Insights, 2018).

One intriguing way that fintech companies are already tapping into this tendency is by creating products that have 'instagrammability' (yes, I realize it's a horrible word!). Fintech disruptors can design debit cards and other physical financial products that are design classics, appealing to millennials in particular with colourful, minimalist designs. Fintechs can distinguish their cards from traditional bank cards via clean layouts, personalization and even distinct and heavier materials. Venmo and SoFi are examples of companies that have chosen a vertical layout, providing a distinctive card orientation that is both fresh and eye-catching.

Square and Acorn have both also incentivized customers to sign up for their services by offering rewards similar to credit cards for their debit card offerings. The Square Cash Card reward programme offers instant 'cash boosts' at a variety of popular high street stores, delivering a range of discounts in the region of 35 per cent. And Square has similarly partnered with a range of top street brands, such as Shake Shack, Whole Foods and Chipotle, to provide similar customer incentives.

But how much market penetration has been achieved by these initiatives? Many fintechs have revealed their customer numbers, and it seems that they are making progress with attracting customers from traditional banks. Thus, recent start-up Starling boasts 210,000 customers, Monzo has nearly reached a million, in common with its US peer Chime. The aforementioned neobank N26 also has more than a million customers, while the well-known Revolut has already attracted over 2 million account holders. And some of the market leaders boast even bigger numbers. TransferWise has over 3 million account holders, Square has 7 million users, and the cryptocurrency exchange Coinbase reports over 20 million accounts.

However, although we have spoken elsewhere of the suspicion with which traditional banks view fintechs, and their reluctance to cooperate with these companies that they view as a threat to their business, there is evidence that this pattern is beginning to shift. According to the PwC Global FinTech Report 2017, fintechs and banks are starting to collaborate less and compete more, as the existing financial aristocracy understands the potential of this transformative technology. PwC (2017) noted that a new era of cooperation is imminent, with 82 per cent of traditional banks expecting to increase fintech partnerships before 2022.

Payments and challenger banking

And when we look at two key areas in which fintechs are making waves, it becomes obvious why banks are, if not running scared, sitting up and taking notice. Firstly, fintechs have particularly disrupted the payment space, delivering a level of speed, convenience, efficiency and multi-channel accessibility that was unimaginable until recently. This has enabled fintechs to achieve significant successes in such areas as retail, payroll, online micropayments and international transfers.

Consumer-focused fintech solutions have already revolutionized payment markets, and more companies are emerging in this sphere all the time. Examples of successful disruptors in this niche include iZettle, which offers small businesses portable point-of-sale solutions, as well as free sales overview tools. iZettle has been particularly successful due to its absence of start-up costs and monthly fees. The Swedish e-commerce provider Klarna has also made a splash, providing payment services for online storefronts. Indeed, 40 per cent of Swedish e-commerce transactions already utilize Klarna, and the company is currently valued at over €2 billion (Shanley, 2016).

In the labour market, Doreming provides a payroll system that offers workers access to their daily incomes through a linked virtual account. This works for both employees and staff, calculating payroll automatically, while also making access to information easier for workers. With millions of people in the workforce required to take expensive forms of credit to make ends meet, Doreming makes budgeting and managing money that much easier.

Payments fintech is also making cross-border payments much easier. Two disruptors leading this market are Adyen and Azimo. Adyen outsources financial transfer services to international merchants, providing them with a single solution to accept payments anywhere. Its end-to-end infrastructure connects directly to Visa, MasterCard and 250 other payment methods, and the company already works with such notable names as Facebook, Dropbox, SoundCloud, Spotify, Uber, Airbnb and Netflix. And Azimo's digital network makes it possible to transfer money internationally to over 190 countries from any internet-connected device.

Further disruptive technologies, such as Apple Pay, have helped to shape the direction of the banking industry in this regard with mobile payment systems, and have become part of the financial furniture as a result. The migration of consumers to payment methods other than cash has occurred with rapidity, leading many to speculate and ruminate on the impending demise of cash as a method of payment.

While this may be slightly premature, the fact remains that bank customers all over the world seek methods of transferring money rapidly, without waiting for the usual cumbersome procedures. And fintech firms have very much filled the void in this respect, with the likes of PayPal and the aforementioned Venmo being prominent examples of companies that enable customers to transfer money via bank account aliases. Such services have set new standards of customer service, in which liberalized access to banking services is the defining quality, rather than the institution being king, which had been the guiding principle previously.

The sea change in the banking sector, and in the way that fintech companies are choosing to provide services for customers, is underlined by the fact that the youthful Zelle accounted for $75 billion across 247 million transactions in 2017, and this was already a 36 per cent and 45 per cent increase respectively over performance in 2016 (Finextra, 2018). This is a rapid change in the way that customers are seeking financial services, and banks are bending to the will of customers. But this process has only just begun.

Finally, in the payment sphere, fintech is perhaps most readily associated with microfinance and micropayments, and several companies are already hugely popular in this area. One of the more innovative recent examples is Flattr, which enables users to 'flattr' creators for their digital content by clicking the Flattr button next to their content. Flattr helps those working in creative industries gain access to income so that they can continue to create great things.

And challenger banking has been another area where fintechs have already become massive market participators. There are already around 75 challenger banks operating in the UK, and these newfound financial institutions have particularly targeted millennials and small businesses. This can be considered something of an oversight for the big banks, as many of them have failed to court the small business community satisfactorily; indeed, they have often ignored it.

Challenger banks appeal to customers who have lost faith with traditional banks and are ready to turn to these new upstarts that incentivize their custom with transparency, lower fees, faster services, and superior user experiences via always-on digital interfaces.

With the so-called 'gig economy' likely to become even more prevalent in the years to come, fintechs will likely mesh with the ethos of these irregular workers, freelancers, independent contractors, early-stage tech entrepreneurs, and small business owners. These self-employed professionals already represent around half of the European labour market, and this segment of society is expected to outpace traditional salaried work in the next decade.

The success of fintechs in capturing this market is reflected in figures obtained by the Accenture banking report, 'Star Shifting: Rapid Revolution Required'. This study revealed that new competitors have already grasped 14 per cent of UK banking market revenue. Accenture also noted that 63 per cent of current financial service operators didn't even exist just a decade ago (Accenture, 2018). These two figures alone show the extent to which fintechs are becoming significant players in mainstream banking.

Progressive legislation in Europe has made it particularly viable for these newfound banks to operate, resulting in the establishment of such leading challenger banks as Atom Bank, Tandem Bank, Monzo, and Starling Bank, along with Revolut and N26 which we've mentioned previously. Each of these institutions has obtained the financial licence necessary to operate, and the UK has become a particular market leader in this new banking space.

It should be noted that challenger banks face some issues in expanding into the conservative US market. While N26, Monzo, and Revolut have been active in hiring US staff, but there are much higher barriers to entry and competition in the United States. Furthermore, already established fintechs, such as Square, Klarna and TransferWise are already operational in the United States. Of course, the fact that there are established players in the US market indicates that fintech is already active and making an impression in this huge economy.

While some may be sceptical that fintechs could become the major banking entities in the world, the history of commerce is replete with examples of changes that seemed impossible, until they became inevitable. Think of Amazon, Uber and Airbnb, and the impact that they had on their respective industries, all of which were jam-packed full of highly established companies. Traditional banks may not be running scared, but they are undoubtedly only too aware of the threat posed by fintechs.

Case studies and success stories 2012–2018

Aside from the companies already mentioned, there have been some particular success stories over the last few years, as fintech has become more established as a publicly accepted concept. So here we're going to briefly examine five of the most prominent fintech players – Square, Stripe, Kabbage, Credit Karma and TransferWise.

Square has been a particularly massive success story, establishing a diverse network of financial services. The company has marketed a range of software and hardware payment products and has also expanded into small business services. Square achieved this by simply delivering a powerful and user-friendly ecosystem, and then pushing it swiftly into multiple territories.

Investors certainly concur with the market potential of Square, with the company's share price having more than doubled during 2018 trading. And in June 2018, Quartz.com reported that Square's market capitalization had overtaken the combined value of established financial players Nasdaq and Cboe (Detrixhe, 2018).

Stripe is another direct payment company that has travelled a long way in a short period of time. Founded in 2010, Stripe rapidly attracted investment, with even PayPal founder Peter Thiel offering capital. Specializing in sending and receiving secure payments over the internet, within six years of being launched Stripe had attained a market cap of $9 billion, and this had ascended further to $20 billion by September 2018 (Bary, 2018).

The general opinion is that Stripe has become so hugely successful because it does not have a direct competitor. Most payment vendors are focused on offering products that have a particular commercial need, such as payment gateways, consumer payments, or recurring billing. Stripe has set itself aside from competitors by delivering a broader solution that provides a foundation for the entirety of a customer's digital strategy. Studies have indicated that this unique value proposition particularly resonates with Stripe customers.

Kabbage has marked itself out as a funder of small businesses and consumers through its unique automated lending platform. Its success has been predicated on making customer access to funding particularly convenient, and also on pulling together multiple sources of data in order to make credit decisions. Thus, Stripe will consider business checking accounts, Amazon, Quickbooks, PayPal, Etsy, Xero, eBay, Stripe and Sage when assessing creditworthiness.

The company established a strong reputation pretty rapidly and was included in the Forbes Fintech 50 in 2018 (Novack, 2018). Kabbage also earned a LendIt Industry Award for being a Top Small Business Lending Platform (deBanked, 2017). And the company is expanding its operation, acquiring the data, technology and analytics expert Orchard in an effort to deliver more sophisticated data-driven services. It seems that Kabbage is here to stay.

Credit Karma was founded in 2007 and has managed to develop a credit and financial management platform that is free to its customers.

This business model is achieved by generating revenue from targeted advertisements for financial products, while the company also earns contributions from lenders when Credit Karma successfully recommends customers to the lenders.

Offering a wide variety of useful credit-related tools, Credit Karma provides free credit reports to customers and goes to great lengths to ensure that users of its service have access to a wide variety of regularly updated data. Credit Karma also hosts user forums and financial product reviews and financial calculator tools. At a time when a credit score is becoming increasingly important, Credit Karma provides both business and home users with everything needed to maximize their credit potential.

Finally, TransferWise is a powerful money transfer service that already has offices in such diverse locations as Tallinn, New York and Singapore. TransferWise has already established over 750 currency routes across the world and supports GBP, USD, EUR, AUD and CAD, among other currencies. The company already enables customers to transfer around $50 billion annually.

And TransferWise uses an innovative system to eliminate currency conversion and reductive fees. The company matches transfers with other users and then deducts a small commission while using the inter-bank mid exchange rate. TransferWise also offers a unique borderless account, which enables customers to simultaneously hold over 40 currencies and convert them at their convenience.

TransferWise was already valued at $1.6 billion in 2017 (Chernova, 2017) and has established itself as a disruptive money transfer service by offering something new and exciting in the sector.

Summary

Any transformative technology or development goes through five essential stages. First, it experiences scepticism and scorn regarding its potential. Then it begins to become adopted. Then it becomes popular. Then the existence and success of this transformative technology or development seem inevitable. Then we can't imagine the world without it!

Indeed, the internet itself experienced the process that I've just described. Oh, it'll never have any impact on commerce, said the 'experts'. There is an old BBC news report where an interviewee hilariously claims that e-commerce is less significant than the elevator. There are countless other examples of innovations that seemed unneeded at first or had odds massively stacked against them ever being successful, and then they became successful!

Fintech is somewhere between stages two and three at the moment. While fintechs still experience some market and consumer scepticism, they have been broadly accepted, and are starting to achieve mainstream popularity and success. In the years to come, we can reasonably expect fintechs to traverse the remaining stepping stones, and become a central part of the financial architecture all over the world.

References

Accenture (2018) Star shifting: rapid evolution required [online] https://www.accenture.com/_acnmedia/pdf-87/accenture-banking-rapid-evolution-required.pdf (archived at https://perma.cc/ZPT5-2FGT)

Amberber, E (2015) 'Banking is necessary, banks are not' – 7 quotes from Bill Gates on mobile banking, *Your Story* [online] https://yourstory.com/2015/01/quotes-bill-gates-mobile-banking (archived at https://perma.cc/2GX3-D5RV)

American Banker (2018) Amazon in talks with JPMorgan over checking accounts, report says, 5 March [online] https://www.americanbanker.com/articles/amazon-in-talks-with-jpmorgan-over-checking-accounts-report-says (archived at https://perma.cc/7ZJA-DLEN)

Bary, E (2018) Payments start-up Stripe is worth $20 billion after latest funding round, *Market Watch*, 26 September [online] https://www.marketwatch.com/story/payments-start-up-stripe-is-worth-20-billion-after-latest-funding-round-2018-09-26 (archived at https://perma.cc/P6DQ-RYKY)

BBVA (2015) The Millennial Disruption Index [online] https://www.bbva.com/wp-content/uploads/2015/08/millenials.pdf (archived at https://perma.cc/5FGP-5N62)

BFSI (2019) BFSI market research report [online] https://www.adroitmarketresearch.com/contacts/request-sample/872 (archived at https://perma.cc/4EN4-FK5G)

Blumberg Capital (2016) Are banks an endangered species? [online] https://www.blumbergcapital.com/news_insights/fintechsurvey/ (archived at https://perma.cc/6PQJ-KDP5)

Burnmark Report (2017) Burnmark Report April 17: Digital Wealth [online] https://www.burnmark.com/research/2 (archived at https://perma.cc/3WEW-KBE7)

CB Insights (2018) Banks on notice: fintechs are coming for checking accounts & debit cards [online] https://www.cbinsights.com/research/fintech-checking-accounts-debit-card-disruption/ (archived at https://perma.cc/RKG9-FE4Z)

Chernova, Y (2017) TransferWise raises $280 million at $1.6 billion valuation, *Wall Street Journal*, 2 November [online] https://www.wsj.com/articles/transferwise-raises-280-million-at-1-6-billion-valuation-1509598800 (archived at https://perma.cc/6VTN-57N9)

deBanked (2017) The top small business lending platform finalists named by LendIt [online] https://debanked.com/2017/01/the-top-small-business-lending-platform-finalists-named-by-lendit/ (archived at https://perma.cc/YV3T-M3ES)

Detrixhe, J (2018) Square is almost as valuable as two of the biggest US exchange companies combined, *Quartz*, 19 June [online] https://qz.com/1309121/squares-market-capitalization-is-nearly-greater-than-the-nasdaq-and-cboe-combined/ (archived at https://perma.cc/PQ8C-5Z4J)

du Toit, G and Cheris, A (2018) Banking's Amazon moment, *Bain and Co*, 5 March [online] https://www.bain.com/insights/bankings-amazon-moment/ (archived at https://perma.cc/WZA2-UE4V)

Finextra (2018) Zelle moves $75bn in 2017, 29 January [online] https://www.finextra.com/pressarticle/72374/zelle-moves-75bn-in-2017 (archived at https://perma.cc/94U2-LZV9)

Morgenstern, S and Williams, T (2018) Doing well by doing good, *Omidyar Network* [online] https://www.omidyar.com/blog/doing-well-doing-good (archived at https://perma.cc/8RSN-H394)

Novack, J (2018) The Forbes Fintech 50 For 2018, *Forbes*, 13 February [online] https://www.forbes.com/sites/janetnovack/2018/02/13/the-forbes-fintech-50-for-2018/#54c471ac5582 (archived at https://perma.cc/J34F-V8BX)

Pilcher, J (2012) Study shows consumers distrust banks more than any other industry, *The Financial Brand* [online] https://thefinancialbrand.com/22896/edelman-banking-financial-services-consumer-trust-study/ (archived at https://perma.cc/XA86-78PS)

PwC (2017) Redrawing the lines: fintech's growing influence on financial services [online] https://www.pwc.com/gx/en/industries/financial-services/assets/pwc-global-fintech-report-2017.pdf (archived at https://perma.cc/W8UU-3NRE)

Sanghera, T (2018) 80% of Indians now have bank accounts. So why is financial inclusion low? *Business Standard* [online] https://www.business-standard.com/article/finance/80-of-indians-now-have-a-bank-account-so-why-is-financial-inclusion-low-118051700150_1.html (archived at https://perma.cc/E5EG-VT6E)

Shanley, M (2016) Swedish payments firm Klarna shifts focus to U.S. as revenues swell, *Reuters*, 24 February [online] https://uk.reuters.com/article/us-sweden-tech-klarna/swedish-payments-firm-klarna-shifts-focus-to-u-s-as-revenues-swell-idUKKCN0VX1W5 (archived at https://perma.cc/C9AQ-VRNA)

Szmigiera, M (2017) Future strategies of banks regarding Fintech companies worldwide 2017, *Statista* [online] https://www.statista.com/statistics/720792/strategies-of-fintechs-regarding-banks-worldwide/ (archived at https://perma.cc/2MGH-ZXBG)

03

Early collaboration models

Collaboration and partnerships are two of my favourite terms when writing about fintech. At the risk of sounding like a broken record, I will be using these terms again and again to emphazise the future of fintech. Fintech is definitely not about disrupting or destroying banks anymore, it is about finding a place in the mainstream financial ecosystem, and collaborating with large financial institutions and regulators in a way that makes sense for every party within that ecosystem. However, before we got to this stage, fintechs began experimenting with early models of collaboration as early as 2012.

The fintech threat

In the early days of fintech, between 2010 and 2013, fintech start-ups posed a huge threat to the existing banking system; however, chipping away at something as established and profitable as the big banks will take some time. Some banks in the UK service families rather than individuals, and more than four to five generations of a family might have banked with them. Indeed, figures published in 2018 indicated that the 'big five' banks in the UK – Barclays, HSBC, Lloyds Banking Group, Royal Bank of Scotland and Santander UK – still account for 80 per cent of the UK retail market (Carey, 2018).

It is useful to remember, though, that they achieved their market status by playing the long-term game and always being ahead of the curve, managing product and business lines through multiple recessions and downward economic cycles. They know that fintech will become increasingly significant in the years to come, and they definitely won't be resting on their laurels. Research by Gartner (2018) suggested that 80 per cent of financial firms will either go out of business or be rendered irrelevant by new competition by the year 2030. Despite this, I genuinely believe that banks will continue to exist, but not in the current form we see today.

This is a pretty radical prediction of the timeline of this transformation, depicting extremely rapid process. And one thing we know from our experience of the digital field is that change can be unbelievably rapid in technology once the first stone is cast. The capabilities in artificial intelligence and quantum mechanics are great examples of this.

In this scenario, traditional banks face a considerable risk of failure if they fail to adapt, and if they continue to rely on traditional business lines and operating models. This means that the focus of established financial institutions must shift, or at least diversify, from merely making profits and growing revenues into placing emphasis on efficiency and productivity improvements as well as innovation and digital servicing. Companies that can leverage a low-cost digital infrastructure, often having the potential to act as service brokers, will thrive in this environment while other less agile firms will flounder.

It should also be noted that the speed and nature of digital transformation will also be hugely dependent on the regulatory environment. When we talk about a digital transformation, though we live in an increasingly globalized world this shouldn't be viewed as a uniform process. Legislation will influence the way that the digital society develops from nation to nation, with the more conservative countries likely to inhibit development, and countries such as Australia, Brazil, China, India, Singapore and the UK likely to lead the way in accelerating the digital economy.

Losing customers

So, it's perhaps not surprising that banks are genuinely worried about fintechs stealing their customers. Already with open banking we are seeing an environment being created in which the established financial players can no longer claim sole ownership of customer data. This will liberalize the marketplace and make it far more plausible for fintechs to grab hold of a significant chunk of traditional banks' business.

The Bank of England (BoE) has noted that the UK banking sector has underestimated the potential – they might describe it as the 'threat'! – of fintech. Reuters reported on this in November 2017, noting that a BoE study found that 'Britain's banks may be overstating their ability to stop "fintech" firms stealing customers and eating into profits' (Jones, 2017). The Bank of England Governor Mark Carney commented at the time that fintechs could disrupt the 'stability of funding of incumbent banks', even forcing the central bank and management of the British economy to 'ensure prudential standards and resolution regimes for the affected banks are sufficiently robust to these risks', the *Daily Telegraph* (Burton, 2017) reported.

Nonetheless, there isn't a comprehensive agreement on the extent to which fintechs threaten the banking hierarchy. But it is broadly agreed that, in the immediate future, fintechs will be of more concern to the retail sector, where they are well placed to gobble up a pretty sizeable slice of the banking cake. This atmosphere then becomes more rarefied when we consider the erosion of trust that has tainted the once unsullied image of the financial sector. Do people trust traditional banks anymore? It would be too strong to say that they do not, as most people still have accounts with the biggest retail banks. But consumer scepticism is quickly growing, which fintechs are happily tapping into, with their transparent pricing and simple interfaces.

The degree to which this is occurring can be difficult to measure, and there is conflicting data, and conflicting opinions, on the level of market penetration that fintechs have achieved over the last 10 years. But a report from consultancy Accenture (2018) suggests that new banking market entrants, including challenger banks, non-bank payments institutions, and tech companies, have captured one-third of new revenue in the niche in Europe. While this still means that other, usually more traditional, sources are responsible for two-thirds of even new banking custom, it does represent a significant figure achieved in a relatively short space of time.

This is very much dependent on the geographical location. Whereas in the UK fintechs have already scooped up 14 per cent of total banking and payment revenues, the picture is very different in the United States. One of the world's largest economies has been far less receptive to the start-ups, and fintech and banking start-ups have only managed to accrue 3.5 per cent of the total $1.04 trillion in revenue generated (Irrera, 2018). However, several regional, community banks have shown a spurt in numbers of customers driven by lack of trust and disillusionment with larger banking groups.

Figures show that 20 per cent of banking industry competitors in Europe are new entrants, with these start-ups having snagged 7 per cent of the overall market (Bambrough, 2018).

In Canada, where new entrants have only captured 2 per cent of the market, there is quite clearly an appetite for change, and perhaps a realization that such change is inevitable. This is reflected by the fact that a staggering 47 per cent of financial institutions operating in Canada in the banking niche are now new entrants (Accenture, 2018). While these more modern companies may not have collectively made a huge amount of headway, it seems inevitable that this will change very soon.

It is figures such as these which have meant that the big banks do fear losing customers to fintechs, and perhaps even accept the inevitability of this to some extent. While there is no danger of some of the most established names in finance worldwide sinking without a trace, nor going down without a fight, it is inevitable that they will be forced to compete in a diversified, liberalized and more challenging marketplace, in which their hegemony is no longer guaranteed. The 2008 financial crisis caused the dam to burst, and there is no way that leak can be corked up now.

When we talk about the fintech revolution, we keep coming back to the same word – agile. The most compelling way that fintechs, finance start-ups and challenger banks have been able to capture custom is by making registering, lending and accessing services quicker, easier and more flexible. This has forced the traditional banking industry to adapt, and this is one quality that we do not seem to associate with big banks. They are accustomed to being treated as the custodians of finance and thus have become notoriously slow to react to shifting market conditions.

With 10 years having passed since the global financial crisis became a media talking point, there has been plenty of time for fintechs to gain ground, and the banking industry now finds itself facing a level of competitive intensity and disruption that is simply unprecedented. There is extreme fear looming ominously over the heads of the big banks, and by now they recognize all too vividly the reality of this accelerating power shift.

We can also expect this process to occur briskly in emerging markets, particularly the tech-dominated India. The Indian government announced a process of demonetization in 2016, which not only saw specific notes eradicated from the public domain but also led to disruption in the economy (Mukherjee, 2017). And in this climate of opportunity, new digital payment systems began to establish themselves.

It is this sort of convenience that is now proving to be a genuine challenge for some of the world's biggest financial institutions.

Learning from fintechs

With this in mind, it's not surprising that banks are beginning to learn from fintechs, and attempting to adopt some of their models, products and working practices. Thus, to help them tap into the increasingly vibrant fintech niche, banks are forging strategies, which have particularly included investments similar to venture capital, and a wealth of incubator and accelerator programmes.

If the early efforts in this area represented banks dipping their toes in the water to test the temperature, then more recent initiatives have seen some of the big players far more committed to jumping on the fintech bandwagon. Innovation centres have even been established, with the goal of establishing fresh ideas and concepts that could enhance business and working processes.

The big banks have become far more interested in understanding how fintech works, and specifically how it will impact the financial industry. Additionally, banks have equally sought to understand where they have advantages over fintechs, and where they may be able to offer partnerships or engage in some form of a reciprocal relationship.

Banks are resetting their mindset of trepidation and adopting a more prudent mentality of embracing digital change, assessing how and where their businesses can be enhanced by implementing the new technologies inherent in the digital revolution.

Indeed, banks can fundamentally learn from the technology model associated with fintechs, particularly the lean technology stacks involved in many start-ups in this sphere, and the agile working methods that they have implemented. There is the feeling that traditional banks and financial institutions are too sluggish and cumbersome in their approach, weighed down by dated architecture and processes, and thus these behemoths of many years' standing are looking to fintechs in order to modernize.

However, it is also becoming apparent that some critical factors need to be addressed if the new fintech solutions are to become truly mainstream and transformative. For example, widespread transactions in cross-border payments will require a firm foundation to be successful. There will need to be a critical mass of consumers, common standards and practices will need to be created, and regulators will have to be comfortable with developments in this area. And each of these will have to develop symbiotically as well.

Considering the cooperation required to achieving this, banks increasingly understand the importance of collaborating with fintechs. Traditional banks and start-ups are working together in order to drive progress towards greater standardization, interoperability, and closer working on industry initiatives and innovations. This is another rapid change in a short timeframe, as it was only a couple of years ago that Stephen Bird, CEO of global consumer banking for Citi, was talking about the significant threat that digital innovators in financial services posed to the traditional business models of retail banks (Pymnts, 2018). Clearly, that initial frost is beginning to thaw.

And this isn't a one-way relationship. Banks unquestionably have several assets that fintechs would benefit from, and therefore, the start-ups in the field are just as willing to encourage cooperation. Although we have spoken about the recession of trust in existing financial institutions, the fact remains that the traditional banks have built up a certain amount of cachet in this department, over decades and even centuries. Virtually all citizens have regular bank accounts, and this provides traditional banks with a substantial competitive advantage, as well as a vast customer base.

This is why fintechs are ready to play ball with the big banks and assist them in the technological transformation process that will be central to their prosperity going forward. Payment systems are undoubtedly a scale business, a risky business, and a 'trust' business, and in this regard, many of the start-ups can benefit from tapping into the cachet of traditional banks. It will undoubtedly take time for the digital economy to establish the seemingly permanent and eternal image that big banks have garnered over their lifecycle, and this means that partnerships make sense, even for the most successful and innovative fintechs.

Equally, if banks are to tap into the potential of the digital revolution, they must design and implement products that emphasize security, innovation, flexibility, skill and all of the qualities that can be readily associated with fintechs. Both sides of this equation have something to gain from the other, and this means that collaboration is already becoming far more commonplace than was the case until recently.

One example of this spirit of collaboration is Banco Bilbao Vizcaya Argentaria (BBVA). Derek White, global head of customer and client solutions at BBVA, commented at Money 20/20 Asia on the fintech-banking relationship that it was 'interaction between two different organisms living in close physical association, typically to the advantage of both' (BBVA, 2018). This is symptomatic of a realization that is now dawning on both 'sides'.

Indeed, the World Fintech Report 2018 indicated that start-ups have already played a significant role in improving customer services in financial services, by delivering the all-important consumer demand for the simplicity, accessibility and personalization that have become defining qualities (Capgemini, 2018). The report suggests that fintechs have already largely succeeded in their central goals of redefining the banking marketplace. Yet, they still face a major problem.

Banking customers still don't have the sort of brand recognition with fintechs that they have long since established with the biggest high street retail banks. In some industries, this isn't a huge issue. However, with banking, brand recognition is particularly important (although it should also be said that there are plenty of other industries other than banking in which some form of brand recognition is critical to success). Traditional retail banks have spent billions on cementing the idea in the public mind that they are venerable institutions, as permanent as the natural landscape, a simple fact of life. Regardless of recent bad press and issues of customer service and high fees, this brand image and levels of trust will not be erased quickly.

Thus, the World Fintech Report concluded that financial sector customers still struggle to trust these new banking players when it comes to parking their investments and savings with them. Traditional financial institutions have some of the most important bases covered with banking, such as risk management, regulatory experience, access to capital, and the backing of governments and the legislative environment.

Conversely, fintech firms have the potential to address many problems within the financial industry. Consumers in this sector have become accustomed to sub-par customer service, but there are other perhaps less obvious issues also lurking under the surface. Banks don't tend to use big data particularly efficiently or intuitively, and they have certainly been guilty of failing to reach out to under-represented and disadvantaged members of the community.

This latter point is one area in which fintechs do promise to revolutionize banking, simply by making it possible for all people to access services, and be treated with more respect than has, sadly, often been the case previously. This liberalizing, democratizing and dignifying impact on banking will be a disruptive influence, as this aspect of the sector is so ripe for transformation.

And this process will only be magnified by the potential of fintechs to reach people and transform lives in unbanked areas of the planet. One example of this is the distributed ledger technology system that has been put in place in Jordan, Syria, by a start-up, Building Blocks.

With backing from the World Food Programme, this company has enabled refugees, displaced by civil war, to use a cashless transaction to purchase much-needed goods, including food, for their displaced families.

Clearly, the fintech revolution has massive transformative potential.

Accelerator programmes from banks

The earliest collaboration models of banks wanting to work with fintechs included ways to watch and learn from them. Most of the accelerator programmes were launched by banks between 2010 and 2016, with the aim of supporting them with small seed investments, but primarily to learn innovation by observing the fintechs' products, culture, processes and team management styles.

The Barclays Accelerator is a great example of an early fintech-dedicated accelerator, launched in 2012, and with programmes running in New York, London, Cape Town and Tel Aviv. Powered by TechStars, the accelerator is dedicated to delivering networking and mentorship from Barclays Bank's executives and offering up to $120,000 as an investment along with other corporate partner perks (Nair, 2019). This accelerator has already become popular with fintech competitors and has achieved an enormous amount for the space.

Some of the other banking accelerator programmes launched around this time include:

Wells Fargo, 2014

Nordea, 2015

Citibank, 2013

UBS+Credit Suisse, 2016

BNP Paribas, 2015

JP Morgan, 2015

DBS, 2015

BBVA, 2014

Level39, on the 39th floor of One Canada Square in London, was one of the few non-bank incubator/accelerator programmes launched in the early days of fintech (in 2012) and has now established itself as something of a market leader, proclaiming itself to be Europe's largest technology accelerator for finance, retail, cyber-security and futures. Run by the Canary Wharf Group, Level39 has evolved from an idea about giving fintech start-ups space to innovate, into a three-floor, 80,000-square-foot accelerator space with strong connections to banks and global hubs around the world. Level39 has been involved with over 1,200 events, which have attracted over 100,000 visitors, and has undoubtedly become a favourite among major global financial players visiting London (Canary Wharf, 2016).

Seed funding and early investments

As much as fintechs had achieved over the last decade or so when they were first attempting to become players in the financial game, one of the biggest challenges they faced was around early-stage funding. Most start-ups spend between two and three years before they start earning regular revenues (after several trials) and start looking at venture capital or later-stage funding. Many governmental programmes did not have fintech funding in place in the early years, thus they had to look for support from those showing interest in them at the time – the banks and large financial institutions. Several early-stage funds soon came about to support this fast-growing industry with angel and seed investments.

In 2014, Barclays' Accelerator programme found start-ups from lending, payments, big data, cash management, compliance and crowdfunding, while the Wells Fargo programme invested in user experience, big data and cyber-security around specific use cases.

In 2015, Barclays' Accelerator programme invested in even more segments like security, brokerage, cryptocurrency and gamification, while JP Morgan's programme invested in expected segments like lending, big data and personal financial management. BNP Paribas also launched its programme this year with start-ups in payments and security featuring in the accelerator.

It's interesting to note how the number of segments and the interest in highly niche areas like gamification and remittance show up only in the second or third iterations of most accelerator programmes. Lending, payments and big data seem to feature across the spectrum of all accelerator programmes.

Outright acquisitions were extremely rare, but one of the earliest examples of this was BBVA Bank's acquisition of Simple in the United States. Simple was founded in Brooklyn in 2009 by a group of technology experts, and the direct bank had soon raised seed capital via angel investor Jerry Neumann. Once Simple had proved the viability of its concept, money began to pour in; $10 million of seed capital was raised by Simple in August 2011, with investors IA Ventures, Shasta Ventures and 500 start-ups all involved. At this time, Simple also chose to relocate to Portland, Oregon, where the company remains headquartered today (Rogoway, 2011).

The company had already attracted 20,000 customers early in 2013, processing over $200 million worth of transactions, and this figure doubled to 40,000 within a matter of months. But arguably the biggest achievement of Simple was attracting the attention of BBVA, which resulted in an acquisition in February 2014. The company was already valued at $117 million at this time and has continued to expand its operation since then. Simple was integrated into BBVA's onboarding process, offering a front end to its customers in certain US markets.

The other acquisitions in the fintech space by banks in the early days included Holvi by BBVA (2016), Honest Dollar by Goldman Sachs (2016), TradeKing by Ally Financial (2016) and Future Advisor by Blackrock (2015).

US banks versus European banks

The United States and Europe led the early innovation efforts in fintech from 2010 to 2016, but the most obvious contrast has been that the fintech revolution was much more enthusiastically embraced in Europe. The way that companies in the two geographical locales have invested in fintech has also been quite different.

While early European investment in fintech has tended to focus on challenger banks and p2p lending, this has not been the case in the United States. Challenger banks arguably face a tougher time in establishing themselves in the US market, due to the lack of regulatory openness and the size of some of the traditional retail and investment engines already established in the country. But there has been considerable investment in the United States in digital front-personal finance management, online trading and payment systems.

Goldman Sachs, Citibank and JPMorgan Chase have been particularly active in the fintech sphere, while Morgan Stanley, Wells Fargo and Bank of America are investing in a diverse portfolio of fintechs across the fields of accounting and tax, automation software, blockchain, data analytics, insurance, personal finance, robo-advisory/wealth management, capital markets, lending, payments and settlement, real estate, regulatory technology and supply chain.

Aside from challenger banks, European fintech investment has tended to focus on data analytics, blockchain, remittances, financial inclusion, lending and regulatory technology. There is definitely some overlap between the United States and Europe in terms of fintech investment, but also a tangibly different strategy seems to have been taken.

The United States saw $6 billion being invested from banks into fintechs, whereas the whole of Europe received $700 million in 2015. Though this amount has improved drastically for Europe in more recent years, Silicon Valley still remains the major funder for payments and lending businesses globally.

Fintechs such as Kabbage, Klarna, Square, Funding Circle, Stripe, Coinbase, Nutmeg, eToro and SigFig were all firmly established in the top 50 fintech innovators by 2014, and have gone on to have multi-million-dollar (and in some of them, multi-billion-dollar) valuations and exits.

By 2013, global investment in fintech had hit $3 billion, with innovation increasingly enabled by new consumer behaviours, technology and regulations. London and Silicon Valley became particular hubs of fintech innovation and investment, with the UK and Ireland hosting more than half of Europe's fintech deals at this time, and attracting nearly 70 per cent of the continent's fintech funding (CB Insights, 2014).

Meanwhile, Silicon Valley was responsible for nearly one-third of global fintech funding during this period, which helps explain why some of the early investors were big technology companies. Google, Amazon and Alibaba were all frontrunners in fintech innovation and investment. This has continued in more recent years, with IBM's acquisition of Promontory Financial Group, a global risk management and regulatory compliance consulting firm, seen as particularly significant with regard to its AI plans.

Meanwhile, the decision of Ping An, Tencent and Alibaba to join forces in 2013 was an important landmark and indication of things to come. Together, they launched Zhong An, China's first truly digital insurer. The cross-industry nature of this partnership was massive for fintechs, as it indicated the sort of collaboration and cross-pollination that could be achieved. Zhong An's online insurance offering has already attracted more than 350 million customers, and shown that emerging markets are embracing fintech enthusiastically as well (McKinsey, 2018).

Selling to banks

It is clear from the ensuing market conditions that banks have been much quicker to invest in early-stage fintech start-ups than venture capitalists. Yet, it has not necessarily followed that fintech start-ups have been successful in selling products to banks; the mass market has been far more receptive.

This is an interesting dichotomy and one that is worth discussing. There could be several possible reasons to explain this phenomenon, but three instantly came to mind:

Are banks investing in fintech firms as a precautionary measure without seeing an immediate integration potential?

Are there specific areas of fintech that banks invest more in, and other areas where they watch and learn, letting fintech firms do the groundwork?

Other than for regulatory reasons, are banks willing to open up their systems for partnerships with fintech firms?

What can be said is that banks have certainly invested enthusiastically in fintechs in recent years, with lending, payments, big data and analytics the major areas of focus. And three early collaboration models emerged as a result of this. Accelerator programmes provided templates for banks to essentially 'watch and learn' – observing how fintech developed and unfolded in a fertile environment. APIs have enabled banks and fintechs to collaborate in technology terms. And banks are also increasingly entering into investment arrangements, as they identify fintechs that are worthy of acquisition.

Incubator programmes have also been hugely valuable, helping to create some of the most important fintech start-ups. This approach by banks hasn't always been about direct profit or assistance, but instead often assisting banks in exploring the latest technologies and learning what works best in the prevailing market conditions. Events such as the BBVA OpenTalent Europe Finals have produced no end of revolutionary operators. For example, previous winners such as EverLedger – which uses blockchain to combat fraud, therefore combining two of the hottest sectors in fintech – and Origin – which offers a marketplace for corporate bond issuance – have both been enthusiastically courted by banks.

This is indicative of the way that banks are using the expertise of fintech firms to plug gaps in their portfolios and knowledge bases. Open banking and the availability of APIs have been particularly prominent in this regard, and there are several interesting examples available. Tryum, a personalized relationship science company, received the Pingit Payments APIs from Barclays, and Namu – a white label mobile banking app – received front-end APIs from Citibank through their respective incubator programmes. Both of these firms have used the experience of working closely with banks to innovate in a rapid way that otherwise may have been impossible, and to develop solutions that immediately appeal to the financial services world.

As the prominence of fintech continues to develop, banks continue to invest significantly in fintech start-ups, which can quickly help improve their products, operations, and customer service. Gamification will be one of the most dramatically different ways of improving customer interactivity, and will help deliver improved customer-centricity and satisfaction. The loyalty that is derived through this improved focus on customer-centricity will be paramount, as traditional banks are increasingly faced with the threat of challenger banks, and competition from alternative business models.

Banks will also launch a wider base of customer touchpoints so that customers have more opportunities to interact as part of their relationship. Banks increasingly offer business units around remittances, currency transfer, peer-to-peer lending and tax advisory services, as the field develops. Meanwhile, customer advisory services will become heavily dependent on data, analytics and machine learning, while also becoming more straightforward and more intuitive at the app level. From my conversations with traditional banks of all sizes, security will also inevitably become an area of increased focus in the years to come, and this is another aspect of operations in which fintechs and banks will collaborate.

Banks' investments vary between short-term and long-term investments, as well as tactical and futuristic approaches. Different strategies are being adopted by banks and venture capitalists today, and that is because there is no singular path that is appropriate to all circumstances. The behaviour of banks in the fintech niche shows that they are enthusiastic about the future of this technology, but the fact that the direction of the industry is still developing and unfolding means that banks are more comfortable with taking a backseat, and helping fintechs to develop, rather than investing with abandon.

Summary

Banks have been much slower to embrace the fintech revolution than technology firms, but we have seen that the tide is not only beginning to turn, but it has already turned quite considerably. There is no doubt that banks have viewed fintechs as a threat to their business model, and even their existence. From their perspective, they already have a highly profitable and well-established series of codes, practices and revenue-generation techniques, so why is there any need to change? In this respect, it was always likely that the big banks would initially view fintechs with suspicion, and often outright hostility.

However, over time, the dust has settled and instead given way to a climate of collaboration. This has not moved fast by any means, perhaps partly due to the fintechs' nascent nature, and partly due to the conservative nature of the largest financial institutions. Indeed, established technology companies have been more enthusiastic about supporting and embracing the fintech revolution in its early days.

There is now quite considerable evidence that banks and fintechs are collaborating constructively. With all of the evidence pointing to this financial sector increasing in size quite significantly in the years to come, we can only expect this collaboration to grow as the youthful but burgeoning relationship settles into a more comfortable phase.

References

Accenture (2018) Banks' revenue growth at risk due to unprecedented competitive pressure resulting from digital disruption, Accenture study finds, 17 October [online] https://newsroom.accenture.com/news/banks-revenue-growth-at-risk-due-to-unprecedented-competitive-pressure-resulting-from-digital-disruption-accenture-study-finds.htm (archived at https://perma.cc/MD94-XDHW)

Bambrough, B (2018) Global fintech warning to traditional banks – the threat is 'real and growing', *Forbes*, 17 October [online] https://www.forbes.com/sites/billybambrough/2018/10/17/global-fintech-warning-to-tradional-banks-the-threat-is-real-and-growing/#3bc82ac62c71 (archived at https://perma.cc/QM89-9EMV)

BBVA (2018) Banks and fintech are looking for the perfect symbiosis, 23 March [online] https://www.bbva.com/en/banks-fintech-looking-perfect-symbiosis/ (archived at https://perma.cc/7C77-GDXB)

Burton, L (2017) Mark Carney warns of fintech threat to traditional banks, *Telegraph* [online] https://www.telegraph.co.uk/business/2017/04/12/mark-carney-warns-fintech-threat-traditional-banks/ (archived at https://perma.cc/272L-BWWG)

Canary Wharf (2016) Canary Wharf Group appoints Ben Brabyn to lead technology strategy, 2 February [online] https://group.canarywharf.com/media/press-releases/canary-wharf-group-appoints-ben-brabyn-to-lead-technology-strategy-240216/ (archived at https://perma.cc/B5RV-3XMA)

Capgemini (2018) The World FinTech Report [online] https://www.capgemini.com/wp-content/uploads/2018/02/world-fintech-report-wftr-2018.pdf (archived at https://perma.cc/VU56-6SLV)

Carey, S (2018) Open banking threatens big banks' most valuable customers, *Computer World UK* [online] https://www.computerworld.com/article/3427523/open-banking-threatens-big-banks--most-valuable-customers.html (archived at https://perma.cc/Y7UP-AQRC)

CB Insights (2014) The boom in global fin tech investment: fin tech grabs $3 billion in 2013, 27 March [online] https://www.cbinsights.com/research/global-fin-tech-investment-accenture/ (archived at https://perma.cc/33CT-R6WR)

Gartner (2018) Gartner says digitalization will make most heritage financial firms irrelevant by 2030 [online] https://www.gartner.com/en/newsroom/press-releases/2018-10-29-gartner-says-digitalization-will-make-most-heritage-financial-firms-irrelevant-by-2030 (archived at https://perma.cc/X672-AUZU)

Irrera, A (2018) Fintech making inroads, but U.S. bank revenues little changed: report, *Reuters*, 17 October [online] https://www.reuters.com/article/us-fintech-banking/fintech-making-inroads-but-u-s-bank-revenues-little-changed-report-idUSKCN1MR0X1 (archived at https://perma.cc/FUU9-K37G)

Jones, H (2017) BoE says banks may be underestimating fintech threat, *Reuters*, 28 November [online] https://uk.reuters.com/article/uk-boe-banks-fintech/boe-says-banks-may-be-underestimating-fintech-threat-idUKKBN1DS18K (archived at https://perma.cc/7Y8V-3MQ6)

McKinsey (2018) Digital insurance in 2018: December 2018 driving real impact with digital and analytics [online] https://www.mckinsey.com/industries/financial-services/our-insights/digital-insurance-in-2018-driving-real-impact-with-digital-and-analytics (archived at https://perma.cc/3QU4-UJXG)

Mukherjee, A (2017) For banks, threat from Fintech start-ups is real, *IndiaTimes*, 22 February [online] https://economictimes.indiatimes.com/small-biz/money/for-banks-threat-from-fintech-start-ups-is-real/articleshow/57285164.cms (archived at https://perma.cc/MZZ3-FZGF)

Nair, A (2019) This US-based accelerator is redefining 'mentorship' for Indian start-ups, *YourStory*, 2 May [online] https://yourstory.com/2019/05/us-accelerator-mentorship-india-start-ups-techstars (archived at https://perma.cc/L73N-P6VE)

Pymnts (2018) Why the bank-fintech relationship is more complicated than conflicted, 1 November [online] https://www.pymnts.com/innovation/2018/fintech-banks-relationship-mobile-digital/ (archived at https://perma.cc/3NLD-MT29)

Rogoway, M (2011) Promising NYC start-up BankSimple moves HQ to Portland, *Oregon Live*, 24 August [online] https://www.oregonlive.com/silicon-forest/2011/08/promising_ny_start-up_banksimple_moves_hq_to_portla.html (archived at https://perma.cc/LEU6-KGCK)

04

Widening of the fintech ecosystem

I like to call the years after the early phase of fintech, post-2016, 'fintech 2.0'. This is the time when we started seeing a mature market, with steady growth in investments and start-up numbers, and most importantly, increased and improved collaboration between all parties in the fintech ecosystem. We are now witnessing a broadening of the entire fintech platform, as big banks and start-ups collaborate on an increasingly frequent basis. Consulting firms, software vendors, universities, research institutes, domain experts, etc are now collaborating with banks and start-ups to drive innovation further. Over the last few years, fintech has become a massive growth area for the financial services industry, and one that promises to become increasingly important as it continues to mature and widen.

Evolution of collaboration models

Many banks and fintechs have now become collaborators, as both sides' initial expectations have shifted somewhat. Banks steadily stopped viewing fintechs as rivals and began to understand that they could enhance their overall business by embracing the fintech revolution. And fintech start-ups, and even established companies in the financial services industry, also realized that changing the banking system would be a potentially slow and arduous process. This is not necessarily a fast-moving industry, therefore, it makes sense for young fintech companies to seek partnerships with established banking players.

Central to this has been the ability of fintechs to unbundle many traditional banking services in a new approach to finance that revolves around improved customer service and experiences. Traditional banks have created a significant amount of friction concerning the customer experience, and many fintechs focused on resolving this issue from day one. So it was only natural that banks would seek to learn from the operational advantages of fintechs, such as lower cost bases, no burdens of legacy systems, emerging technology adeptness, and a culture of being willing to take risks to serve customers.

By about 2016, banks had begun to realize that the fintech model was one that would not only be sustainable for the industry but actually necessary from a business perspective going forward. Indeed, the CEO of ANZ – the third-largest bank by capitalization in Australia – commented that fintechs 'certainly spell the end of banks which don't rapidly adapt, which have leaders lacking flexible mindsets, or which lose sight of what their customers value' (Bajkowski, 2018). Thus, many partnerships between banks and fintechs have been formed in recent years, as banks increasingly recognize this necessity.

Cooperation in the fintech space can take many forms, and it is, therefore, useful to discuss some of the more common models. The first of these most commonly involves fintechs selling products directly to bank customers. Banks benefit from it by being able to offer new products and services, while investing relatively small amounts of time, effort and capital in delivering them. Banks also gain immediate insight into whether customers enjoyed the offering and can then make a decision on whether to expand or walk away.

Equally, I think fintechs gain access to new customers and revenue, while their brand recognition is also improved significantly. Another obvious benefit is the market insight that fintechs gain from such an arrangement, while it is also a natural booster to credibility to be associated with a well-respected bank. This is also a popular arrangement as there are few risks for either party. One such example of this approach to collaboration is the cooperation between The Royal Bank of Scotland and Funding Circle to deliver SME loans (Funding Circle, 2015).

A second popular arrangement involves banks engaging with fintechs as if they are suppliers, in what could be described as a satellite model. New positions are created by integrating the abilities of the fintechs with the bank's existing products. This data effectively appears to customers if the bank is providing the service, while in reality, it is a genuine collaboration. Indeed, the contribution of the fintech is usually contained within the terms and conditions.

This is another way for banks to explore new propositions with customers, while also obtaining certain flexibility, as banks can always remove their cooperation with relatively low expenditure. Often the banks involved in this sort of relationship also make investments in fintech firms. An advantage for the fintechs of this sort of arrangement is that they are not necessarily exclusive, leaving the possibility of collaborating with other banks open. This sort of model has been utilized in the partnerships that Swedish firm Tink has created with SEB, ABN Amro and Paribas Fortis.

The third approach to collaboration involves a bank acquiring a fintech but enabling the company to still operate in a relatively independent fashion. Immediately, a glaring example of this for fintechs is that the companies involved receive an injection of capital, along with implicit validation of their business models. Banks are also able to investigate a potential area of business, without suffering any detrimental impact from problems with the arrangement. Banks gain strong market intelligence, and ensure exclusivity, while fintechs will find it easier to retain their existing staff, who often prefer working within the confines of a smaller company, rather than a monolithic bank.

Banks do take more of a financial risk in this form of investment, but it hasn't prevented several from taking the plunge.

Finally, the most traditional form of collaboration between banks and fintechs is a straightforward merger. Such transactions are undertaken with an understanding that the fintech company will be wholly integrated and rebranded as a result of the arrangement. Fintechs retain absolutely no independence under such arrangements, and indeed effectively cease to exist. However, the financial rewards can be massive, and banks benefit by acquiring a form of technology and by effectively making it their own. We will see many more examples of this type of collaboration in the coming years, but a notable recent acquisition of this nature was the purchase of Final by Goldman Sachs' consumer bank Marcus.

As the field continues to develop, it is becoming clear that the fintechs do not necessarily face a simple choice between disruption or collaboration. Fintechs rather have the potential to plug gaps in the service offerings of banks and help them to provide a superior and more innovative customer experience, which is also significantly more inclusive.

Beyond banking accelerator programmes

'Collaboration between start-ups and corporates: a practical guide for mutual understanding' was published by the World Economic Forum in January 2018, and examined the collaboration process between corporates and fintech start-ups. In the paper, the distinguished organization explained why the process of collaboration had taken a while to evolve, suggesting that both banks and fintechs have preconceived ideas of how working with the other group will operate; however, these ideas are not necessarily founded in reality. The World Economic Forum (2018) suggested that start-ups need to establish a better understanding of corporate structures and incentives, while corporate players need to avoid viewing start-ups as innovation units, or sources of free consultancy, which ultimately distract them from their core activities. As the forum concluded, 'Mutual understanding depends on each side appreciating the risks and the differences the other faces in embarking on collaboration.'

Adam Carson, managing director of global technology strategy and partnerships at JPMorgan Chase, has also commented on how bank and fintech partnerships should ideally operate. Carson suggests that large companies such as banks usually want to see tangible proof that business models are working, and that products are being effectively placed in the hands of customers, before considering a partnership to be viable, let alone committing to one. Carson particularly notes that large banks really have the ability to indulge in unproven product or strategy (JPMorgan Chase, 2018).

With this in mind, banks now often want to see real use and business cases before engaging with start-ups. What has effectively occurred is that the fintech space has become more competitive as it has matured, and as with any field, this has meant that only the standout examples of fintech operation have attracted bank partnerships. This process will indeed become more established in the coming years, as the future direction of fintechs becomes more established, and banks have a stronger understanding of what does, and indeed does not, work.

But when new business models are put in place appropriately, banks certainly have no hesitation in collaborating with fintechs.

One such example is Symphony Communications, which received backing from legendary investment bank Goldman Sachs in its initiative to replace secure messaging. In October 2014, Goldman Sachs, along with 14 other financial institutions, created and invested $66 million in Symphony Communication Services LLC and acquired Perzo, a secure communication application that provided end-to-end encryption messaging (Miller, 2015).

Another good example is CommonBond, which received investment from NelNet. As a result of this arrangement, NelNet agreed to finance $150 million worth of CommonBond's annual loan volume. This collaboration was initially announced in February 2015, and marked the first time that a public financial services company had invested in a student loan marketplace company (CommonBond, 2015).

BlendLabs is an innovative fintech company that has managed to attract a lot of backing from banks and financial institutions. BlendLabs is currently working to replace mortgage origination software with several corporates, working closely with Wells Fargo and US Bancorp among others.

LendingClub is another company that is partnered with several banks, enabling the banks to purchase loans and offer new LendingClub products to their customers. LendingClub first began partnering with banks in 2014 and today proudly proclaims on its website that it has been able to procure 54 banks as partners. These range in total assets from less than $100 million to more than $100 billion, and, at 45 per cent, banks represent the largest share of the company's investor base (LendingClub, 2019).

BBVA has also been highly active in the fintech space, and its BBVA Compass brand has begun referring customers who are unlikely to qualify for a loan over to the fintech OnDeck. BBVA Compass has also partnered with Dwolla, through which it has launched real-time payments. Dwolla also uses FiSync to enable the use of secure authentication and tokenization, ensuring that BBVA Compass account holders aren't required to share their account info with Dwolla.

This just scratches the surface. Yes Bank has forged a significant partnership with Flipkart for UPI transactions, with the two very openly offering their products as a partnership to customers. Yes Bank has also partnered with PhonePe, with over 30 million customers created through the app (Bhakta, 2018). Tez and WhatsApp Payments are similarly trying to cash in on this market. Moven is another company working with many banks around the world. In this climate, it's not surprising that 82 per cent of banks, insurers and asset managers intend to increase the number of partnerships they have with fintech firms in the coming years (PwC, 2017).

A recent example of this is Nivaura, a fintech focused on automating the issuance and administration processes for financial instruments. This company was able to raise £20 million in seed capital in March 2019, with several prominent partners wading into the investment (CityAM, 2019). As the fintech niche has developed, so institutional investors have better understood the potential of the sector, and the level of money now being pumped into numerous fintech start-ups underlines this succinctly.

Hackathons and a focus on technology

As banking accelerator programmes are becoming increasingly generic and spread widely across all segments within fintech, banks have felt the pressure to find solutions to specific problems or use cases business units are facing. One of the ways innovation teams are supporting business units in this solution-finding exercise is hackathons. I feel that hackathons based on real use cases within the bank have been far more effective in bringing tangible results and significant collaboration than incubator or accelerator programmes not targeted at specific use cases. As banks look to accelerate their technological and financial investment in the fintech space, more and more hackathons are emerging, with banks, consulting firms and vendors like IBM running them on a regular basis with the help of universities, developer groups and the testing community. These vibrant congregations of technology experts are critical for the future of fintech, to drive further collaboration and results.

Defrag the Dinosaur is a colourfully named hackathon that draws together developers, designers, data scientists, and analytics experts. Its organizers call on its innovative participants to 'find, capture, defrag, rethink and rebuild the dinosaurs of the banking system'. With 48 hours of coding taking place, a prize pool of over €15,000, and major hiring opportunities available, Defrag the Dinosaur represents an exciting opportunity for talented IT experts (Hackathon. com, 2019a).

Hackgrid is a 36-hour spectacular, in which participants consider innovative solutions that can be applied to real-world problems. Fintech technology is at the heart of this event, and Hackgrid has hosted over 1,000 developers since its inception (Hackathon.com, 2019b).

Another example of the hackathon is Hack it Together, with this particular event aimed at talented women in the sphere. Posted in New York City, Hack It Together offers an opportunity for participants to network with banks and companies in the world of fintech. The organizers encourage talented women in technology to form teams and get hacking to create awesome projects that can be presented at the end of the evening.

WhatTheHack is one of Europe's most prominent student hackathons, while SmallBizHack is aimed at the small business community. Really, it was possible to pick dozens of other examples, as the hackathon phrase is growing rapidly, and providing value to banks, fintechs and IT professionals interested in the financial world.

HACKATHON CASE STUDY
DBS Bank

The stiff competition faced by banks from fintech companies and other non-financial companies requires them to reinvent their processes to stay relevant by making the best use of emerging technologies. The global Hackathon launched by DBS is a case of innovation addressing two common challenges: hiring and new product development for problem solving. The bank revolutionized the process of product development without altering the core code[1] for easy integration into the system, by bringing quality talent through a collaborative process. It partnered with universities, fintech start-ups and technology providers to provide the right ecosystem for product creation. It launched technology initiatives to bring banking into the everyday life of its customers, and its largest banking API platform[2] made possible partnerships with government agencies, fintechs, start-ups and its SME customers. Innovative rollouts include the 'POSB Smart Buddy' – the world's first in-school wearable tech savings and payments programme – and the 'Digibank', a mobile-only bank available in India and Indonesia. It also acknowledged the critical role of HR in helping the bank execute its priorities. Several career development programmes were introduced to future-proof its employees across multiple markets, empowering them for technology-powered change.[3] A transparent, competitive and unique hiring process was used. No additional investments were made, and no hiring partnerships were implemented.

The bank began with pioneering global Hackathons to develop innovative cutting-edge services for today's 24/7 connected and digitally savvy customers and to attract developer talent from all over the world to solve banking problems. Partnering with Amazon Web Services (AWS), Capgemini, Microsoft, Quantum Black and Telstra for the technology and cloud services,[4] the thrust was on sharing of expertise, mentorship and global outreach. The participating teams were expected to work on a prototype with given data, with a focus on technology use for better customer experiences and efficiencies. After a successful Hackathon in 2015, DBS has continued the process with the 2019 'Paradigm Shift'.[5]

The DBS global Hackathon is a model for sowing the seeds of next-generation fintech solutions built on the Microsoft platform. This event is an industry first for a bank providing the team, technology and ideation support to revolutionize banking product creation and talent development. The end-to-end collaboration empowering participants to build code on Azure is a unique proposition for building working models with minimal resource allocation. This initiative is also unique because it gives developers an opportunity to create working models for agility in prototyping solutions. The model of using a Hackathon for building products not only future-proofs talent but also lays the foundations of collaboration for fintech development. By sharing real banking data and real-life problems with the participants, the bank ensured the success of the prototypes. The bank's Hack2Hire programmes[6] for recruiting people[7] from the Hackathons is another revolutionary concept in hiring.

Digitization of financial services lies at the core of the banking industry. The joining of forces of a leading bank and collaborative platforms is an example of how the synergy of talent and technology support can help solve real banking problems. The focus on technology with the support of partner companies empowered higher levels of output, to prototype quickly and reduce time to solutions. This laid the foundation for future collaborations in fintech development, leveraging talent, technologies, tools and processes. Developing profitable products and customer satisfaction is the ultimate goal and a driver of success[8] for a bank, as proven in this case. More than 2,000 employees benefited from the Hackathons,[9] with the human-centred design and agile methodology processes ultimately enriching internal talent.

NOTES

1 Bizenius (nd) From regulation to innovation: new product development in banks [online] https://bizenius.com/from-regulation-to-innovation-new-product-development-in-banks/ (archived at https://perma.cc/Y7RM-BLW3)

2 DBS (nd) Reimagining banking, DBS launches world's largest banking API developer platform [online] https://www.dbs.com/newsroom/Reimagining_banking_DBS_launches_worlds_largest_banking_API_developer_platform (archived at https://perma.cc/9DEC-U7TW)

3 Phua, T (2016) Case Study: how DBS trained more than 2,000 employees on innovation, *Human Resources* [online] https://www.humanresourcesonline.net/case-study-dbs-bank-can-fill-26-vacancies-via-internal-transfers/ (archived at https://perma.cc/7PLN-BG8Z)

4 DBS (2019) DBS breaks new ground with global hackathon [online] https://www.dbs.com/newsroom/DBS_breaks_new_ground_with_global_hackathon (archived at https://perma.cc/C49L-ZJR6)

5 DBS (2019) Virtual global hackathon: hack the future of banking [online] https://www.dbs.com/pshift/index.html (archived at https://perma.cc/48VX-XXMR)

6 DBS (2019) DBS Hack2Hire 2019 launches inaugural Hack2Hire-Her to double female technologists intake this year [online] https://www.dbs.com/newsroom/DBS_Hack2Hire_2019_launches_inaugural_Hack2Hire_Her_to_double_female_technologists_intake_this_year (archived at https://perma.cc/4Q5P-H546)

7 CNBC (2019) DBS Bank to hire 100 techies via hackathon [online] https://www.cnbctv18.com/finance/dbs-bank-to-hire-100-techies-via-hackathon-2224611.htm (archived at https://perma.cc/RWA4-WB5B)

8 Khuram, F (2017) 4 challenges faced in new product development, *IQVIS* [online] https://www.iqvis.com/blog/4-challenges-faced-in-new-product-development/ (archived at https://perma.cc/A3B6-69NC)

9 Phua, T (2016) Case Study: How DBS trained more than 2,000 employees on innovation, *Human Resources* [online] https://www.humanresourcesonline.net/case-study-dbs-bank-can-fill-26-vacancies-via-internal-transfers/ (archived at https://perma.cc/7PLN-BG8Z)

Venture capital funding

As collaboration and innovation in the fintech niche advances, venture capitalists have begun to sit up and take notice.

One of the big investors in this area has been Citi Ventures. The New York-based firm has been investing particularly actively in payment companies, with Chain, Betterment, Square, DocuSign, and Trade It all benefiting from venture capital. Citi Ventures continues to invest in start-ups and a pile of new technologies, investigating innovative business models through its Citi Innovation Labs and Citi businesses.

A stated goal of the company is 'to accelerate product roadmaps and expedite commercialization opportunities within Citi' (CitiBank, 2016) meaning that fintechs are very much seen as part of the bank's teacher strategy. Citibank has placed innovation at the centre of its ethos and particularly emphasizes the customer experience in delivering exciting new lending platforms. Aside from fintech, the investment arm continues to pursue opportunities in big data and analytics, commerce and payments, and security and enterprise information technology.

Another major investor has been Santander, through its Santander InnoVentures vehicle. The Spanish bank has enthusiastically embraced the fintech space, offering venture funding capital for a number of start-ups and innovators. For example, in 2017, Santander added Pixoneye, Curve and Gridspace to its expanding line-up of fintech companies, with the three innovators delivering predictive personalization, connected finance technology and conversational intelligence, respectively.

This is indicative of the fact that the venture capital fund set aside by Santander for fintech has been named as the most active bank-backed corporate venture on the planet by CB Insights. Santander InnoVentures has a particular interest in artificial intelligence, with the banking group believing that this will be a key technology in the financial landscape in the years to come. Aside from the companies already mentioned, Santander has already invested in other AI-related start-ups such as Elliptic and Socure. In the six months leading up to the investment in Pixoneye, Curve and Gridspace, the number of fintech investments made by Santander reached 15.

Europe has definitely been a major player in venture capital investment for fintech, with growth of over 120 per cent between 2017 and 2018. This has meant that hackathons such as Startupbootcamp have become increasingly prestigious and high profile, attracting some of the most recognizable and wealthy banks in the world.

Another financial sector powerhouse entering the fintech space in a venture capital capacity is the Swiss financial technology house Avaloq. The company has set up a venture fund with the intention of targeting the fastest-growing fintech businesses and most innovative start-ups. Avaloq Ventures is led by Minho Roth, a former executive at FiveT Capital AG and Baader Bank, who intends to invest heavily in the coming years.

As mentioned previously, digital payment services and online lending platforms have been the foremost recipients of venture capital funding. The ability to deliver user-friendly financial services and products through innovative technology in these spheres is considered particularly valuable. This is accelerating confidence in fintech along with the most prominent financial players, resulting in the surety that global investments in fintech will touch $50 billion in 2020.

And the geographical regions in which this growth is being achieved are quite clear. It is interesting to note that China, Russia, Middle East nations and other emerging economies have been investing heavily in the fintech space. This has particularly driven growth in the United States and the UK, with the UK continually topping the European league for venture capital funding. With its strong links with the financial services industry, and the strength of the City of London, there is no doubt that the UK is already a global leader in this niche.

And British start-up companies were able to attract $7.7 billion from the nearly one-third of the $24 billion raised by all start-ups across the European continent (Henry, 2018). Venture capital investment in the fast-growth businesses in the UK was thus over 2.5 times the level of France and 1.5 times the level seen in Germany. Challenger bank Monzo and peer-to-peer lender Zopa have been among the British success stories in terms of intake of venture capital funding.

Start-up collaboration programmes and private accelerators

There are prominent examples of the trend for start-up collaboration programmes and private accelerators in fintech, as incubation spreads rapidly. For example, Techstars in New York has proved hugely successful, enjoying a tie-in with Barclays. During the time that they have collaborated, Techstars and Barclays boast that they have become two of the most active fintech investors in the world, demonstrating the enthusiasm of established and recognizable names for investing in the fintech sphere.

Techstars is a potent accelerator programme, as it is built on the outstanding track record of the company for working with technology firms. When this is married with the banking expertise and phenomenal distribution and resources of Barclays, there is no surprise it has become one of the most prominent accelerator programmes in the world. Equally, the involvement of Barclays means that standards are very high, with the bank calling for tenacious, resilient and innovative participants. The investment bank actively seeks companies and innovators that are 'pushing the known boundaries' in capital markets, consumer banking, InsurTech, risk management, payments/credit, lending, RegTech, credit solutions, and more besides.

There are dozens of other accelerator programmes for fintechs now being run globally. Again, it is impossible to even touch upon the vast majority of them, but here are some of the more exciting examples.

The FinTech Innovation Lab was co-founded by Accenture and the Partnership Fund for New York City, and runs an annual accelerator programme in New York City, bringing together fledgling fin/entrepreneurs, experienced technology business people, and senior bank executives. A raft of workshops, panel discussions, user-group sessions, networking opportunities and meetings take place before final presentations are made in front of venture capitalist financial industry executives. This is truly a hugely prestigious event, with supporting institutions including Bank of America, Barclays, Citi, Credit Suisse, Deutsche Bank, Goldman Sachs, JPMorgan Chase, Morgan Stanley and Wells Fargo.

Deutsche Bank Innovation Labs also now runs out of New York City, having previously set up accelerator venues in Silicon Valley, Berlin and London. The labs have been set up in order to help the banks evaluate and adopt emerging technologies, fundamentally driven by fear, but fuelled by the desire to innovate quickly enough to have substantial impact on their digital transformation strategy.

The Wells Fargo Start-up Accelerator involves one of America's largest banks, and is hosted on a six-monthly basis in San Francisco. This prestigious accelerator programme brings together entrepreneurs with industry experts, mentors, and other major players, all of which brings back potential customers and venture capitalist investors.

BNY Mellon Innovation Center is a Silicon Valley project that focuses on fintech, cloud computing, big data science, cyber-security, the Internet of Things, mobile and wearable computing. The Silicon Valley Financial Services Cloud is also a collaborator in this accelerator programme, which hosts a variety of networking events for innovative young companies and banks.

Another exciting collaboration initiative is undoubtedly the FinTech Sandbox. This is a non-profit organization from Boston, which has backing from such prestigious organizations as Fidelity Investments, F-Prime Capital, Thomson Reuters, Silicon Valley Bank, Amazon Web Services, EY and Intel. Fintech start-ups gain invaluable access to financial data and resources at this event, with mentorship and introduction to potential clients and investors also a huge pull factor.

London is also a major hub for accelerator programmes, meaning that there is a whole host of interesting events going on in England's capital city. The first of these is FFWD, which was launched by the Accelerator Academy and City University. This incubator is responsible for Ziffy, OneFineMeal and Coffee Munch, and calls itself a pre-accelerator, with a focus on preparing start-ups for their very first funding round. Start-ups focused on technology, marketing and finance are particularly welcome, and FFWD has become a fixture in Shoreditch in recent years.

The Tech City Tub is held in Bethnal Green and is considered one of the most vibrant incubators on the London scene. The Tech City Tub represents a dynamic community of innovators, with a desk-based, heavily subsidized range of professional services available. Another interesting programme is Escape the City, which is focused on helping fintechs and other innovators get their initial ideas off the ground. Escape the City is noted for its particularly high level of innovation and has attracted a wide range of corporate clients.

IncuBus is particularly notable for being held on the top deck of a double-decker London bus! Designed in collaboration with YC and Techstars employees, this programme is already known as the world's best accelerator, helping start-ups track investment, and offering mentorship, workshops and desk space.

And Activate Capital, held in Ealing, offers six weeks of exciting accelerator action. Digital start-ups are welcome to participate in the programme, which has a net value in excess of £30,000. Activate Capital has helped many budding entrepreneurs in the technology and finance spaces to ensure that ideas are developed into investor-ready propositions.

With fintech having achieved real credibility in the contemporary world, it is perhaps only natural that the field is broadening beyond its initial parameters and remit. Parties beyond banks and start-ups are also involved, as the process of developing viable fintechs becomes more involved, layered and complex. This means that regulators, universities, and consulting firms are all investing in their own fintech programmes, while vendors such as IBM are also getting involved. This all adds up to an increasingly vibrant and viable space, into which valuable investment is rapidly pouring.

With this in mind, artificial intelligence has become a hot topic in fintechs over the last year or so, which has probably been helped by its increasingly prominent media presence. The achievements of Google, particularly in building a world-class Go-playing machine in the shape of AlphaZero, have probably helped this process.

This has encouraged some of the biggest names in finance to get involved with the fintech space where it overlaps with AI. Thus, Bank of America has already partnered with HighRadius to launch the Intelligent Receivable System, a new service which utilizes artificial intelligence in order to improve straight-through reconciliation of incoming payments.

While this is a prominent example of artificial intelligence impacting on the fintech space, it is certainly not the only one. Westpac Banking Corp has also been working with a start-up, Hyper Anna, for some time, with the technology produced from this collaboration used to conduct data analytics and visualization. This is certainly one field in which AI will become, if not dominant, undoubtedly extremely prominent in the coming years.

NAB's Digital bank Ubank has created RoboChat with IBM Watson, intended to respond to questions on home loans. And ANZ Banking Group has created biometric voice capabilities with the technology company Nuance, allowing customers to access banking services by talking directly to the software. We are going to see more of this type of innovation in the future, as people become more accustomed to AI playing a role in their lives. The popularity of home speaker systems produced by the likes of Amazon, Google and Apple will only contribute to this process.

For financial institutions, there are a variety of significant benefits of getting involved with some of the pioneers in this field. Bank of America has particularly sought to invest in intake operations that are customer- and operations-focused, to improve customer-centricity and operational efficiency. The likes of BNP Paribas, Credit Suisse and Goldman Sachs have invested heavily in fintechs intended to enhance their trading and portfolio functions, with the overarching aim of improving the level of automation in their businesses. And Wells Fargo and Citibank have looked to the fintechs to assist them with regulatory compliance and supervision issues.

Another interesting area of artificial intelligence that relates to the acquisition niche is chatbots. These have become extremely popular with some of the best-known banks, with several big names investing heavily in the concept. Chatbots can make a massive contribution to customer service, saving both time and money for banks that deal with a huge amount of people.

Axis Bank has already partnered with active intelligence to launch intelligent banking chatbots. American Express is working closely with Facebook to provide an Amex bot for its card members. HDFC Bank already uses a chatbot developed by Niki.ai for its foray into commerce on social media, while Bank of America has finalized its chatbot Erica, which is now available within the bank's mobile banking app.

Other banks and institutions investing in chatbots include DBS, ATB in Canada, Russian-based Tochka Bank, Barclays Africa – the first bank to do so on the continent – and Canadian online lender Thinking Capital. In this latter case, there is again a tie-in with Facebook, with the company having already announced the launch of its 'Lucy' chatbot on the social media platform.

Another major new area where banks are beginning to collaborate significantly with fintech start-ups is blockchain. This is an area that has made banks aware of the significant disruption potential that can happen through the power of decentralization. Despite the hype around cryptocurrency, banks have realized that the true power lies with the underlying blockchain technology, rather than the actual currency being used. Blockchain has supported banks in their ambition to remove archaic processes and systems from the organizations, and have clear, transparent, consent-driven data exchanges. Banks see the power of the cost savings it can offer in the long term. There was also the negative association caused by connecting cryptocurrencies to blockchain (which is really only the infrastructure), creating further fear about bringing in blockchain within banks. However, this changed quickly and currencies such as Ripple have been of particular interest to financial sector participants, offering significant cost and time benefits in cross-border payments.

Companies as diverse and significant as Westpac, ANZ, JPMorgan, ING and Credit Suisse have invested in blockchain technology, with a variety of benefits being derived. Bank guarantees, payments, securities lending, corporate lending, and trading have all been of interest to these major financial industry players, with improvements in operational efficiency, faster settlements, risk reduction and faster dispersal. Aside from the aforementioned Ripple, major corporates have invested in such names as Circle, Axoni, Cobalt, Setl, Chain and r3, as the blockchain niche becomes ever more diversified and credible.

Another area where we will undoubtedly see developments in fintech is open banking, even though monetization has proved hard to deliver correctly. Nonetheless, there are still some interesting companies already involved in this space, such as Token, TrueLayer and Plaid. The latter two of these companies are both offering API tools, while Token is a pure open banking platform on the blockchain.

Meanwhile, Zopa has worked with TrueLayer, an income verification project which removes the need to manually upload documents in order to verify income, instead replacing this process with open banking data. And Plaid has already gained a raft of highly attractive customers, including Chase, Citibank, Simple, Stripe, Capital One, and

Coinbase. Citi Ventures has also invested heavily in the potential of open banking.

Digital Landing is an area that is obviously suitable for fintech collaboration, and it is thus not surprising that banks are already partnering with start-ups in this field. For example, C2FO and Citi have partnered to offer an end-to-end trade finance solution that includes dynamic discounting among a suite of bank-provided payables solutions.

ING-Kabbage is a major banking–fintech partnership, with Kabbage offering SMP loans in partnership with ING, but also involving Santander and Scotiabank. JP Morgan Chase also collaborated with OnDeck, one of the leading providers of online small business lending, although this partnership ended in July 2019. It enabled the company to offer a propriety credit score based on loans granted to small and medium corporates.

Another interesting partnership is the tie-in between TD Bank and nCino. This has enabled the former to digitalize its entire consumer lending process from start to finish. And DBS has also joined forces with peer-to-peer lending sites, Funding Societies and MoolahSense, enabling them to offer better service for businesses. In return, the two leading platforms refer borrowers with good credit to DBS for commercial banking solutions such as cash management.

Banks are also frequently partnering with fintechs now in order to automate their treasury operations. There are several prominent examples of this; a great illustration is the collaboration between Capital One, Bill.com and Gusto. This has enabled the credit provider to simplify cash flow for small businesses and integrate HR into the overall business processes, to ensure that Capital One runs more efficiently.

KeyBank has also partnered with AvidXchange to provide a software-as-a-service solution as part of KeyBank's treasury management platform. This solution replaces paper-based invoicing with digital capabilities. And BBVA has acquired Holvi – an online business banking service. BBVA has been one of the major investors in the fintech industry and has been particularly enthusiastic about Holvi, which is geared towards entrepreneurs. Offering small and medium-sized businesses a sales platform and cashflow tracker, Holvi delivers a one-stop shop for retailers and businesses.

By now, the level of investment collaboration with beta fintech platforms is so prominent that a vast number of major banks are involved on some level. For example, if we look at four of the most successful platforms in this area, we see that a raft of major investment banks has got involved with each of them. So here are the full details:

- Visible Alpha – this B2B platform has managed to partner with Morgan Stanley, Goldman Sachs, Citibank, UBS and HSBC among others.

- Droit – Wells Fargo, Goldman Sachs and DRW have all got involved with Droit.

- Acadia Soft – this B2B platform has been particularly successful in attracting corporate investment, with Morgan Stanley, Citibank, Goldman Sachs, UBS, Bank of America, HSBC and Deutsche Bank all involved.

- Symphony – this is another fintech B2B solution that has attracted some of the biggest names in banking, with Goldman Sachs, JP Morgan, Deutsche Bank, Credit Suisse, Citibank, Bank of America and BNY Mellon all involved.

And banks are getting involved with fintechs thanks to the outstanding customer experience that digital banking collaboration offers them. Mobile-first bank subsidiaries are able to catch niche customers segments, especially young people and millennials. This has led to such companies as Pepper, Digibank and Hello Bank establishing themselves in this space.

Fintechs also offer intelligent financial assistance and no-conversation interfaces, which help to improve customer engagement and enhance channel partnerships. Such companies as K-Assist, finn.ai and TalkBank are actively involved here. Similarly, technology partnerships are frequently being made with white-label modular and API-driven platforms from challenger banks, again helping to improve customer experience. Fidor, Railsbank and solarisBank are all good examples of this phenomenon.

Customer-facing challenge banks' platforms help deliver improved onboarding experiences and enhanced self-server capabilities. Go, Simple and MovenBank are all examples of this type of company. And challenger banks' data-driven personalized products not only frequently deliver better rates than the traditional banking industry, but also help to improve transparency. SoFi and Qapital are further examples of this trend.

COLLABORATION CASE STUDY
Scotiabank–Kabbage

In Canada, small businesses represent 97.9 per cent of employers.[1] In 2014, borrowing activity by Canadian small businesses fell continuously, according to data from PayNet,[2] and more than 80 per cent of Canadian SMBs lacked the credit history or collateral to secure a loan.[3] In Mexico, where SMBs are an important engine of the economy, generating 40 per cent of GDP, small businesses represent more than 90 per cent of business profiles.[4] Only 12 per cent of these were granted loans from financial institutions, and the loan process was lengthy and manual. The loan validation and risk assessment were asymmetrical, and coupled with the banks' tilt towards larger loans, most small business owners were left without loans. At the bankers' end, it was not cost-effective to provide loans to owners of businesses making less than $200,000 annually. The costs of business validation, loan approval and loan scoring were also phenomenal.

The 2016 bank–fintech partnership[5] of Kabbage[6] and Scotiabank[7] is a case of financial innovation in banking deliveries. It serviced a market segment that it hadn't targeted traditionally: the small business customer segment.[8] It was a baby step in financing loans to small business owners without deploying an auxiliary platform or developing a new product. No additional investments were made by the bank, and no new products were designed; Scotiabank used its existing small business owner accounts for the project. It leveraged the seamless customer experience and automated decision making of the Kabbage business model to bring the bank's small business customers under lines of credit. Applications for business loan, payroll loan, lines of credit or merchant cash advances were approved and sanctioned within minutes, which tapped the small business owner segment. The Kabbage platform uses advanced metrics, social media analytics, and FICO's Origination Manager Decision Module for the task of credit scoring.[9] This automated risk assessment was further supplemented with data culled from 30 different data sources, and 50 different models to maximize loan de-risking. The bank used the Kabbage scoring system for dedicated repayment terms.

The platform partnership was an industry first for an international bank based in Canada.[10] It was implemented specifically to launch Kabbage's product of automated loans. Without re-branding it into the bank's product, the scheme was cobranded[11] as 'Scotiabank Fastline for Business'[12] – Scotiabank's first digital product for their small business department.[13] While the bank did not use the Kabbage name in all the branding for its small business lending solutions, it was explicitly mentioned in all press releases that Scotiabank for Business was powered by Kabbage® loan. The bank made adjustments to small business bank profiles to render easy setting up of pre-approval accounts for provision of loans. No product customization was undertaken. As the Fintech platform had licensed its technology to the bank, a suite of APIs integrated directly into the existing backend of Scotiabank, while assimilating on the front end for customer experience. This case is an example of a bank partnering with a fintech start-up instead of building digital solutions from scratch. It used the data and technological support of Kabbage to fuel its future plans for small business lending operations.

Scotiabank had more than 120,000 non-borrowing small business customers in its launch markets in Mexico. They had CA$2 billion in deposits but limited loans. With this automated lending format, the bank was able to phase in its lending programme to SMEs in Canada and Mexico. The partnership led to the bank subsequently rolling out its own dedicated lines of credit to small businesses with Scotia Running Start for business.[14] Kabbage provided the bank with valuable data on businesses seeking capital, and also trained staff to help onboard the platform. With alternative lending seen as a high growth area in recent years, the Scotiabank–Kabbage partnership model brought innovation into small business lending. The joining of forces of a leading bank and a Fintech platform brought together the existing infrastructure of a bank and a digital lending platform for rapid evaluation and sanction of loans.

NOTES

1 Government of Canada (2016) Key small business statistics [online] https://www.ic.gc. ca/eic/site/061.nsf/eng/h_03018.html (archived at https://perma.cc/4NY8-Z5G5)

2 Innovation, Science and Economic Development Canada (2016) Key Small Business
   Statistics, June 2016 [online] https://www.ic.gc.ca/eic/site/061.nsf/425f69a205e4a
   9f48525742e00703d75/0084a61ef063217785257fcb0042d60b/$FILE/
   KSBS-PSRPE_June-Juin_2016_eng.pdf (archived at https://perma.cc/
   5RFU-LFQG)

3 Cision (2016) Scotiabank and Kabbage partner to provide small business customers
   with a new, streamlined digital lending experience [online] https://www.prweb.com/
   releases/2016/06/prweb13505107.htm (archived at https://perma.cc/YZM3-Y7SJ)

4 Scotiabank (nd) News releases [online] https://scotiabank.investorroom.com/index.
   php?s=43&item=53 (archived at https://perma.cc/T8RL-T6SN)

5 Marous, J (2016) How small banks can partner with fintech firms, *Financial Brand*
   [online] https://thefinancialbrand.com/58829/small-community-banking-
   partnership-fintech/ (archived at https://perma.cc/D522-PDDP)

6 https://www.kabbage.com/ (archived at https://perma.cc/Y55S-37LF)

7 https://www.scotiabank.com/global/en/global-site.html (archived at https://perma.
   cc/35HQ-UUVH)

8 https://www.strategyand.pwc.com/media/file/Small_Business_Growth.pdf (archived
   at https://perma.cc/L3B4-S9RR)

9 Jackson, B (2016) How Kabbage knows if it can lend you $100,000 in just seven
   minutes, *itbusiness.ca* [online] https://www.itbusiness.ca/news/how-kabbage-knows-
   if-it-can-lend-you-100000-in-just-seven-minutes/78573 (archived at https://perma.
   cc/A33V-7J5R)

10 Scotiabank (nd) News releases [online] https://scotiabank.investorroom.com/index.
   php?s=43&item=53 (archived at https://perma.cc/T8RL-T6SN)

11 Muhn, J (2016) Kabbage and Scotiabank ink partnership, *Finovate* [online] https://
   finovate.com/kabbage-scotiabank-ink-partnership/ (archived at https://perma.cc/
   DKJ4-N5NG)

12 Scotiabank (nd) Scotiabank Fastline for business Credit Agreement [online] http://
   www.scotiabank.com/eExprienceTC/NPA/EN/LOANTC/tc.pdf (archived at https://
   perma.cc/N6E8-NTT5)

13 Scotiabank Business Centre [online] https://www.scotiabank.com/ca/en/small-
   business.html (archived at https://perma.cc/2TAX-A7TX)

14 Scotiabank Running Start for Business tool [online] https://dmts.scotiabank.com/tools/
   runningstart/Eng/Index.html (archived at https://perma.cc/UC7K-D8HK)

Summary

So it should be clear from this chapter that Fintechs are indeed
becoming part of the mainstream financial architecture. There is an

enthusiasm among the big culprits for this technology, and fintech is definitely something that is here to stay, and that will indeed expand in the years to come. Perhaps the most exciting aspects of the fintech revelation are its diversity and plurality, with the technology now impacting multiple areas of the financial system.

References

Bajkowski, J (2018) ANZ CEO says robots can't replace bankers, *ITNews*, 22 October [online] https://www.itnews.com.au/news/anz-ceo-says-robots-cant-replace-bankers-514312 (archived at https://perma.cc/29RA-PWZP)

Bhakta, P (2018) The UPI bandwagon: banks to partner with fintech start-ups, *India Times*, 1 June [online] https://economictimes.indiatimes.com/small-biz/start-ups/newsbuzz/standing-on-the-shoulders-of-start-ups/articleshow/64410422.cms (archived at https://perma.cc/87DG-273B)

CitiBank (2016) Citi launches innovative analytical tool to help institutions optimize banking connectivity and automate and digitize treasury and shared service center operations [online] https://www.citibank.com/tts/about/press/2016/2016-1107.html (archived at https://perma.cc/3GJH-44QP)

CityAM (2019) London Stock Exchange Group leads $20m Nivaura funding round [online] https://www.cityam.com/london-stock-exchange-group-leads-20m-nivaura-funding-round/ (archived at https://perma.cc/QZG5-R6DU)

CommonBond (2015) Marketplace lending in 2015: from the margins to the mainstream, 7 November [online] https://www.commonbond.co/post/marketplace-lending-in-2015-from-the-margins-to-the-mainstream (archived at https://perma.cc/U93J-NZ2T)

Funding Circle (2015) RBS partners with Funding Circle to support thousands of UK businesses, 22 January [online] https://www.fundingcircle.com/blog/press-release/rbs-partners-funding-circle-support-thousands-uk-businesses/ (archived at https://perma.cc/N4QT-MMHV)

Hackathon.com (2019a) SGEF Digital Factory presents: Defrag the Dinosaur Hackathon 2019 [online] https://www.hackathon.com/event/defrag-the-dinosaur-5c61ac16ad437b001b288324 (archived at https://perma.cc/Q7J9-2KBK)

Hackathon.com (2019b) Hackgrid [online] https://www.hackathon.com/event/hackgrid-5c78254da4bcbd001bded35c (archived at https://perma.cc/F44G-SFB5)

Henry, Z (2018) Research suggests Brexit has had little impact on UK companies, Inc. [online] https://www.inc.com/zoe-henry/forget-brexit-uk-start-up-investment-rises..html (archived at https://perma.cc/6LSM-ZCDX)

JP Morgan Chase & Co (2018) Tips for fintech start-ups on partnering with banks [online] https://www.jpmorganchase.com/corporate/news/stories/acarson-tips-fintech-start-ups.htm (archived at https://perma.cc/N3SV-ETA3)

LendingClub (2019) Banks and LendingClub [online] https://www.lendingclub.com/investing/institutional/banks (archived at https://perma.cc/3GLW-UX4L)

Miller, R (2015) Wall Street-backed symphony wants to revolutionize financial services communication, *TechCrunch* [online] https://techcrunch.com/2015/02/21/wall-street-backed-symphony-wants-to-revolutionize-financial-services-communication/ (archived at https://perma.cc/DT8U-FLR9)

PwC (2017) PwC: 82% of banks, insurers, investment managers plan to increase FinTech partnerships; 88% concerned they'll lose revenue to innovators [online] https://www.pwc.com/bb/en/press-releases/fintech-partnerships.html (archived at https://perma.cc/C93B-N9SE)

World Economic Forum (2018) White paper: collaboration between start-ups and corporates, A practical guide for mutual understanding, 19 January [online] https://www.weforum.org/whitepapers/collaboration-between-start-ups-and-corporates-a-practical-guide-for-mutual-understanding (archived at https://perma.cc/4M2W-K3QX)

05

Emerging markets driving innovation

Emerging markets have always had an advantage with disruptive technologies. With no legacy systems in place in traditional banks in these markets, along with a high adoption of phones and social media, countries in Africa, Asia and Latin America have played host to some of the world's most impressive fintech innovations, and are playing a prominent role in the development of the sector. The consumers in these countries don't need to be trained for using technologies – they have skipped the traditional route to banking and have gone directly to social media-friendly disruptive technologies, being very comfortable with paying friends and borrowing money through basic mobile phone apps or Twitter. They don't need to be retrained away from using credit cards or debit cards; they are converting in an exponential rate from using cash to mobile wallets and app-based banking.

Why are emerging countries so good at fintech?

There are several reasons why countries like Mexico, India, South Korea, Turkey, Kenya and Indonesia are doing so well with innovation compared to some of the more mature banking markets:

- *Lack of legacy banking systems.* The banks in Europe and the United States have been transforming their systems by putting in complex core banking systems and customer management systems since the 1980s, whereas most of the banks in emerging countries started similar transformation initiatives only in the 2000s. Due to the lack of legacy systems and mainframes in place at the time of transformation, the banks in these countries have been able to implement highly innovative, social media-friendly, big data-friendly systems with a superb customer experience across all touchpoints. Fintechs, who came about bang in the middle of this transformation have been able to integrate themselves easily into the decision making around core systems at these banks.

- *Smartphone penetration and internet costs.* Countries like Singapore, South Korea, Taiwan and Malaysia have over 70 per cent penetration of smartphones (Burnmark, 2016) whereas countries like the Philippines, India and Brazil have a low smartphone penetration (under 40 per cent) but a very high mobile phone penetration. This population is tech-savvy, and demanding apps that make their lives easier through the most used device in their communities – the mobile phone. These countries also have a very low cost of accessing mobile-based internet, with India at $0.3 for 1 GB of mobile data and Chile at $1.9 (cable.co.uk, 2019).

- *Poor confidence in banks.* Several of the emerging countries exhibit common characteristics around not having trust in the traditional banking system, either due to an experience of severe economic crisis or to the poor customer service the population has experienced. Countries like Mexico, Malaysia and South Korea have low to moderate mistrust of the banking establishment

- *The level of unbanked.* A large unbanked population indicates high cash usage in the country which, in turn, drives lack of monetary transparency for governments as well as individuals, poor money management options and high potential of theft or loss. Technology has been welcomed in countries like Somalia, Nigeria and Colombia to eliminate cash and to offer superior education and access around money management to the unbanked population.

- *The level of underbanked.* Countries like India and Indonesia have had a fairly well-established traditional banking infrastructure despite the unbanked population, but have failed to adequately service niche groups like SMEs, entrepreneurs and freelancers and the fast-rising middle-class population.

Africa

Africa is not one homogeneous region, but several countries in Africa are showing significant growth in both fintech investments as well as the launch of new start-ups. The growth of fintech in Africa is indicative of the general technological spurt in the continent, including in other sectors like healthtech, edtech and retailtech. Fintech has been particularly successful in this continent in which only 17 per cent of the population have bank accounts. The value of fintech services in this environment is obvious, and in 2017, over 30 per cent of the funding raised by African start-ups was in the fintech sphere. And last year, venture funding increased by 51 per cent, reaching $195 million, according to figures from Disrupt Africa (Letsebe, 2018).

There are many examples of successful fintech start-ups in Africa, and several areas in which companies are achieving economic and user penetration. M-pesa has been one of the most successful companies, with the mobile payment system already boasting 30 million users in 10 countries in this largely unbanked continent. As mobile money has become more established, Africa has established itself as a pioneer in the field, with mobile money now surpassing bank accounts in the region. Sub-Saharan Africa is the only region in the world in which 10 per cent of GDP transactions occur via mobile payment (Sy, 2019).

Not only is fintech having a significant economic impact in Africa, but it can still have a significant influence over the structural development of the continent, in a future in which many countries remain dependent on a relative handful of industrial sectors. This will almost certainly have a considerable impact on the economic potential of Africa.

And the ensuing climate will result in an increasing number of unbanked Africans gaining access to financial products. For example, there are 37 million Kenyans who currently possess a text-capable mobile phone, which vastly exceeds the number of ATMs (Ramadan, 2018). This means that companies offering mobile money and wallet solutions in African countries such as Kenya can really reap the reward of technology in money management. With 525 million smartphones in sub-Saharan Africa expected by 2020 (Ramadan, 2018), these opportunities for innovators and consumers alike are only likely to expand.

With the potential for fintech in Africa becoming increasingly high, there is equally an increasing number of mainstream financial institutions getting involved with fintech. For example, Standard Chartered has already launched its Africa innovation lab, which serves as a platform to collaborate with fintechs in Kenya and the broader African region.

With other labs located in Singapore and Hong Kong, Standard Chartered is continuing to invest strategically in emerging economies. Indeed, Standard Chartered Kenya's Chief Executive Officer, Kariuki Ngari, describe the company as a 'connector bank', indicating that they look to connect 'clients, markets and products with networks and facilitating trade and investment across a global footprint across some of the fastest growing markets' (Standard Chartered, 2019).

Mastercard Engage is another example of a major financial sector player partnering with fintechs in Africa to broaden partnership opportunities in the region. Initially launched in Nairobi and Lagos, Engage is a global partnership and development programme which builds digital payment technology ecosystems, and helps to enhance speed to market. The adoption of this scheme in Africa underlines how seriously the major financial players are taking the development of fintech in the continent.

CASE STUDY
Mobile wallet success story in Africa: M-pesa

Poverty rates in Kenya are among the highest in the developing world; national poverty in 2007 was estimated at 45 per cent.[1] The structure of the economy is agrarian, with a rapidly expanding informal sector and a stagnant manufacturing sector.[2] Inequality in wealth distribution and poverty levels were very high, and the population is largely poor and rural. More than 55 per cent of the people lived below Kenya's poverty line, and 58 per cent lived on less than $2 a day.[3] Most citizens had no bank accounts, and small businesses could not avail themselves of credit or loans. The banking network had not penetrated to rural areas, as banks did not find it feasible to serve the poor segment whose accounts barely held any money. In this scenario, M-pesa's entry with micropayment facilities by way of an integrated account on a mobile device emerged as a solution for the poor and unbanked. Small businesses could use the M-pesa money transfer services and loans through the mobile wallet.

M-pesa, launched in 2007 by Kenyan mobile network operator Safaricom, is a mobile wallet and microfinancing success story from Africa. It serviced market segments that had traditionally been ignored: the unbanked individual and small business. Further, this case study looks at how a mobile banking service that originated in Kenya, expanded its footprint to several other countries, including India,[4] where the mobile wallet landscape was highly competitive. The earliest prototype, developed for small money transfers, was subsequently repositioned with an added value proposition: microfinancing. The pilot launch had a simple mechanism of texting small money transfers between users. A network of agents, airtime resellers and retail outlets served the users, who could deposit money and make payments using PIN-secured text messages. A small fee was charged for sending and withdrawing money. The success of the model resulted in the gradual introduction of new services like international transfers, loans, third-party integration through the API, overdraft facilities and vendor partnerships. The geographical reach widened to Tanzania, South Africa, Mozambique, Lesotho, Egypt, Afghanistan, India and Romania. As of March 2019, there were more than 30 million subscribers.

The M-pesa model of mobile wallet-enabled financial services is distinctive because of its 'social' role in an underdeveloped region like Kenya. It gave financial resilience, which in turn became the engine of long-term poverty reduction, growth and women's empowerment. The expansion of mobile money lifted 2 per cent of households in the country above the poverty line.[5] It targeted the market segment that bankers across the world have always ignored because of the non-viability of serving the poor and rural sectors. The case study is unique because the mobile wallet enabled greater financial inclusion[6] across Kenya and other African countries where it was introduced. Since its rollout in Kenya, daily per capita consumption levels have increased by 6 per cent. Women, who are usually secondary income earners, were empowered by mobile money services; an estimated 185,000 women moved from farming to business occupations and became financially independent.[7] The focus on the bottom of the pyramid transformed the lives of Kenyans and brought into focus the dominance of a traditionally ignored section of society that nevertheless forms the core of economic growth. The M-pesa case study has proved that servicing the bottom of the pyramid can also power commercial viability of fintech operations.[8] M-pesa's annual revenue has registered an 18.2 per cent jump from last year, rising to $889.33 million.

Easy and secure storage of money leads to better financial management and savings, especially among women, and this was proven by M-pesa. Micropayments are at the core of economic growth because they serve the broadest swathe of society and the economy. Digitization of financial services has enabled a positive ecosystem for small businesses and covered every corner of rural Kenya. Underserved individuals, entrepreneurs, and SME business owners have benefited from being incorporated into the formal economy. Reciprocally, banks and governments have benefited from incorporating the underserved into the formal economy. Poor clients and small business owners who lacked access to conventional banking now are part of the formal financial system.

NOTES

1 Kenya National Bureau of Statistics (2007) Basic report on well-being in Kenya [online] http://catalog.ihsn.org/index.php/catalog/1472/download/42105 (archived at https://perma.cc/9V4Z-NRBF)

2 Arndt, C, McKay, A and Tarp, F (2016) Growth and poverty in sub-Saharan Africa, *Oxford Scholarship Online* [online] https://www.oxfordscholarship.com/view/10.1093/acprof:oso/9780198744795.001.0001/acprof-9780198744795-chapter-15 (archived at https://perma.cc/H7SK-4FVD)

3 Library of Congress (2007) Country profile – Kenya [online] https://www.loc.gov/rr/frd/cs/profiles/Kenya.pdf (archived at https://perma.cc/BRZ3-T6ZN)

4 Sen, S (2014) Inclusion by mobile, *Business Today* [online] https://www.businesstoday.in/magazine/case-study/case-study-vodafone-mpesa-mobile-cash-transfer-service-future/story/211926.html (archived at https://perma.cc/MNK4-8T7L)

5 Matheson, R (2016) Study: mobile-money services lift Kenyans out of poverty, *MIT News* [online] http://news.mit.edu/2016/mobile-money-kenyans-out-poverty-1208 (archived at https://perma.cc/2ZGQ-B3H7)

6 Adams, T (2018) Why financial inclusion matters (blog post) *Center for Financial Inclusion* [online] https://www.centerforfinancialinclusion.org/why-financial-inclusion-matters/ (archived at https://perma.cc/E9CE-M5YF)

7 Jack, W and Tavneet, S (2011) Mobile money: the economics of M-pesa [online] http://faculty.georgetown.edu/wgj/papers/Jack_Suri-Economics-of-M-PESA.pdf (archived at https://perma.cc/JU5Y-DH94)

8 Monks, K (2017) M-pesa: Kenya's mobile money success story turns 10, *CNN* [online] https://edition.cnn.com/2017/02/21/africa/mpesa-10th-anniversary/index.html (archived at https://perma.cc/CW2D-UBUY)

Asia

There is even less homogeneity in Asia across countries ranging from Bahrain and UAE to India to Indonesia to China. However, this is another region of the world where the fintech revolution has had a dramatic and enduring impact. Naturally enough, this technology-focused continent is particularly well suited to contributing to the development of fintech, and several countries within Asia have certainly achieved this.

Asia has very much led the way with the adoption of fintech products in payments and e-commerce. The fact that the continent contains the two most populous nations on the planet has had a significant impact on this process, and surveys in China and India have indicated that more than half of adult consumers with internet connections regularly use fintech services, making it a mature fintech market of over 1 billion users, just between these two countries. With over 80 per cent of Chinese respondents indicating that they have used mobile money transfer and payments systems, this is a region in which such consumer-focused fintech can achieve massive market penetration. But there is also diversity inherent in the Asia fintech experience, with around half of both Chinese and Indian consumers indicating that they have accessed a fintech insurance product.

Funding for fintech start-ups continued to climb rapidly throughout 2018, with both private equity and strategic investors interested in the sector. $12 billion was invested in venture capital-backed fintechs in that year, and over one-third of this was directed to companies based in Asia. Meanwhile, six fintech unicorns – venture capital-backed private companies with valuations of at least $1 billion – were based in Asia, namely China's Tuandaiwang, Tongdun Technology, 51Xinyongka, and Lu.com, and India's Policybazaar and Paytm.

CASE STUDY

Mobile wallet success story in Asia: Paytm

The internet user base in India in 2010, prior to the launch of Paytm, was 51 million active users, with a reach of 10 per cent and one in every four internet users having mobile access.[1] The number of smartphones crossed 8.5 million in 2010. The e-commerce trend was taking off as internet usage and market penetration increased, and the emergence of m-commerce was a foregone conclusion. Paytm leveraged the increasing mobile phone usage for facilitating prepaid phone recharges. It tapped the wide subscriber network by adding value-added services for enhancing the ease of living quotient. The payment wallet extended to an online payment gateway and digital wallet. In the aftermath of the demonetization exercise by the Indian government in 2016, it became the go-to payment system for every service, from phone bills and utilities to m-commerce.

Paytm is an e-commerce payment system and digital wallet success story from India. It services a highly cash-based economy and a market segment that was traditionally uncovered: small payments users. This case study looks at how a mobile payments service, which started out as an e-payment platform, expanded to include a range of merchant services, mobile recharges, utility bill payments, travel and entertainment bookings, as well as in-store payments at partner institutions. The earliest prototype, developed for a mobile recharge platform, was subsequently repositioned as a mobile wallet with multiple services using both the mobile app and the QR code. Paytm began with mobile recharge and gradually upscaled to include DTH, bill payments, bus tickets, e-commerce, payment gateway, deals and coupons. Customers could make credit and debit card payments and bank transfers via the Paytm app. The 'Paytm for Business' app in 10 regional Indian languages allowed local merchant partners to track payments and make daily settlements. Merchants accepted Paytm, UPI and card payments directly into their bank accounts at 0 per cent charge. As of May 2019, the merchant base is 12 million partner merchants:[2] 60 per cent of the market share.[3] With more than 100 million app downloads today, the Paytm model's success story is down to a constantly evolving service offering. It expanded its user base amongst individuals, small businesses, merchants, utilities and even travel and entertainment platforms. The mobile banking space was extended to small investment schemes: Paytm Gold Savings Plan and Gold Gifting. The Payments Bank brought banking and financial services access to half a billion unserved and underserved Indians. Online payments come with no maintenance charge but a commission on each transaction. The Paytm Mall app further allowed consumers access to a Paytm-certified marketplace.

The Paytm model of payments disintermediation has helped its fast-paced diversification into a wide range of payment and wallet services. Its focus on providing an easy mobile-based alternative to cash transactions made it a trusted payment platform. By paying even educational fees, utility bills and taxes, the model powered ease of living. As it was convenient, safe and secure to use on mobile applications for both consumers and marketers,[4] it became an engine of transformation in the Indian economy. The unified dashboard[5] API makes every transaction seamless, instant and cashless. This case study is unique as the revenue is not sourced from users, but from interests received from escrow accounts, advertisements, subscriptions and sales commission from sellers.[6] It has proved that strong partnerships with a wide consumer base can increase the user base without the need for advertising campaigns. The company's partnerships with Indian Railways, cab aggregators, and travel and entertainment companies have become a role model for digital wallets.

The mobile platform's high trust rating and range of services including banking facilities have made it a pervasive platform for mobile, e-wallet and commerce across India. It is not only revolutionizing the payments space but also complementing the Indian government's push for a 'Digital India' and a cashless economy.[7] The case study has proved that bringing digital payments mainstream can increase financial inclusion and battle the menace of black money.

NOTES

1 India Microfinance (2010) India online landscape 2010 – internet usage statistics for India [online] https://indiamicrofinance.com/india-online-landscape-2010-internet-usage-statistics-india.html (archived at https://perma.cc/7MGC-KTCM)

2 Economic Times (2019) Paytm dominates UPI merchant payment segment with 60% share [online] https://economictimes.indiatimes.com/small-biz/start-ups/newsbuzz/paytm-dominates-upi-merchant-payment-segment-with-60-share/articleshow/69724483.cms?from=mdr (archived at https://perma.cc/SF85-A95U)

3 Livemint (2019) Paytm dominates UPI merchant payment segment with 60% share [online] https://www.livemint.com/companies/start-ups/paytm-dominates-upi-merchant-payment-segment-with-60-share-1560160951172.html (archived at https://perma.cc/NJ3G-QNBF)

4 NazimSha, S and Rajeswari, M (2018) A study on Paytm services in promoting cashless economy after demonetization in India and an outline on its support towards making India digital, *International Journal of Pure and Applied Mathematics* **119** (7) [online] https://www.researchgate.net/publication/324994017_A_Study_On_Paytm_Services_In_Promoting_Cashless_Economy_After_Demonetization_In_

IndiaAnd_An_Outline_On_Its_Support_Towards_MakingIndia_Digital (archived at https://perma.cc/DR5Z-GRLJ)

5 Delhi School of Internet Marketing (2015) Case study: Paytm, journey from mobile recharge to e-commerce market [online] https://dsim.in/blog/2015/05/08/case-study-paytm-journey-from-mobile-recharge-to-e-commerce-market/ (archived at https://perma.cc/7E5P-6HEN)

6 Sharma, H (2017) Pay through mobile: a case study on Paytm, *Academia.eu* [online] https://www.academia.edu/32150913/_PAY_THROUGH_MOBILE_A_CASE_STUDY_ON_PAYTM (archived at https://perma.cc/6J88-ARAZ)

7 NazimSha and Rajeswari (2018)

The move towards a cashless economy has been swifter in Asia than in other continents, perhaps due to the cultural willingness of the continent's citizens to embrace innovation. Figures in China indicate that cash transfers are declining rapidly, with third-party payment systems and digital transactions resulting in an almost rapidly evolving cashless society. Mobile is key in this process, with the estimated level of mobile transactions in China expected to nearly triple from 120 trillion yuan ($17.4 billion) in 2017 to 354 trillion yuan by 2020.

Already there is a fintech aristocracy emerging in China, with the niche dominated by three big providers. Ant Financial's Alipay, Tencent Holding Ltd's Tenpay, and ChinaPay had established a market share of 66 per cent by the end of 2017, while investment in other Asian locations is also increasing. For example, investments in fintechs in Hong Kong reached $546 million last year, a dramatic rise from $216 million just two years ago (Moroccan Trader, 2018).

All of the evidence points to Asia being a vital region in the development of fintech, and China is unquestionably a major player in this. Four of the very largest fintech industry unicorns hail from the world's most populous nation, with the aforementioned Alibaba being the largest fintech unicorn in the world, with a total valuation of over $150 billion.

India is also moving towards cashless quite rapidly, particularly since the government adopted its demonetization strategy at the end of 2016. This is also being reflected in the number of people in China and India that utilize fintech regularly, with a 2017 survey discovering that 69 per cent of the Chinese population and 52 per cent of the Indian population have used some form of fintech technology or product (Govind, 2018).

While fintech is undoubtedly becoming a major competitor for banks in the UK, US and Europe, this is far more true for Asia. Tech giants are, in fact, powerful competitors for the big banks in Asia. Having entered the financial markets through payment platforms, fintechs are leveraging big data, which establishes the basis for expansion to a wide variety of financial areas. And there are specific aspects of the social and political climate in Asia that will lend themselves to the technology basis of fintech.

In particular, the increasing prominence of social credit scoring will have an impact on the way that financial transactions are dealt with in Asia. Major fintech players have been established as government partners in the growing social credit system, and although this is undoubtedly a controversial aspect of the Chinese society, it is one that is likely to become more ingrained in the future. This trend is extending to other territories as well, with Singapore-based start-up Lenddo currently providing social credit scores to over 50 leading institutions in more than 20 countries.

Meanwhile, there is a general appetite, on the part of both financial institutions and consumers, to improve security, and this is being achieved via facial recognition and fingerprint technology. Facial recognition has already been installed in bank cash machines in China since 2015, and is now being tested across several aspects of Chinese society, with everything from making retail purchases to boarding flights in airports being involved.

In India, fingerprints and iris scanners have already replaced ID cards, with 1.17 billion Indians having registered in the government-based identity database, known as Aadhaar (Hays, 2017). Despite its own set of privacy concerns around Aadhaar and security concerns around its implementation, it has tremendous power to change the lives of billions of people who have access to financial services and utilities thanks to this identity programme.

Another major factor in the growth of fintech innovation in Asia is that the technology has had such a rapidly transformative impact that major banks are relying on open collaboration in order to survive. Traditional financial sector players understood this extremely quickly in Asia, and it is already leading to an extensive scope of collaboration. Thus, all of the five biggest banks in China have already allied with fintechs and other technology innovators, building lasting partnerships. One such example is the work of Tencent with the Bank of China. The two financial sector giants are building a new cloud platform that will provide internet banking and funding solutions for customers of the retail bank.

Fintech in Asia also has the huge advantage of having an existing digitally native, highly skilled workforce on the continent. The Asia-Pacific region, in particular, is fortunate enough to possess a huge amount of technology graduates, who are ideally suited to understand and embrace the financial disruption that fintech is causing. It seems almost inevitable that fintech will continue to expand across the region, as more and more young people embrace innovation, from both consumer and employment perspectives.

One Asian country that doesn't get mentioned quite as much as some of the others in terms of fintech adoption, is Japan. This is partly because the culture of adoption in this nation is slightly more cautious than in India and China, perhaps since consumers have a high expectation of technology due to the almost intrinsic relationship that Japan has with this aspect of contemporary society. However, fintech is beginning to break through in Japan, even if the total investment in the country pales next to China. Nonetheless, in 2018, the value of the investment in fintech increased five-fold, exceeding $500 million (Accenture, 2019). Tokyo-based mobile payment provider Origami is one example of a fintech start-up that is driving innovation and growth in Japan, and the experienced financial players in the country are beginning to collaborate with fintech newcomers.

There is no doubt that Asia is driving fintech worldwide, with financing in the region having more than doubled over the last two years alone. Asia is responsible for approximately 43 per cent of global fintech investment, while, as mentioned previously, six of the seven largest fintech companies are based in Asia. It seems evident that this technology-focused continent will continue to play a massive and influential role in the growth of this innovative and significant technology.

Latin America

Several countries in Latin America, along with Mexico, have been quick to embrace innovation in lending, payments and digital banking. Fintech activity in Latin America has already spread to 18 countries, and this has been another part of the world that has enthusiastically embraced the potential of disintermediating technology.

During 2018, 1,066 fintech ventures were identified in the Latin American region, which represented a staggering increase of 66 per cent in just 12 months, according to the report Fintech en América Latina 2018: Crecimiento y Consolidación (Fintech in Latin America 2018: Growth and Consolidation), published by the Inter-American Development Bank and Finnovista (Finnovista, 2018).

And this fintech trend has reached a later period of maturation than would perhaps be expected. The same report noted that nearly two out of every three fintech ventures were already at advanced stages of development, indicating that the pace of growth in the region has indeed been rapid.

As would be expected, the Latin American economic powerhouse of Brazil has dominated the fintech field, with 380 start-ups in total, but other countries have racked up impressive numbers as well. Mexico with 273, Colombia with 148, Argentina with 116, and Chile with 84 are following hot on the heels of Brazil, as fintech expands in the region.

And there is no more palpable manifestation of this expansion process than the fact that many Latin American fintech providers are already looking beyond the region. One in three Latin American fintech companies has already expanded their operations beyond the borders of their home country, with initiatives identifiable in every country in Latin America.

Indeed, Juan Antonio Ketterer, Division Chief of the Connectivity, Markets and Finance Division of the IDB, noted that 'there is also a growing trend toward internationalization [in Latin America]. This shows the opportunities that entrepreneurs are seeing but also the importance of strengthening dialogue and harmonization at the regional level' (IADB, 2019).

As has been prevalent in fintech across the planet, payments and remittances have played a significant role in the development of technology in Latin America. Of the initiatives identified in the region, 24 per cent have been focused on this sector, with lending also being a major part of the fintech sphere. But digital banks have also sprung up in Latin America, with a sudden boom in credit scoring, identity and fraud protection becoming apparent.

With fintech becoming part of the financial scene in Latin America, venture capital has begun to sit up and take notice. Record levels of investment have poured into Latin American fintechs in recent months, as the market shows convincing signs of maturity. Further indications of the maturity of the fintech marketplace in Latin America come from close examination of major international investors in the market, and the first governments in the region adopting specific regulatory frameworks.

Interestingly, it has also been noted that women are particularly active in the fintech space in Latin America. Research indicates that 35 per cent of fintech companies in the region were either founded or co-founded by women, which is massively above the global average, estimated to be around 7 per cent (Ammachchi, 2019). It seems that these particular fintech companies also target segments of the population that are treated poorly by, or outright excluded from, the traditional financial sector, meaning that the development of fintech in Latin America shares characteristics with the unbanked population of Africa.

The financial system of Latin America has often stood apart from other regions, but fintech is helping to change this impression, promoting much more internationalism and reducing isolationism. This isolationist aspect of the financial landscape of Latin America has often been attributed to the challenging and complex nature of the region. But thanks to fintech, venture capital start-ups and even traditional banks are beginning to understand the incredible growth opportunities available in the region. This has led to estimates that the fintech market in Latin America will be worth $150 billion in just two years.

While the level of unbanked citizens in Latin America is still quite high, it nonetheless remains an area of change as addressed by governments. It is estimated that around 45 per cent of the entire Latin American population is currently unbanked, while only 113 million people of a total regional population of 625 million now have access to credit cards (Patschiki, 2019a). Even those who do carry credit cards are often denied international access, with their existing products only appropriate for domestic use.

Clearly, this lack of access to consumer credit means that it is difficult for the Latin American population to participate in the global economy, and even in some instances travel with confidence. This is where fintech has helped people in the region hugely, as it begins the process of penetrating this significant unbanked population.

This means that neobanks, which enable users to create mobile digital accounts, are ideally suited to the culture of Latin America. Thus, this innovative concept has already begun to penetrate the likes of Brazil, Mexico, Chile and Argentina. Considering the logistical difficulties that governments face in Latin America, several governments have already made attempts to reduce the level of banking sector regulations in an effort to ensure that fintech can thrive in the Latin American continent. A report published in 2018 found that 85 per cent of banks in the region are already considering fintech as potential partners, with another 6 per cent expressing interest in acquiring fintech competitors (Patschiki, 2019b).

Clearly, the penetration of fintech services in Latin America is already having a major impact on the mainstream financial architecture. Furthermore, the process of acquisition has already begun, with one of Colombia's largest national banks having acquired a Colombian neobank in 2018. This partnership now allows the users of the fintech service to withdraw cash from their account at the bank's branches and cash machine (ATM) locations.

In short, the reach of fintech is such that it has already created a sizeable footprint in Latin America. And this is just one of many locations in which this fintech influence can be expected to grow in the years to come.

Fintech hubs and interesting start-ups

As fintech emerges as a significant aspect of the financial system in emerging economies, a variety of interesting and illustrative case studies have also emerged. The following case studies show us that fintech has some specifically regional influences and features, but is truly global in nature in terms of innovation.

Mumbai

Incred has made massive leaps and bounds in India with its intelligent web-based financial services platform. Having launched just a few years ago in April 2016, this technology platform provides personal, consumer, home and education loans, while also lending a significant amount of funds to SMEs, making excellent connections in the business realm as a consequence.

At the heart of the Incred operation is technology and data science, which is utilized to ensure that lending can take place in a much smaller timeframe than has typically been the case with traditional banks. This level of convenience resonates with customers, as Incred has become hugely popular in Mumbai, as well as attracting a vast amount of equity funding. Indeed, the latest funding round associated with the company has increased its total equity capital to over $13 billion; certainly not a figure to be sniffed at.

Singapore

Singapore is another region particularly associated with technological innovation, and it is this climate which has led to huge success stories such as BetterTradeOff. This company, founded in Singapore, has delivered a fascinating and innovative life-planning solution, which the company refers to as Aardviser.

Aardviser uses a platform called BetterTradeOff to offer digital financial advice to financial institutions. BetterTradeOff users benefit from statistical models and sophisticated artificial intelligence, ensuring that customers of the company can make better decisions when attempting to plan their financial future. BetterTradeOff is able to provide flexible and modular advice, which captures the financial situation of a client and then digitizes the process of data capture, which has traditionally been associated with financial advisors.

Not only does this reduce the amount of time that is required for a financial health check to merely minutes, but also results in more sophisticated decision making. BetterTradeOff is able to adjust the financial plans of clients via investment products dynamically and do so in virtually real time. This highly impressive system has established itself as a significant part of the financial planning architecture of Singapore, and we're sure to see similar solutions delivered in other parts of the world as well.

Another advantage of such fintech innovations is that they can deliver outstanding results when partnered with experienced humans. It has been noted in several fields that the combination of machine learning and human intuition can achieve exceptional results, and conventional financial advisors are increasingly partnering with BetterTradeOff to deliver the ultimate in fiscal planning.

Hong Kong

Blue Fire AI has been one of the big fintech innovators in Hong Kong, enabling businesses to achieve transformation through sophisticated machine learning-based algorithms. This capital market intelligence engine can map information via advanced algorithms, allowing the system to rapidly understand profitable human behaviours, which then directly impact on asset performance.

This highly sophisticated technology already covers over 75,000 securities, and increasingly understands the impact on the future cash flows of underlying assets. Dealing with equities, rates and credit, the system has established itself as the first on the planet to algorithmically map information that is based in Mandarin to capital markets.

The other key thing to understand about Blue Fire AI is that it can continue to become ever more accurate in its predictions over time, thanks to its machine learning abilities. AI has the ability to deal with shifting market conditions and use data for trend predictions much better than current technological capabilities in banks, and thus is a useful tool for digital advisory.

Having already received prestigious awards in Hong Kong, Blue Fire AI is a pioneer in the artificial intelligence field and another demonstration of the power of fintech in developing markets.

Beijing – Baidu

We have already seen in this chapter that China is undoubtedly a global leader in the fintech sphere. And Beijing has, naturally enough, been a major part of this success story, meaning that initiatives such as Baidu have gained traction.

Baidu delivers integrated financial services, including consumer finance, financial management, e-wallet payment, internet banking and insurance. The company is taking a particularly strategic approach to the development of fintech and is thus able to deliver identification, big data risk control, smart investment consulting, and intelligent customer service products, alongside financial cloud services and blockchain.

This is another company that is embracing the AI revolution in the financial industry and attempting to promote the concept of inclusive finance in a nation in which some segments of the population can be ostracized. Baidu is making waves in China, and can already be considered part of the mainstream financial picture in the world's most populous nation.

Sao Paulo – Geru

Geru employs well over 100 people in this vibrant Brazilian city and has established itself as one of the major fintech players in a country that is undoubtedly embracing this transformative technology. Geru has been able to establish itself in the financial system in Brazil by providing loans at rates which are extremely competitive compared to those offered by traditional banks.

This start-up has also created a diverse company culture and has tapped into the prominence of female interest in fintech in Latin America by employing a majority of women in its major management positions. Geru is proving itself to be a thoroughly modern business and one that appeals to consumers across a range of demographics in Brazil.

Cape Town – Yoco and JUMO

Cape Town in South Africa is one of the best examples of a city located in a leading emerging economy that has embraced fintech, as the city has particularly sought to establish itself in the technology sphere. With this in mind, it is worth looking at two particular fintech start-ups that are changing the way that people in the country think about financial services.

Yoco has specialized in delivering mobile card processing machines, and these have already appeared in countries all over the world. The company has been listed in the top 250 fintech firms on the planet, which prompted CEO Katlego Maphai to muse on the global mindset of the business, and its plans 'to build and deliver something world-class to small business in Africa and beyond' (Global Ethical Banking, 2019).

Elsewhere, JUMO is another fintech that has made a huge splash across the African continent, by providing businesses in emerging markets with the potential to facilitate digital financial services such as credit and savings. JUMO allows customers in emerging markets to obtain financial services that they would otherwise struggle to access, meaning that financial products are becoming more available to some of Africa's disadvantaged people.

JUMO is addressing a theme that continues to be rather prevalent in both the developing world and emerging economies, but one for which fintech is forming a prominent part of the solution.

There has also been a huge amount of innovation in the fintech space in emerging economies. So in this section of the chapter, we will examine some case studies of companies that are particularly pushing the envelope in developing markets.

Kenya – BitPesa

BitPesa is one such company, headquartered in Kenya, which provides a cryptocurrency trading platform, enabling the conversion of digital currencies such as Bitcoin, Ethereum and Ripple into more traditional African currencies. This makes it easier for both consumers and businesses to receive and send payments both to and from sub-Saharan Africa.

The company has also made it easier for such transactions to take place by reducing the cost of remittance fees. With offices also established in London and Lagos, BitPesa is being widely adopted by people and businesses in the region and would seem to have an incredibly bright future.

Hong Kong – WeLab

WeLab is a Hong Kong start-up that was founded in 2013, and which became the first peer-to-peer lending platform in the country. WeLab enables users to borrow money as personal loans from other individuals while delivering lower interest rates than traditional banks. WeLab makes this process as easy as possible, with an online application form and relatively short assessment process being the only barriers to accessing credit.

One of the fascinating initiatives implemented by WeLab is Wolaidai, a mobile peer-to-peer lending platform for top-tier university students in China. With the founder of WeLab, Simon Loong, having experience in the commercial banking industry at Citibank and Standard Chartered, this fintech solution draws on experts in the traditional financial system, while taking on some of its biggest proponents. We will undoubtedly see more of this in the years to come.

India – ToneTag

ToneTag is a brilliant piece of software development that has allowed mobile payment solutions to initiate in-store purchases, using either sound or NFC (near-field communication). Unlike such systems as

Apple Pay, ToneTag can work on any smartphone or mobile device, making it a flexible solution for all consumers. ToneTag is quite possibly the most all-encompassing mobile payment system in the world and has already partnered with 14 financial sector operators across a diverse range of companies.

It seems that this innovative mobile payment system is here to stay, particularly in a climate in which mobile payment systems will undoubtedly continue to grow in popularity.

Hong Kong – 8 Securities

8 Securities is one of the most successful fintech companies in Asia, as well as being hugely innovative and pioneering. 8 Securities has already established itself as the leading mobile trading and investment platform on the Asian continent. It has achieved this by launching the very first robo-investing service in the shape of 8 Now, which enables consumers from all over the world to access a sophisticated global investment portfolio.

With the company already holding over $800 million in assets, 8 Securities is already a massively successful business and is expected to grow in the years to come as robo-advising becomes a more significant and accepted part of the trading environment.

Kenya – Kopo Kopo

Kopo Kopo is another solution that is already making a big impact in Kenya. This web-based mobile payment gateway enables owners of small and medium-sized enterprises to accept mobile payments through a variety of electronic methods. The company has also partnered with other major fintech players in the region, such as M-Pesa, to open up its offering.

This Kenyan fintech generates several million dollars in transactions every month, while the business has also launched innovative additional services. One of these, branded as GROW, enables customers to take cash advances, with borrowers paying a mere 1 per cent interest-free to the company. Kopo Kopo has partnered with mobile money service providers to expand this service and roll out merchant payments.

With big business already engaged with Kopo Kopo, it seems that this Kenyan fintech will continue to make big strides with its innovative approach to mobile payment and credit.

Indonesia – Crowdo

Crowdo is a company headquartered in Singapore, Malaysia and its native Indonesia, which has conducted some particularly interesting operations in the crowdfunding sphere. Crowdo offers a portfolio of crowdfunding solutions, including equity crowdfunding and peer-to-peer lending.

Having been established in 2012, Crowdo has grown to become the largest platform on a membership basis of its type, with a massive community that now exceeds 25,000 members. Crowdo has helped to launch crowdfunding campaigns across five continents, facilitating financial support from over 50 countries around the world. With a management team with huge experience in both the finance and technology spaces, it seems the Crowdo will continue to grow and innovate in the crowdfunding niche.

The Philippines – Lenddo

We mentioned Lenddo earlier in the chapter, and this is a business which has branched out rapidly in a relatively short space of time, having established offices in the Philippines, Colombia, New York and India. The reason for this is quite simple – Lenddo developed an innovative algorithm that can determine the creditworthiness of a consumer based on their social media presence. This is undoubtedly an ideal way for fintech to attract the millennial generation while providing young people with access to credit that may not otherwise be available.

In addition to its basic credit service, Lenddo also enables employers to validate employee and applicant information rapidly. Lenddo has considered its market carefully and has thus optimized its services to emerging markets, within which additional credit scores and collateral frameworks often do not exist.

With Lenddo having earned its stripes and proved is worth, banks, card issuers, telcos, and peer-to-peer lenders have begun to sit up and pay attention, with several third parties now partnering with Lenddo. This business is another example of the way that machine learning and artificial intelligence can revolutionize the fintech space enabling start-up companies to do incredible things and reach broader markets.

Latvia – ZoomCharts

The Latvian company ZoomCharts is doing something particularly interesting with big data, having developed visualization software which accompanies this interesting aspect of contemporary society. ZoomCharts is a highly interactive and responsive software package, which enables users to drill down into vast swathes of information, identifying the absolutely necessary data. This is proving highly useful for a wide range of corporates, with ZoomCharts having already established partnerships with companies in numerous nations.

India – IndiaLends

Finally, IndiaLends is an online marketplace that connects consumers and SMEs looking for low-rate loans with investors seeking good returns. The reciprocal connections that IndiaLends have set up have resulted in excellent working relationships, with the company already dealing with over 10,000 loan requests every month. Having partnered with 10 financial institutions, and established offices in Mumbai, Bengaluru and Delhi, this start-up is helping to change the financial climate in India.

IndiaLends has particularly innovated in this sphere by using a combination of analytics and judgemental oversights to screen potential borrowers. This creates a premium list of loan products, which is continually updated, as IndiaLends is another fintech company utilizing a range of big data, deep analytics, and machine learning algorithms. This helps borrowers secure better loans, and lenders to make more informed credit risk decisions.

Not only has IndiaLends proved successful, but mainstream providers will increasingly adopt its whole approach to the field of lending and credit. And over time, fintech innovators that resemble IndiaLends will indeed become mainstream providers, offering a template that appeals to a wide range of borrowers.

Summary

Developing countries are playing a central role in the development of fintech, even if they weren't necessarily the pioneers and the first ones developing some of the technologies. Social, political, economic and cultural factors are combining to ensure that the Asian region, in particular, has embraced fintech at a pace that exceeds Western nations; the spirit of innovation has truly gripped some of these emerging economies. As the future of fintech looks increasingly bright, it is clear that start-ups in emerging economies will play a key role in developing the direction of the industry.

References

Accenture (2019) Global fintech investments surged in 2018 with investments in China taking the lead, Accenture analysis finds; UK gains sharply despite Brexit doubts, 25 February [online] https://newsroom.accenture.com/news/global-fintech-investments-surged-in-2018-with-investments-in-china-taking-the-lead-accenture-analysis-finds-uk-gains-sharply-despite-brexit-doubts.htm (archived at https://perma.cc/WH7X-HCW8)

Ammachchi, N (2019) LatAm fintech market is buzzing with start-ups, *Near Shore Americas*, 23 January [online] https://www.nearshoreamericas.com/latam-fintech-market-buzzing-start-ups/ (archived at https://perma.cc/M3GN-Y85Y)

Burnmark (2016) Challenger Banking Report [online] https://www.burnmark.com/research/7 (archived at https://perma.cc/MWF7-8TNT)

cable.co.uk (2019) Worldwide mobile data pricing: The cost of 1GB of mobile data in 230 countries [online] https://www.cable.co.uk/mobiles/worldwide-data-pricing/ (archived at https://perma.cc/MJ43-82LY)

Finnovista (2018) The Inter-American Development Bank (IDB) and Finnovista release the second edition of the greatest report on Fintech innovations in Latin America, 11 June [online] https://www.finnovista.com/informe-fintech-2018/?lang=en (archived at https://perma.cc/KRA6-MNTP)

Global Ethical Banking (2019) Fintech 250 Report: Cape Town-based start-ups JUMO and Yoco made the list, 10 November [online] https://www.globalethicalbanking.com/fintech-250-report-cape-town-based-start-ups-jumo-yoco-made-list/ (archived at https://perma.cc/VA9E-BQBW)

Govind, D (2018) How fintech firms are disrupting the ecosystem, *Livemint*, 20 July [online] https://www.livemint.com/Industry/qUvIjAew6YcIWqnQsM1pNI/How-fintech-firms-are-disrupting-the-ecosystem.html (archived at https://perma.cc/8K47-HV76)

Hays, P (2017) India's Aadhaar programme and the future of biometrics, *Global Risk Insights*, 10 October [online] https://globalriskinsights.com/2017/10/aadhaar-future-biometric-databases/ (archived at https://perma.cc/KQE8-W62R)

IADB (2019) Fintech activity in Latin America spreads to 18 countries, 17 January [online] https://www.iadb.org/en/news/fintech-activity-latin-america-spreads-18-countries (archived at https://perma.cc/W76Y-3QW6)

Letsebe, K (2018) African start-ups bag $195m in funding for 2017, *ITWeb*, 22 January [online] https://www.itweb.co.za/content/kYbe9MX6aAJvAWpG (archived at https://perma.cc/UL78-GG2W)

Moroccan Trader (2018) HK a thriving cultural hub, 29 September [online] https://moroccantrader.wordpress.com/2018/09/ (archived at https://perma.cc/4CXH-GC2U)

Patschiki, A (2019a) Fintech is transforming Latin America's financial sector. Here's how, *Brinknews*, 12 February [online] https://www.brinknews.com/fintech-is-transforming-latin-americas-financial-sector-heres-how/ (archived at https://perma.cc/V6ZC-JQ76)

Patschiki, A (2019b) Why fintech start-ups are rapidly becoming unicorns in Latin America, *Payments Journal*, 29 March [online] https://www.paymentsjournal.com/fintech-start-ups-unicorns-latin-america/ (archived at https://perma.cc/S9UH-JT5H)

Ramadan, A (2018) The unbanked in Africa could be one of the biggest opportunities in fintech history, *Plug and Play* [online] https://www.plugandplaytechcenter.com/resources/hottest-african-payments-start-ups-fintech/ (archived at https://perma.cc/QG26-X7GL)

Standard Chartered (2019) We've launched our Africa eXellerator innovation hub in Kenya, 8 April [online] https://www.sc.com/en/media/press-release/weve-launched-our-africa-exellerator-innovation-hub-in-kenya/ (archived at https://perma.cc/7MQK-RESD)

Sy, A (2019) Fintech in sub-Saharan Africa: a potential game changer, *IMF Blog*, 14 February [online] https://blogs.imf.org/2019/02/14/fintech-in-sub-saharan-africa-a-potential-game-changer/ (archived at https://perma.cc/J42S-648F)

06

Governments and fintech hubs

One of the most interesting trends I have noted in fintech is the ability of governments and supervisors to influence the movement of fintech in their country. It is almost counter-intuitive to say this – that a government is capable of driving or destroying levels of innovation which have pretty much come about as a contra-authoritarian disruptive voice. Most of the fintechs who fought against traditional infrastructure and policies in their country (be it the UK or Nigeria) are now warmly embracing the potential of working closely together with them to achieve scale, spread the impact of innovation and, simply, ensure survival.

Governments, on the other hand, have also been keen to promote fintech. India, Finland and Turkey have embraced fintech start-ups to support them with payment disruption in their cashless journeys. The supervisors in countries like the UK and Singapore have set up separate teams to foster innovation through fintechs. Most countries have established fintech hubs in their most innovative cities, ensuring the hubs have access to skills, resources and capital.

In the early days of fintech, certain geographical areas and fintech hubs (Silicon Valley in the United States and Old Street in the UK) saw the biggest spread of fintechs. However, this is changing quickly and the geographical spread of fintech throughout the world is now quite complete.

India is indeed one of the best case studies of how central and state governments have supported the rapid rise of fintech through multiple fintech hubs. MEDICI figures (2018) indicate that 1,216 new fintech companies were founded in India in just the five years from 2010 to 2015. And the success of India in this period is underlined by the fact that 454 of the start-ups were founded in India during 2015, while, by comparison, just 364 were founded in the United States during the same calendar year. These hubs did not spring up just in the largest cities of India like Mumbai and Bengaluru; they are spread across tier 2 and tier 3 cities now, with each of the 28 states driving their own individual innovation programmes. Fifteen per cent of fintech start-ups are today based in tier 2 and tier 3 cities in India whose populations range from 6 million to 2 million per city. The small beach-side city of Trivandrum, where I was born, is now a massive AI hub and hosts the global R&D centres for Nissan, United Nations tech innovation lab, Airbus and Finastra.

As fintech has developed in India, payment, lending and invest-ment platforms have steadily developed to support the smaller start-ups. Successful start-ups include FTCash for small cash-based merchants, ProfitBooks, offering simplified billing and payments software, FineTrain, which delivers small business credit enabling, and Shiksha Financial, lending to low-income students. Kyash is another success story, focusing on payment point network and lowest cost payment gateway. The company delivers a fully automated and secure system, enabling merchants to collect cash in digital payments via such sources as Pay2vpa, Pay2Account, and KyashCode. The payment networks now offer a set of national standards across India, meshing with the existing business, and making the collection of payments secure and straightforward. The government of Maharashtra and the administration of Andhra Pradesh have also both been involved in intriguing strategies to build innovative ecosys-tems for fintech at Fintech Valley Vizag. Both particularly emphasize the importance of adopting an ecosystem approach to creating an environment for innovation and sustainable business.

Israeli fintech hubs have been hugely successful, with 500 compa-nies emerging in the Middle Eastern nation, and funding at an estimated $600 million. Payments have become the largest market segment in the country, with Payoneer achieving huge success in cross-border payments, CreditPlace excelling in peer-to-peer investments, and Fundbox making waves in small business cash-flow management. Meanwhile, a raft of fintech hubs has also emerged in Israel, including the Israeli Bitcoin Embassy, which promotes the use, development and regulation of the blockchain. Barclay's community space Rise Tel Aviv has also partnered with fintech start-ups, while The Floor is aimed at connecting the Israeli fintech industry with Asian markets. B-Hive Tel Aviv also emerged in 2017, connecting Israeli and Belgian fintechs.

Australia is also increasingly becoming a hive of fintech activity, with investment rapidly escalating from $53 million in 2012 to over $675 million in 2016 (Nathani, 2018). There are now nearly 600 fintech companies operating in Australia, while fintech hubs such as the Victorian initiative the Goods Shed North in Docklands are being used to bring together start-ups, investors, corporates and researchers (Kumar, 2018). Stone & Chalk is a major fintech hub with presences in Sydney and Melbourne, and works closely with the supervisors, ASIC, on regulatory sandboxes and with other countries in Asia for pan-Asian collaboration.

As fintech continues to grow around the globe, other areas that have attracted a large number of important hubs include Singapore, Hong Kong, Berlin, Luxembourg, New York and Austin. There are multiple cities in China that are strong fintech hubs, including Beijing, Shanghai, Hangzhou and Chengdu. However, in a further validation of how governments and regulations have the power to break or make fintech, the funding levels in China for fintechs have plunged from $70 million in Q2 2018 to $29 million in Q1 2019 due to tighter controls on lending regulation in the country (CBInsights, 2019).

What makes a good fintech hub?

There are a variety of elements that go into making the ideal environment for a fintech hub, but we at Burnmark (2018) have identified five particularly important factors. The first of these is the policy environment, with three separate factors contributing to this overall ecosystem. The regulatory environment must be suitable for fintechs to develop, and this means explicit support for such initiatives as sandboxes, help desks, funding assistance and licensing.

One of these elements, funding access, is key, with policies and initiatives that assist in tech start-ups being particularly important. Recruiting the best talent is also vital, and among the best ways to achieve this is to allow tax benefits for fintech start-ups and entrepreneurs. A fertile economic environment can enable fintechs to germinate rapidly.

The second plank of an ideal environment for fintechs involves growth capital, enabling innovative companies to gain access to their financial requirements. This can be broken into two separate segments, with the first being access to risk capital from angel investors, HNIs and government. Secondly, it is vital to ferment a culture of innovation, enabling fintechs to gain access to growth capital from VCs and technology ventures alike.

The third key area in the development of fintech hubs is investing in future skilled human capital. We have seen all over the world that fintechs will burgeon if the talent is nurtured and allowed to develop. This means that it is vital to enable fintechs to gain access to local talent from academic institutions, technology firms, and financial sector players. Domestic labour may not be satisfactory to meet all of the needs of an innovator in the fintech sector and it is therefore vital for the company to have the ability to obtain visas for talented individuals from overseas. Another aspect of human capital is ensuring that talented people are appropriately rewarded for what they are doing. This will then enable fintechs to hire experts from global banks, BigTechs, Fortune 500 firms etc; this knowledge and expertise are critical in enabling fintechs to grow. Finally, in terms of human capital, it is vital to understand retail demand and pay heed to macro factors such as internet and smartphone penetration, retail banking generation, and retail savviness.

The fourth important aspect required for fintechs to grow and fintech hubs to develop is sustained market development, and this particularly requires demand from the SME sector. Understanding and responding to SME segment size, growth rates within the industry, and delivering per demand for financial products and services, will all be vitally important. Equally, this then needs to be balanced with the demands of established financial institutions. Responding to the size of the banking segment can help with delivering appropriate legacy infrastructure, and understanding and reacting to trends in collaboration will have an impact on the effectiveness of fintech hubs.

Finally, the environment that is created for fintechs to operate in will be of absolutely critical importance. Accelerators and other supportive innovation programmes must emerge that are independent of government, and which enable talented people to innovate. Bank-sponsored accelerators have been particularly successful, while the frequency and quality of the fintech events available will have a massive impact on the success of the emerging technology within a particular nation.

Market access should also be seen as critically important, as the global connectedness of fintech hubs will be paramount in the success or otherwise of a nation's approach to the sphere. If start-ups can gain access to foreign markets rapidly and without obstruction, they are simply far more likely to be successful. Unicorns have also been shown to be necessary within various countries that have experienced fintech success stories, with pioneers in the field offering both established knowledge bases and pools of talent, while also providing expertise in networking for other start-ups.

Successful fintech hubs

Perhaps the two most prominent examples of successful fintech hubs are London and Singapore, with the two innovative locations rocketing to the forefront of this booming industry. Both of these regions have been investing heavily in further research to identify the best practices for the fintech industry.

A joint report from the Institute of Chartered Accountants in England and Wales (ICAEW) and the Institute of Singapore Chartered Accountants discovered that the five elements needed for a region to foster fintech success are markets, talent, capital, progressive regulation and strong government support; very much in line with the Burnmark findings. The research discovered that both London and

Singapore have been able to exhibit all of these characteristics, while also benefiting from 'mature and successful financial services sectors' (McCance, 2018; ICAEW, 2018).

The regulatory environments in the two locations have also been helpful and supportive, and increasingly this is recognized as a defining factor in whether or not a fintech hub becomes successful. The strength of a tech hub is directly related to the ability of organizations within the sector to access talent, capital and demand, as well as the effectiveness of progressive policies and regulations, ultimately designed to enable fintechs to prosper. Governments that have oiled the wheels of growth have benefited from strong fintech hubs that have enabled the fintech revolution to develop, while those that have obstructed it have, almost without exception, caused difficulties.

If all parties of the ecosystem do not work smoothly it can cause huge complications for smaller start-ups as well. The long and complicated journey that fintechs face through the licensing process can be sometimes very difficult without the overt support of the regulator. Many start-ups have little understanding of the process involved, especially in countries without regulatory sandboxes, nor often the protracted timeframes that can result from legal applications for financial services. Considering and having security licences approved within suitable timeframes can be a crucial factor in achieving market readiness. Security and privacy around customer and employee data, especially in light of new regulations like the GDPR, are also important for start-ups to consider and cater to the laws of every single one of the countries and states they operate in.

Fintech market players have also experienced problems with raising capital, compliance and even failing to protect intellectual property adequately. Indeed, obtaining global patent protection for fintech can be extremely complex, yet this process is also often overlooked by companies wishing to establish themselves as quickly as possible. Although copyright protection covers areas such as computer code and audio-visual features, patents are required to protect core innovation. And this has been a murky area, with the likes of the Supreme Court ruling against companies on the grounds of their particular patents being abstract ideas.

How are governments supporting fintech?

With fintechs and fintechs hubs cropping up all over the world, the support of governments has become increasingly important. While creating an appropriate legislative environment has undoubtedly been hugely challenging, it is encouraging to witness governments beginning to assist fintechs, instead of getting in their way.

For example, the UK Government's first Fintech Sector Strategy was published recently (GOV.UK, 2018), and the highlights of this programme included a Cryptoassets Taskforce, advances in RegTech and a UK–Australia start-ups support programme. Then-Chancellor Philip Hammond suggested that the programme will make a major contribution to the British economy in the foreseeable future. The Cryptoassets Taskforce consists of HM Treasury, the Bank of England, and the Financial Conduct Authority, and this trifecta of powerful influences will continually scrutinize issues related to digital currencies while seeking to harness the benefit of the underlying blockchain technology.

While the United States has arguably been a little slower to get on board with the fintech revolution, the 2018–19 federal budget did set aside $138 million for open banking, digital identity programmes, blockchain and the fintech sector (Yun, 2019). With the United States containing several financial sector behemoths, support for fintech has been a little slower than in some other comparable economies, and thus the United States government has been a little reticent to reveal details around legislative support, at least in open documents. But it does seem that there is now at least the will to help fintechs and enable innovators in this arena to reach their potential.

Elsewhere, in the Middle East, the government of Bahrain has become one of the major innovators in the fintech sphere. The Bahraini government has already implemented a number of initiatives intended to help the country become a major fintech hub. With this in mind, the central bank of the kingdom has launched a dedicated fintech and innovation unit, which includes a regulatory sandbox. Supporting this initiative has been the announcement of a national cloud-first policy in Bahrain, which provides the foundation for an ambitious national digital strategy. The Bahraini government has also established the Bahrain Fintech Bay, which bills itself as a one-stop shop for fintech companies. Other countries in the Middle East are now following this lead, but Bahrain has undoubtedly been something of a pioneer.

I previously mentioned Singapore as being one of the most significant territories in the fintech revolution, and it is perhaps not surprising then that the Singaporean government has made every effort to support fintech development, including in immigration policy. In particular, a private–public partnership between the EDB and the Singapore-based FinTech Consortium has helped provide a physical co-working space for local fintech companies, aided and abetted by corporate incubation and other initiatives.

And the continent of Oceania has also seen fintech hubs emerge, as all geographical regions embrace this coming technology. The two major cities in Australia, Sydney and Melbourne, have both made significant efforts to become active in the area of fintech. The State Government of Victoria has called for 'experienced innovation hub operators' to help the administration establish a fintech hub in Melbourne, with talks ongoing with operators to initiate this as soon as possible (Business Insider, 2018). This hub will aim to connect businesses with investors to strengthen the fintech ecosystem in Melbourne.

Eastern Europe has also seen its fair share of fintech players and hubs sprout up, and the Estonian government has been one of the early supporters of these initiatives. The government in Estonia has supported the fintech ecosystem, enabling it to gain momentum, via such efforts as the e-Estonia Initiative. This is a public-sector movement to help citizens to interact with the state through the use of automated solutions. E-services created under the initiative include i-Voting, e-Tax Board, e-Business, e-Banking, e-Ticket, e-School, and University via the internet. However, perhaps the best-known example of fintech innovation in Estonia is the e-Residency programme, which helped Estonia become the first country in the world to offer electronic residency for non-natives in 2014. This programme enables non-residents to apply for smart ID cards, providing access to the various electronic services that have been established in Estonia. Finnish online-only business bank Holvi has already announced a partnership with this programme, helping provide digital business banking for e-residents. The Estonian government has also created Start-ups Estonia, which is intended to support the local start-up ecosystem. It provides training programmes for start-ups, concentrates on educating local investors, helps to attract overseas investment, and delivers a raft of other benefits. This programme has been financed with €7 million of funding from the European Regional Development Fund.

Regulator–fintech collaboration and support

Regulators have been very forthcoming to offer support and collaboration for fintech as the field has developed and matured. Regulators in some of the most successful fintech markets, such as the UK, Australia and Taiwan, have recognized the need for larger and longer sandboxes from an early date. But others have been slower to move, with the Securities and Exchange Commission (SEC) in the United States warning against the dangers of potentially cosy relationships between regulators and non-bank lenders such as fintechs. Consequently, the regulatory and legislative environment varies quite considerably from one country to another, but there are still several regulators with a collaborative attitude towards and policies around fintech.

In particular, the International Organization of Securities Commissions (IOSCO) is playing a growing role in fintech regulation, with the European Securities Regulator, the SEC, and the China Securities Regulation Commission also prominent. There is an increasingly coordinated effort between such bodies as it becomes clear that the fintech environment will pose international challenges. Following an IOSCO Report in 2018, regulators agreed to create the Fintech Network to facilitate the sharing of information, knowledge, and experiences. Joint regulation and fintech frameworks should be forthcoming, and a more unified international community and environment will steadily come into focus. Global regulators are expected to promote the constructive use of fintech to internationalize regulation and compliance, for example, in the blockchain sphere.

Other regulators have also demonstrated their willingness to collaborate with fintechs, among them the Autorité des Marchés Financiers (AMF) in France. This organization established itself as a game changer by setting up an entire department dedicated entirely to putting fintech regulatory foundations in place. It has also demonstrated an outward-looking perspective by entering into joint agreements with overseas organizations, such as Japan's Financial Services Agency (FSA). The AMF has made an effort to communicate directly with the French business community, advancing the cause of fintechs, and has both supported and attended the Paris FinTech Forum, a location at which hundreds of chief executives and industry experts have congregated in recent years. And in 2016, the IMF joined forces with the Autorité de Contrôle Prudentiel et de Résolution (ACPR) to launch a consultation body. This new organization enables heads of fintech firms and industry experts to garner a clearer picture of the regulatory and supervisory challenges of financial innovation.

Other countries that have also benefited from collaboration between regulators and fintechs include Sweden, where the government has focused on implementing fairness and equality in the financial sector as much as is practically possible. Already many international regulators are looking to Sweden as an example, with the regulatory framework in the country considered to be mature and all-encompassing.

The US Office of the Comptroller of the Currency has also moved to accept national charter applications from fintech companies, while the Saudi Arabian Monetary Authority has announced the start of a sandbox regulatory environment for local and international financial technology firms to test new digital solutions. Frameworks by the Australian Prudential Regulation Authority are also viewed as a model for regulators in the region.

Attempts to engage with fintech and encourage innovation are emerging rapidly. A report by the credit card firm American Express noted in 2018 that there were already over 30 agreements between regulators and fintechs, in countries including the United States, UK, Australia, Singapore, Hong Kong and Canada.

There are also attempts underway to create a global sandbox environment, although regulators and experts warn that this will be a highly complex process. Christopher Woolard, the Financial Conduct Authority Executive Director of Strategy and Competition, noted that 'establishing a global sandbox is an immense undertaking and we have to be realistic about the task at hand' (Law360, 2018). The fast-moving nature of fintech means that establishing such standards and moving with the industry will be a difficult logistical task, even for experienced regulators and industry experts.

Regulatory frameworks

Regulatory sandboxes are probably the most common initiative delivered by regulators around the fintech space and have aided fintech development in many cases. Sandboxes particularly help regulators to observe and understand the boundaries of appropriate fintech solutions. They have been a way to encourage and support innovation in the fintech industry, making data and banking/regulatory APIs readily available for those fintechs that are interested; in most cases, this has been those interested in being actively regulated.

It should be noted, though, that RegTech (regulatory technology) has not been a particularly popular entrant to the sandbox environment, as RegTechs usually need to work directly with banks, rather than through the regulatory channels. Nonetheless, there have been some successful examples, such as Tradle, a DLT (distributed ledger technology)-based identity firm. There were further entrants into the 2017 FCA programme, one of the earliest focused on regulatory start-ups, like the Swiss artificial intelligence firm nViso and facial recognition payments start-up Saffe (Lee, 2017).

Indeed, Burnmark research (2018b) indicates that regulatory sandboxes are more popular with regulators in Asia than anywhere else on the planet – and by some distance as well. Asia is responsible for 80 per cent of the regulatory sandboxes launched by regulators in the last few years. This research also unearthed the fact that a relatively small number of RegTech firms are currently in regulatory sandboxes – only 15 per cent currently. Sandboxes instead primarily provide an environment for fintechs and regulated entities that operate outside of RegTech.

However, regulators across the globe are upbeat about RegTechs, with a wide variety of regulators having invested energy in the concept. Some of the regulatory agencies working with RegTechs to help advance the space are as follows:

· United States: The Office of the Comptroller of the Currency, the Securities and Exchange Commission, and LabCFTC.

· United Kingdom: Financial Conduct Authority.

· Australia: Australian Securities and Investments Commission.

· European Union: European Securities and Markets Authority.

· Germany: Federal Financial Supervisory Authority.

· Hong Kong: Securities and Futures Commission.

· Singapore: Monetary Authority of Singapore.

· Lithuania: Bank of Lithuania.

· Bahrain: Central Bank of Bahrain.

REGULATORY SANDBOX CASE STUDY
Monetary Authority of Singapore (MAS)

Growing prosperity in the ASEAN region, increased flow of funds from advanced countries, liberalized financial markets, and sophisticated offshore banking created the foundations for Singapore as Asia's financial centre and a global financial hub.[1] With a well-developed infrastructure, a highly skilled workforce and a strategic location, Singapore saw the emergence of high-tech start-ups in the fintech sector. However, 2016 saw an almost 50 per cent slide in global fintech investment from the previous year, with Singapore seeing one of the steepest drops, from US $605M to US $186M.[2] Despite Singapore being an established centre of innovation, the impact of venture capital funding was barely perceived. Singapore had crafted the vision of a 'Smart Nation'[3] in 2014, in which the Singapore Smart Financial Centre was created as part of the Smart

Nation roadmap for pervasive use of technology in the financial industry. The MAS introduction of the Regulatory Sandbox in 2016 was a follow-up to create a safe, regulated ecosystem for fintech maturity and to nurture fintech experimentation and innovation for financial inclusion. It facilitated financial institutions (FIs) as well as small non-financial players to experiment with innovative financial products within a well-defined space and duration. The Regulator guidelines provided a platform for rapid evaluation of projects in partnership with FIs. The ultimate direction was a safe and conducive space for experimentation with fintech. It enabled wider adoption of success stories, in Singapore and abroad.

MAS implemented various initiatives that worked in cohesion to advance the fintech industry. The Regulatory Sandbox[4] approach provided a favourable environment for fintech experiments and innovations to take root. The Fintech Innovation Lab[5] was created to support collaboration between MAS, financial institutions, innovators and technologists.[6] A Fintech Innovation Village[7] was rolled out as a dedicated physical working space for start-ups. Data from the MAS Monthly Statistical Bulletin was made available as APIs for ease of working. Regulations for venture capital funds were reviewed to incentivize investments, and an amount of US $160 million was set aside for the Sandbox.

The model is a leading example of a successful Sandbox approach by a Regulator. Fintech was leveraged as the instrument of transformation for financial inclusion,[8] job creation and ease of living. The Sandbox was the driver to open up opportunities for trailblazers and improve the lives of Singaporeans. It also created opportunities for corporates to explore and experiment with new-fangled business models and presented opportunities for successful fintech innovation by being at the intersection of start-ups, FIs and regulatory bodies. What further makes it unique is that, instead of a standalone Sandbox approach, MAS used several parallel initiatives that gave traction to Singapore's plans of becoming the fintech hub in Asia.

The MAS case study proves that Regulatory Sandboxes have the potential to benefit customers, fintech start-ups and Regulators as well as investors. The Sandbox aligned compliance and regulation with a rapid spur in fintech innovation. Different players like banks, private equity and venture capital funds were attracted to secure investment. Earlier innovations were often stifled and opportunities lost because investors were prone to exercise caution. As MAS did not compromise on key requirements like customer security or anti-money laundering, the investment landscape became regulated. Regulatory certainty in turn consolidated investor interest. Being a Regulator-driven Sandbox model, it inspired investor confidence in an innovator's ability to be compliant while developing disruptive products and services.[9] Fintech companies could work with MAS while testing their products in a live market. Customer interest was protected, as products were tested in a controlled environment before commercial implementation.

NOTES

1 Yew, L K (2017) Singapore's Transformation into a Global Financial, National University of Singapore [online] Hubhttps://lkyspp.nus.edu.sg/docs/default-source/case-studies/entry-1516-singapores_transformation_into_a_global_financial_hub.pdf?sfvrsn=a8c9960b_2

2 KPMG (2017) Global fintech investment sees sharp decline in 2016 despite record VC funding: KPMG Q4'16 Pulse of Fintech Report (press release) [online] https://assets.kpmg/content/dam/kpmg/sg/pdf/2017/02/global-fintech-investment-sees-sharp-decline-in-2016-despite-record-vc-funding.PDF (archived at https://perma.cc/K2EL-Y5M7)

3 Liang, F S and Pan, G (2016) Singapore's vision of a smart nation, *Asian Management Insights*, **3** (1), pp 76–82 [online] https://cmp.smu.edu.sg/sites/cmp.smu.edu.sg/files/pdf/12.AMI_Issue5_SmartNation.pdf (archived at https://perma.cc/YU4Z-LGLW)

4 MAS (2016) MAS Proposes a 'Regulatory Sandbox' for fintech experiments [online] https://www.mas.gov.sg/news/media-releases/2016/mas-proposes-a-regulatory-sandbox-for-fintech-experiments (archived at https://perma.cc/6JM4-67XE)

5 MAS (2016) MAS establishes FinTech Innovation Lab [online] http://www.mas.gov.sg/News-and-Publications/Media-Releases/2016/MAS-establishes-FinTech-Innovation-Lab.aspx

6 Tan, R (2017) Singapore's 'disrupt yourself first' strategy for fintech innovation, *Innovation is Everywhere* [online] https://www.innovationiseverywhere.com/singapore-fintech-innovation/ (archived at https://perma.cc/P5WS-X7LS)

7 Lattice80.com (nd) https://www.lattice80.com/ (archived at https://perma.cc/YTB6-XSDC)

8 Demirgüç-Kunt, A, Klapper, L and Singer, D (2017) What do we know about the link between financial inclusion and inclusive growth? *World Banks Blogs* [online] https://blogs.worldbank.org/allaboutfinance/what-do-we-know-about-link-between-financial-inclusion-and-inclusive-growth (archived at https://perma.cc/SPM8-ST5R)

9 Finextra (2018) The role of regulatory sandboxes in fintech innovation [online] https://www.finextra.com/blogposting/15759/the-role-of-Regulatory-Sandboxes-in-fintech-innovation

SupTech

Another key aspect of the regulatory environment is SupTech, or supervisory technology, where regulators collaborate directly with RegTech start-ups for market monitoring solutions. Innovators are also supplementing this process. For example, Vizor has developed a technology that enables financial regulators to automatically monitor financial institutions to determine whether they are meeting regulatory requirements. Vizor serves several central banks, as well as regulators in England, Canada, Ireland, Saudi Arabia and more than a dozen other countries.

Regulators and supervisors are choosing to work with start-ups directly for a host of different reasons. In the second phase of RegTech, regulators, especially in those regions with prominent fintech hubs, will become significant users of RegTech themselves. This differs from the first phase, during which direct involvement with RegTechs was minimal, except via accelerator programmes.

This will benefit regulators by helping them to keep up with supervisory challenges. SupTech will be a major part of this process, enabling regulators to take a data-driven approach to the supervisory process, and shift from a retrospective to a forward-thinking approach. SupTech deployed by regulators will also allow them to take more information-driven approaches to supervision, and potentially facilitate the shift from retrospective reviews to more forward-looking supervisory procedures.

Government as a catalyst to collaboration

The government can also be a catalyst to collaboration in fintech, and the Aadhaar Stack in India (sometimes simply referred to as the India Stack) is one example of this process. The Aaadhaar Stack has been a significant government initiative to create a unified software platform that will bring India's population into the digital age. 'India Stack is a set of APIs that allows governments, businesses, start-ups and developers to utilize a unique digital infrastructure to solve

India's hard problems towards presence-less, paperless, and cashless service delivery', its website notes (IndiaStack, 2016).

The Indian government intends for Aadhaar to serve as a foundation of the digital economy, with the platform providing a range of digital services for citizens. There has been controversy, though, over the storage of biometric data in the system, and this is something that would need to be treated far more sensitively in western countries in particular.

Essential skills development

As we have noted in this chapter, one of the defining characteristics of the fintech space is its rapid evolution. This is pretty much inevitable for any industry as tech driven as fintechs undoubtedly are. What this means is that people working within the fintech space will need to 'future skill' themselves. Future skill sets of human capital in the fintech centre will define the niche going forward, and the depth of talent that is skilled enough to work on emerging technologies is a key enabler of any fintech hub.

The delivery of most fintech solutions involves future technologies such as artificial intelligence and blockchain. These, of course, require specific knowledge and expertise of technology, so this needs to be recruited adequately if initiatives in this area are to be successful. There are also other challenges related to assembling this knowledge base. The lean team size required by most fintechs, along with the limited pool of trainers and managers, not to mention funds, means that it is vital to hire, train, and retain the right talent; future skilled human capital will likely be the difference between success and failure.

Burnmark research (2018a) indicates that technology-focused employees and coders form the core of fintech start-ups, with 87 per cent of founders identifying employees focused on technology development as being critical to their overall workforce. Within the fintech space, 32 per cent of total employees are coders, with this number as high as 67 per cent in idea and pre-revenue-stage start-ups.

However, the currently available talent pool may be rich in technology graduates, but there is a real gulf of knowledge in terms of future tech skills. Countries such as India have extremely rich and strong talent pools in the STEM field, boasting 2.4 million graduates, including 1.5 million engineering graduates, and 300,000 Masters of Technology. This creates a huge prospective employee pool for fintech start-ups and helps to explain why India has already made a significant impression in this field.

But other countries aren't so lucky. Many fintechs feel that there is a significant gap in the technical expertise required by them. When Burnmark surveyed fintechs, 71 per cent of respondents stated that the lack of deep technology expertise is a key impediment to their growth, and this figure rises to 81 per cent for B2B fintechs. This finding has been further substantiated by fintechs working in the blockchain sector, with many acknowledging that the availability of coders is particularly low. This has necessitated fintechs working in this field to recruit from areas with strong skill bases in this sphere, such as Russia, Poland and Silicon Valley.

Another recruitment issue for fintechs is that skilled tech talent retention presents a major challenge for those companies that are non-funded and bootstrapped. There is unquestionably a limited technology talent pool, and this means that hiring and retaining available talent will be key going forward. Respondents to the Burnmark survey highlighted this as a particular challenge, especially for pre-Series A start-ups. Sixty-three per cent of pre-series A and 83 per cent of pre-revenue fintechs consider the retention of skilled technology talent to be a major area of concern.

This means that education will be key for the fintech revolution. Lawrence Wintermeyer, the Principal of advisory business Capstone, noted that 'incentivizing STEM education, knowledge and research for the next generation will be key to an equipped and adaptable workforce in the future.' Wintermeyer went on to discuss the sort of skills that will be key in the fintech industry in particular, and the tech/finance space in general (YesFintech, 2018):

It is important that STEM education also adapts to the changing needs of the industry. Financial technology and new age technology have very different requirements compared to traditional industry, with proficiency in data analytics, new-age coding and database management skills like blockchain coding and Python database management gaining importance. Hence it is important to include these in STEM courses as well as create R&D labs to hone these skills. There is also a clear need for fintech organizations to liaise better with academia. Also, education in STEM, financial literacy, innovation and design should begin in early school.

It is also interesting to note that mature companies continue to rely on referrals for recruitment in the space. Major players in the fintech industry are increasingly taking advantage of digital channels, but most are still relying on references to a great extent. Ninety per cent of the respondents to the Burnmark study were hired through referrals from other fintech firms or co-founders, meaning that talent recruitment is still very much reliant on communication among fintechs.

This means that networking and matchmaking events and initiatives have retained particular importance in the industry. Nonetheless, methods of hiring are also maturing, with 77 per cent of successful start-ups and 83 per cent of those with Series A funding stating that online channels such as job portals and LinkedIn have become the preferred source of hiring. The industry continues to evolve, so this trend will become more prevalent.

Funding also remains a major issue. Burnmark (2018a) discovered that 71 per cent of pre-revenue and 81 per cent of idea stage fintechs had reported severe difficulties in raising funds. This problem escalates further still when seeking proof-of-concept funding. Interestingly, the educational background and experience of fintech founders appear to have some influence over the funding process, with 84 per cent of start-ups founded by postgraduates able to raise funds relatively easily; this also applied to 85 per cent of founders with over 15 years of experience. What this implies is that new fintech entrants and start-ups will find the funding process more obstructive, which must change if new ideas and innovation are to be supported.

The extent of the financial struggle for some fintechs is underlined by the fact that 74 per cent of start-ups have a burn rate between $10,000 and $50,000 annually, while only 7 per cent of these companies are profitable (Economic Times, 2018). Funds are increasingly being made available, as administrators all over the world recognize the importance and transformative potential of fintech. But respondents to Burnmark research and industry experts alike note that the process and criteria for acquiring funds can be ambiguous. Several governments have established funds intended for direct investment into fintech statements, yet disbursement remains relatively low, perhaps partly due to the complexity of the sector.

Summary

Fintech hubs are now popping up all over the world, in every continent and across diverse geographical locations. The fintech sector is beginning to mature, and both government and regulators are starting to recognize the legitimacy of this industry. However, fintechs continue to face many challenges, particularly those that are start-ups. There are still regulatory and funding obstacles that need to be hurdled and steadily removed, while fintechs will also face increasing educational and recruitment demands in the near future.

It should also be noted that while regulators have attempted to assist fintechs, the complex and rapidly evolving nature of the industry means that they face challenges as well, and collaboration between fintechs and the authorities shouldn't be viewed as a one-way process, with regulators also needing assistance from fintechs.

References

Burnmark (2018a) The Indian Fintech Report [online] https://www.burnmark.com/research/4 (archived at https://perma.cc/QC9S-DMYN)

Burnmark (2018b) RegTech Report [online] https://www.burnmark.com/research (archived at https://perma.cc/AS2W-CQ7T)

Business Insider (2018) The two Australian cities that have built global reputations as fintech hubs, 29 August [online] https://www.businessinsider.com.au/fintech-snapshot-australia-2-2018-8 (archived at https://perma.cc/T98T-U78J)

CBInsights (2019) Global Fintech Report Q2 2019 [online] https://www.cbinsights.com/research/report/fintech-trends-q2-2019/ (archived at https://perma.cc/X4EA-FNRN)

Economic Times (2018) Managing burn rate a worry for fintech start-ups, 12 March [online] https://economictimes.indiatimes.com/small-biz/start-ups/newsbuzz/managing-burn-rate-a-worry-for-fintech-start-ups/articleshow/63264615.cms (archived at https://perma.cc/NY65-2S7N)

GOV.UK (2018) Fintech Sector Strategy launched at International Fintech Conference [online] https://www.gov.uk/government/news/fintech-sector-strategy-launched-at-international-fintech-conference (archived at https://perma.cc/7EK7-AUQQ)

ICAEW (2018) ICAEW: Fintech innovation: perspectives from Singapore and London [online] https://www.icaew.com/technical/technology/technology-and-the-profession/fintech-innovation-perspectives-from-singapore-and-london (archived at https://perma.cc/Q79W-9D2K)

IndiaStack (2009) What is IndiaStack? [online] https://indiastack.org/about/ (archived at https://perma.cc/J9XE-WHGH)

Kumar, S (2018) Increasing financial inclusion in Australia through fintech, *Borgen Project*, 20 November [online] https://borgenproject.org/increasing-financial-inclusion-in-australia-through-fintech/ (archived at https://perma.cc/CR54-7UMU)

Law360 (2018) Regulators teaming up on global fintech sandbox, FCA says, 19 March [online] https://www.law360.com/articles/1023530/regulators-teaming-up-on-global-fintech-sandbox-fca-says (archived at https://perma.cc/LP5T-8WUZ)

Lee, J (2017) Selfie payments firm accepted into FCA's 'regulatory sandbox', *Biometric Update* [online] https://www.biometricupdate.com/201706/selfie-payments-firm-accepted-into-fcas-regulatory-sandbox (archived at https://perma.cc/74A2-9MVR)

McCance, D (2018) London and Singapore named top fintech hubs, *ICAEW*, 31 October [online] https://economia.icaew.com/news/october-2018/london-and-singapore-named-top-fintech-hubs (archived at https://perma.cc/R674-3ZEK)

MEDICI (2018) The story of India's emergence as a leading fintech hub, 19 March [online] https://gomedici.com/story-of-indias-emergence-as-leading-fintech-hub (archived at https://perma.cc/XT9P-5DXQ)

Nathani, K (2018) Why this 201-year-old bank is building Asia–Australia economic corridor, *Entrepreneur*, 5 December [online] https://www.entrepreneur.com/article/324348 (archived at https://perma.cc/YS24-T98X)

YesFintech (2018) Yes Bank India Fintech Opportunities Review 2017–2018 [online] http://burnmark.com/uploads/reports/Burnmark_Report_YesBank_India.pdf (archived at https://perma.cc/JVA9-DSTE)

Yun, J (2019) Government sets aside $138m for innovation and fintech, *Fintech Business*, 9 May [online] https://www.fintechbusiness.com.au/industry/1017-government-sets-aside-138m-for-innovation-and-fintech (archived at https://perma.cc/ET84-PN57)

07

Fintech segments at play

The word 'fintech' first appeared in the British press in the 1980s and '90s, but did not gain popularity until after the 2008 financial crisis. Fintechs, between 2008 and 2012, were start-ups that competed directly with the traditional banks disrupting and disintermediating the way they offered products and services to their customers.

In this early era of emergent fintech, most public and expert attention went to B2C (Business-to-Consumer) segments like neobanks, B2C robo-advisors, money transfer services, digital brokerage and P2P (Peer-to-Peer) lending companies. The customer needed a much better experience, and quickly.

However, increasingly, the early definition of fintech has widened. A fintech today is any innovative company utilizing technology to improve efficiencies, costs or processes and includes a significant number of tech firms who do not deal directly with consumers. The B2B (Business-to-Business) fintech segments like RegTech and B2B robo-advisory did not receive much attention until 2017, especially from strategic investors and venture capitalists, due to their apparent lack of customer growth curves. However, we have seen increasing recent venture capitalist interest in B2B fintechs, driven by:

- shifts in the regulatory landscape;
- increased bank and fintech collaboration;
- the need for better and stronger revenue models in the fintech industry;
- business model expansion/pivoting;
- the emergence of enabling technology such as blockchain and artificial intelligence.

One example is cross-border B2B payments, which are projected to exceed $218 trillion by 2022, up from $150 trillion in 2018 (Juniper Research, 2018). This growth can be credited to the emergence of disruptive technology coupled with the transparency and efficiency that B2B cross-border transfers provide.

Another example is electronic invoicing, or e-invoicing, a form of electronic billing that allows two or more parties to exchange invoices in integrated electronic format. The global e-invoicing market is experiencing steady growth and will be worth an estimated €16.1 billion by 2024 according to research by Billentis (Office Torque, 2017). The fact that both the EU and the United States have made e-invoicing mandatory starting in 2018 has helped facilitate the market growth, fuelled by regulatory pressure.

The primary difference between B2B and B2C fintech is the higher customer acquisition costs associated with B2C fintechs as compared to B2B fintechs. B2C fintechs need to rely heavily on venture capital funding to scale. They, however, have a very clear view of user-related milestones and can make a market impact quickly and effectively. Innovation is easier to achieve for B2C fintechs with a heavy focus on customer journeys and both front-end and back-end disruption. On the other hand, a B2B fintech can get revenues quickly but could be heavily dependent on traditional banks or enterprises for collaboration or funding. The impact they make may seem marginal due to the enormous scale of challenges that are usually ahead of them when working with legacy systems and processes in a large bank.

For example, a P2P payment process takes a few hours on average from start to finish because it has no dependence on any external processes. A B2B payment process, on the other hand, may take up to 90 days from start to finish; it can be heavily complex since it requires multiple inter-dependent processes to take place.

Some fintechs are even shifting from B2C to B2B models. One such company is Burrow, a UK-based mortgage tech start-up. Burrow started as a consumer business in 2016 but decided to shift to B2B in 2018 and will offer its technology to brokers and mortgage networks. Burrow attributed its pivot to high customer acquisition costs and long sales cycles, and commented that 'the unit economics were not stacking up', indicating how severe some of the customer acquisition challenges and costs are in the fintech industry (O'Hear, 2018).

Getting new customers to use new financial products is quite expensive, with the minimum cost ranging from $150 to $350 to acquire a single consumer. For P2P lending spaces, this cost can be 10 times higher. Until recently, challenger banks' cost of acquisition ranged from $5 to $50, but it is projected to increase significantly due to high competition and a large number of challengers being launched in the same geographies, targeting a similar customer base. B2C start-ups have come up with ways to reduce their customer acquisition costs by partnering with bigger brands and by using creative content marketing. B2B customer acquisition costs vary from segment to segment, but most investors and experts agree that the acquisition cost for B2B is much lower than that of B2C.

Crowdfunding

Crowdfunding, though not a part of fintech, is widely considered an important precursor to the fintech revolution, helping create the first disintermediation model of peer-to-peer fundraising instead of going through traditional channels. The success and impact of crowdfunding websites like Kickstarter led to several fintech websites finding trust, interest and investment.

Crowdfunding is the practice of funding a project by raising small amounts of money from a lot of different people. The crowdfunding business model comprises three players:

- **Project proposers:** these are the brains behind the venture. They provide the blueprint or idea of the project that requires financing.
- **Potential investors:** these are people who are interested in the venture. They are willing to invest their money in the idea.
- **An internet platform:** this acts as the medium that brings the project proposers and potential investors together to kick-start the venture.

Based on the business model, the crowdfunding market is divided into different segments like:

- peer-to-peer (P2P) lending;
- reward-based funding;
- equity investment;
- donation;
- hybrid-based funding;
- royalty-based funding;
- other types of funding.

The term crowdfunding has been exclusively associated with the funding of tangible products, but equity crowdfunding is gaining momentum as an attractive way to raise money for start-ups and SMBs. According to the annual Massolution Crowdfunding Industry Report, the total worldwide equity volume peaked at $2.56 billion in 2015 (Galkiewicz and Galkiewicz, 2018). In 2017, more than $12 billion was invested into equity or reward-based crowdfunding projects globally with a projected revenue growth of 32 per cent in the next five years.

Payments

Digital payment services are relatively simple compared to other products, making it easy for fintechs focusing on payments to acquire customers rapidly and at lower cost. Fintechs focusing on payments are also able to proliferate in innovation and adoption of new payment capabilities.

Innovation in mobile wallets has been driven by the huge market penetration of smartphones, which has enabled customers to make payments via their phones. According to Forrester's Mobile Payment Forecast, P2P mobile payments are gaining momentum and are forecasted to grow to nearly $282 billion by 2021 in the United States alone (Parisi, 2017). This growth will, however, still be 50 times less than what we could see in countries like China. Some of the key players in mobile payments include Samsung Pay, Android Pay, Google Wallet, and PayPal. Since 2010, the worldwide remittance flows have risen from \$466.7 billion to \$615 billion in 2018. The cost of sending money continues to be very high, and most start-ups in the payment segment aim to reduce these costs by using real-time payments and digital currency solutions. In wholesale and corporate payments, the most innovation has been observed in alternative finance, supply chain finance, and cryptocurrency adoption.

Lending

Traditionally, lending players were mainly credit data providers, banks, and IRA custodians. In recent years, however, P2P consumer and business lending has emerged as a significant trend in fintech. P2P lending fintechs have enabled individuals and businesses to borrow between each other; those with an efficient structure offer low interest rates and a faster lending process for both lenders and borrowers. The difference between these fintechs and banks is that the fintechs are not involved in the lending. They instead play matchmaker between borrowers and lenders and collect a small fee for themselves. An excellent example of a lending fintech is the UK-based lender, Zopa, which started in 2005. Other big lending fintechs are US-based Prosper Marketplace and Lending Club which began in 2006.

According to EY, there were over 1,300 lending fintechs in the world at the end of 2016, although the number might have been higher, since according to DBS, there were more than 2,000 P2P lenders in China alone in 2015 (Sender, 2015).

Business models for lending fintechs have evolved since the first P2P lending fintechs started appearing in the early 2000s. Early firms were referred to as P2P lenders because their business models involved using technology to match borrowers with retail investors directly. The market, however, evolved and the P2P lenders were relabelled to marketplaces as firms broadened their funding sources by marketing their loans to institutional investors like hedge fund companies, banks, and asset managers. Loan types have also evolved to include mortgages, student loans, point of sale financing, and other consumer instalment debt. Small businesses have also become an area of focus for fintech lenders. Firms are now leveraging technology to tailor-make loan packages and repayment terms for small companies with revenues that would not be profitable to traditional lenders such as banks. The key distinguishing feature for lending fintechs is the use of the internet and emerging data-analytics technologies to improve customer experience through a simplified loan approval process, funding process, and loan extension. Customers can now deliver all the supporting information electronically when applying for a loan.

The growth projection for alternative lending for the EU is €2.8 billion by the end of 2018, a year-on-year increase of 73 per cent. The strongest growth, however, is due in property and consumer, with estimated growth rates of 102 per cent and 79 per cent respectively (Brismo, 2018). China's P2P loans reached RMB1.2 trillion (US $185 billion), growing at 128 per cent CAGR from 2014 to 2017. They represent 3 per cent and 21 per cent of retail and credit card loans, making the Chinese P2P lending market the largest in the world (DBS, 2018).

Robo-advisory

Robo-advisory is a fast-growing application of digital solutions to asset and wealth management. Robo-advisors have user-friendly and automated processes, low-cost portfolio management, and reliable performance, making them a threat to conventional financial advisory services. Robo-advisors leverage technology to apply digital client onboarding, which is a crucial step in delivering convenience and efficiency. They mainly invest in exchange traded funds (ETFs) to provide diversified and low-cost investment solutions.

Robo-advisors first started appearing in 2008 in the wake of the global financial crisis as online interfaces used by financial managers to manage and balance clients' assets. Between Q1 2012 and Q1 2017, private robo-advisors raised over $1.32 billion globally across 119 equity investments, according to CB Insights (2017). The United States led with 57 per cent of deals, followed by Germany, the UK and China. Assets under the robo-advisors segment amounted to US $401.9 billion in 2018, and these figures are expected to show an annual growth rate of 37 per cent to $1.4 trillion in 2022.

The next big targets for robo-advisors seem to be retirement assets – especially in the United States and China, with China projected to overtake the US in retirement assets – and millennial investors who stand to inherit $30 trillion of potential assets from baby boomers. Robo-advisors, however, need to offer sustainability, clean energy, and socially impactful investing strategies to retain this new generation of investors. A group of robo-advisors including Motif Investing and Wahed Invest are creating low-fee investment products aligned with investors' social, religious or economic values. Start-ups are well positioned to establish credibility among young investors, since most of them do not trust banks after the 2008–2009 global financial crisis. Low fees and better digital interfaces further incentivize these young investors.

RegTech

Several firms referred to RegTech as a 'buzzword within fintech' in 2015. However, it has existed as a separate, focused space since 2010. RegTech is technology that seeks to provide configurable, easy-to-integrate, reliable, secure, and cost-effective regulatory solutions. The 2008–2009 financial crisis saw banks across the world having numerous new regulations imposed upon them that required them to hire several compliance officers. These reforms increased challenges and costs for the financial sector in relation to compliance, reporting and supervisory requests. These regulatory challenges created the need for players to step up and provide more efficient and tech-enabled solutions, hence the emergence of RegTech companies.

Since 2008, RegTech companies have provided solutions for regulatory reporting, risk management, KYC (know your customer) and onboarding, compliance monitoring, and fraud detection. Between 2018 and 2013, RegTech companies raised over $6.2 billion across an approximated 680 equity investments, and as of July 2018, there were over 800 RegTech start-ups in the world. Growth in the number of players in each of the RegTech segments between 2010 and 2018 was distributed as follows:

- regulatory compliance: 23 per cent growth;
- risk management: 23 per cent growth;
- financial crime: 13 per cent growth;
- identity management: 7 per cent growth;
- compliance support: 6 per cent growth.

InsurTech

InsurTech is the variety of emerging technologies and innovative business models that can transform the insurance business. InsurTech started emerging in 2011 and saw a brief momentum until 2015, when it died down due to the volatility of large deals. A clear shift towards larger deals in 2017, however, jumpstarted it again. Over $8 billion was invested in an InsurTech start-up, Zhong An, in just one year – this is clearly a sign of things to come (Yan, 2016).

Blockchain as an efficiency enabler

Blockchain is a public register where transactions between two users within the same network are stored in a secure, verifiable and permanent way. The transaction data is saved in cryptographic blocks connected to each other in a hierarchal system. This mode of data storage creates an endless chain of data blocks (blockchains) that allow you to trace and verify all the transactions that you have made. Blockchain's primary function is therefore to certify transactions between users.

Blockchain can be used to save money by eliminating the huge amount of resources needed for record keeping, and it has the potential to disrupt IT in ways that have never been seen since the arrival of the internet. The blockchain architecture enables users to create unchangeable records for the transactions they make. Fintechs can use blockchain technology for paramount security, enhanced information validation, and rapid transaction validation.

Payment, settlement and clearance are full of inefficiencies because each organization stores its own data and must communicate with others for reconciliation purposes. As a result, transactions are slow, typically taking about two days to clear. Blockchain technology makes it possible to share data and reduces the need for reconciliation instantly, and adopting this technology promotes efficient and effective clearance and settlement processes.

Blockchain fintechs such as Sentbe have emerged to lower the costs of P2P micro-payments by 60 to 80 per cent. You see, cross-border micro-payments are still being controlled by big players such as Western Union and MoneyGram, who charge sizeable transaction fees. Blockchain technology can be utilized to lower those transaction costs while reducing clearing time. The global fintech blockchain market size is expected to grow from $370.3 million in 2018 to $6.2 billion in 2023 at a CAGR of 75.9 per cent.

Artificial intelligence as the backbone of fintech

Artificial intelligence (AI) is a computer's ability to do things that can only normally be done by humans, such as pattern recognition, reasoning and speech. It also refers to machines' ability to 'learn' and make decisions based on what they have 'learnt'. The main types of AI include:

- Cognitive automation: automating tasks from deep domain-specific expertise.
- Cognitive engagement: cognitive technology focused on creating personalized engagement with people.
- Cognitive insights: extraction of concepts from various data streams to generate personalized and relevant answers.

Machine learning (ML) is a subset of AI that focuses on computers' ability to be self-adaptive and learn without being explicitly programmed. ML enables computers to change their algorithms when exposed to new data and is good at handling repetitive functions, crunching large data, and detecting anomalies in patterns.

AI emerged in the 1950s, and since then it has seen two boom cycles as well as cycles of disillusionment. One of those disillusionment cycles lasted from the 1990s until recently, but we are now entering into a new boom. The AI fintech space was worth $1.27 billion in 2017 and is projected to reach $7.28 billion by 2023, with a CAGR of 33.8 per cent over the period 2018–2023 (Business Wire, 2018). Some of the applications of AI will be explainable predictions, early detection and containment of cyber-security threats, visual identification and verification, and more human-seeming chat bots. Applications of machine learning in finance include digital advisors, security and fraud detection, underwriting, customer service, sentiment analysis, etc.

Data analytics is the core of AI and has helped in many ways such as risk evaluation, fraud detection, transaction and payment records, better value for customers, and asset management. One of the big users of big data analytics is the wealth management industry. Customer acquisition, customer retention, and customer experience and service are processes that can be improved significantly with big data analytics.

Most banks around the world have started using AI and ML technologies and tools for improving customer-facing front-end experiences, as well as for reducing costs and building new capabilities into backend systems. For example:

- **Bank of America**: planning to roll out a virtual assistant chatbot to customers in 2018 to provide 24/7 financial guidance.
- **JP Morgan**: has launched a contract intelligence program to reduce loan-servicing mistakes. This ML technology will save an estimated 360,000 hours of human work.
- **Wells Fargo**: launched an AI-driven chatbot on Facebook messenger in 2017 to deliver information to customers and help them make better financial decisions.
- **The Royal Bank of Scotland (RBS)**: using an automated AI-driven lending process to approve commercial real estate loans up to $2.7 million in less than 45 minutes. The process would normally take days.

APIs as the building blocks of fintech

An API (application program interface) is a set of formalized commands that allow seamless communication between software applications. APIs allow innovative applications to leverage on existing services to create improved customer-centric services. They help financial institutions create customer-focused initiatives by enabling quick and responsive application development.

Using APIs as building blocks to build applications is increasingly being recognized as the best way to keep up with business and economic challenges facing the financial industry. Mobile apps created by fintech start-ups are posing a serious challenge to those of the established banking industry, leading to the domination of the landscape by these start-ups. Dominant banks and financial institutions are unable to duplicate the agility and speed with which fintech start-ups, with the help of APIs, can innovate. This has forced banks to start playing catch-up by investing heavily to improve the ability to create innovative mobile apps while participating in developer sandboxes and API economy.

Security and authentication as a necessity in fintech

Out of 2.4 billion poor people worldwide, 1.5 billion are unable to prove their identities to formal economies, creating a need to connect to this massive 'invisible' global population (MEDICI, 2018). The use of biometrics is the solution to this problem, which puts the biometrics market in a position to experience substantial growth in the coming years. In fact, estimates suggest that by 2021, the market value will have reached $30 billion, with primary revenues shifting from the government sector to banking (MEDICI, 2016).

Biometrics have found the widest adoption in the financial services industry, with fingerprint logins becoming more common and secure ways to access one's mobile banking account. Samsung and BBVA took biometrics a notch higher when they presented an iris-scanning feature in 2016 which allowed BBVA customers with Samsung smartphones to log on to the bank's Spanish mobile banking app by just looking at their displays. Other big players that have adopted biometrics technology are Visa, which has put biometrics at the centre of its security road map, and Mastercard, which aims at ensuring that every customer has access to biometric authentication services in the next few years.

Biometrics contains:

- voice recognition;
- fingerprint identification;
- face recognition;
- ATMs iris scanners;
- palm vein recognition.

TSB in the UK is one of the first banks in the world to take advantage of iris scanning instead of passwords. The service was rolled out in September 2017. In the United States, Wells Fargo and 30 other smaller regional banks and credit unions are implementing biometrics as a security measure. Asia has also not been left behind, with DCB bank in India using iris scanning to help rural customers authenticate customer identity. Mastercard aims to create fingerprint-enabled cards that use fingerprint scanning to authenticate transactions.

Upcoming innovations

Quantum computing harnesses the law of quantum mechanics to carry out complex data operations. While conventional computers use bits represented as either binary 1s or 0s, quantum computing harnesses quantum bits known as qubits. They can be read as 1s or 0s or both, surpassing traditional computers in power by creating shortcuts in the computing process. For years, technology leaders in the banking industry have shown an interest in quantum computing, but that interest is now turning into involvement. According to IBM, JP Morgan Chase plans to explore quantum computing to use it for trading strategies, asset pricing, portfolio optimization, and risk analysis (Castellanos, 2019). March 2017 saw Google announce its Bristlecone chip design capable of 72 qubits. IBM also successfully tested out a 50-qubit quantum computer in November of the same year. Although the mainstream use of quantum computing is unlikely for the next few years, it is projected to enhance the following:

- modelling of financial data;
- AI/ML;
- high-frequency trading (HFT);
- pricing of complex financial derivatives;
- portfolio optimization (Monte Carlo Simulation);
- security of data and communication;
- fraud and risk analysis.

Visa's proof of concept around augmented reality in 2016 was an interesting example of how technology can change the way we shop. Although augmented reality technology is still relatively new, we can expect to see its applications in:

- data visualization;
- Immense Financial Learning;
- enhanced client service;
- new payment opportunities.

IMPORTANT FINTECHS TO KNOW

Ant Financial: $150 billion valuation

Formerly known as Alipay, this Hangzhou-based company is an affiliate company of the Chinese Alibaba Group. The latest $14 billion funding round in June 2018 made it the highest-valued fintech and most valuable start-up in the world.

Adyen: $20 billion

This is an Amsterdam-based global payment company that allows businesses to accept e-commerce, mobile and POS payments. Some of its biggest customers are Netflix, Facebook and Spotify. They have raised $266 million in funding, and in June 2018 they had a successful IPO with the share price doubling in the following month.

Lu.com/Lufax: $18.5 billion

Based in Shanghai, Lu.com is one of China's biggest online P2P lenders, with $1.7 billion raised in funding.

Paytm: $10 billion

Noida-based Paytm is an Indian e-commerce payment system and digital wallet with $1.9 billion raised in funding.

Stripe: $9.2 billion

Stripe is an online payment platform that has attracted funding from Elon Musk, Peer Thiel, American Express and Visa, totalling $450 million.

Robinhood: $5.6 billion

This is a free stock trading app based in Menlo. Robinhood closed a series D funding round that raised $363 million in May 2018. It has raised $539 million in total.

Credit Karma: $4 billion

This is a provider for free online credit reports based in San Francisco. They have raised $868 million in funding

Oscar Health: $3.2 billion

A digital insurance start-up based in New York. They have raised $892.5 million in funding.

Unlike earlier when the United States dominated in fintech valuations, the top five most valued start-ups today feature one company from the US, two from China, one from Europe, and one from India.

References

Brismo (2018) 2018 origination volumes – USA set to approach $40Bn, UK nearly £8Bn, and EU almost EUR2.8Bn. 25 January https://brismo.com/2018-origination-volumes-usa-set-approach-40bn-uk-nearly-8bn-eu-almost-eur2-8bn/ (archived at https://perma.cc/92AW-AKWP)

Business Wire (2018) AI in the global fintech market to 2023 – a $1.27 billion market in 2017; projected to reach $7.28 billion by 2023, 28 September https://www.businesswire.com/news/home/20180928005176/en/AI-Global-Fintech-Market-2023—1.27 (archived at https://perma.cc/T58J-U5CL)

Castellanos, S (2019) JPMorgan years away from seeing quantum-computing dividends, *Wall Street Journal,* 11 June [online] https://www.wsj.com/articles/jpmorgan-years-away-from-seeing-quantum-computing-dividends-11560275316 (archived at https://perma.cc/WY8A-E9TG)

CB Insights (2017) A wealth tech world: mapping robo-advisors around the globe, 21 April [online] https://www.cbinsights.com/research/robo-advisor-global-fintech-map/ (archived at https://perma.cc/68V4-PNPW)

DBS (2018) China Fintech Sector, 28 September [online] https://www.dbs.com.sg/corporate/aics/pdfController.page?pdfpath=/content/article/pdf/AIO/092018/180924_insights_bargain_hunting_opportunity.pdf (archived at https://perma.cc/NRB4-L4RW)

Galkiewicz, D and Galkiewicz, M (2018) Crowdfunding Monitor 2018 [online] https://www.fh-kufstein.ac.at/content/download/3537648/file/Crowdfunding_Monitor_2018.pdf (archived at https://perma.cc/J9QT-CE86)

Juniper Research (2018) Fintech innovation propels B2B money transfer market to $218 trillion by 2022, 26 March [online] https://www.juniperresearch.com/press/press-releases/fintech-innovation-propels-b2b-money-transfer (archived at https://perma.cc/8FTD-GY6L)

MEDICI (2016) The biometrics market is expected to reach a value of $30 bn by 2021, 25 May [online] https://gomedici.com/the-biometrics-market-is-expected-to-reach-a-value-of-30-bn-by-2021 (archived at https://perma.cc/326M-QJPX)

MEDICI (2018) The rise of biometrics in Finance, 27 April [online] https://gomedici.com/rise-of-biometrics-in-finance (archived at https://perma.cc/3TRY-PPT9)

O'Hear, S (2018) Online mortgage advisor Burrow pivots to B2B, cites unit economics issue, *TechCrunch*, 12 February [online] https://techcrunch.com/2018/02/12/b2b-burrow/ (archived at https://perma.cc/P7AV-RHHY)

Office Torque (2017) E-invoicing/e-billing significant market transition lies ahead, https://www.officetorque.com/wp-contentuploads201708billentis-report-2017-officetorque-pdf/ (archived at https://perma.cc/S9L4-MBKL)

Parisi, D (2017) Mobile payments volume in US will triple by 2021: report, *Retail Dive*, 6 February [online] https://www.retaildive.com/ex/mobilecommercedaily/mobile-payments-volume-in-us-will-triple-by-2021-report (archived at https://perma.cc/4LD3-ESK9)

Sender, H (2015) China's loan sharks come under attack from P2P lenders, *CNBC*, 7 July [online] https://www.cnbc.com/2015/07/07/chinas-loan-sharks-come-under-attack-from-p2p-lenders.html (archived at https://perma.cc/VJN2-YB4H)

Yan, C (2016) The insurance tech equation, *TechCrunch*, 3 April [online] https://techcrunch.com/2016/04/03/the-insurance-tech-equation/ (archived at https://perma.cc/K8XC-BJME)

08

B2B fintech

We have already seen the massive shift of fintechs from a heavily B2C focus in the early part of the fintech revolution, to a B2B focus, primarily due to the high customer acquisition costs associated with B2C models. Fintechs have experienced extensive evolution, from being seen as enemies of the banking industry to collaborating with the same sector to ensure better customer service provision. This collaboration between fintechs and banks is the major contributor to the exponential growth observed in B2B fintechs in the last few years. For example, the number of European fintechs shifting towards the B2B market has been growing in recent years. Most of the European B2B fintechs are focused on better service delivery to previously neglected customers like small and medium-sized businesses (SMBs), freelancers and students, a group of fast-growing and evolving customer segments who did not receive special offerings or customer service from banks.

The total capital invested in B2B fintechs has increased compared to the amount of capital invested in B2C fintechs. In Europe, the total capital investment grew from $660 million in 2015 to $948 million in September 2017. B2B fintechs in Europe went from taking 26 per cent of the total fintech funding in 2015 to 49 per cent in 2017 (Innovate Finance, 2017). One of the things that has made B2B fintechs such a huge success is their role in commercial payments. You see, B2B payments had been a significant pain point to buyers and sellers alike before fintechs came into play. B2B payments included complex, expensive, and sometimes unsafe processes, and without the current digital solutions, this proved to be a huge hurdle, especially for small businesses. Since the emergence of B2B payment fintechs, all the payment processes have been streamlined to make them safer and easier to use.

There are several reasons why B2B fintech is poised to be the most significant aspect of the fintech industry:

- B2B fintechs are centred around significant market drivers, which are cost, control, capital and compliance. This makes B2B fintechs critical players in all aspects of the value chain.

- B2B fintechs are centred around providing banks and other major financial players with innovative technological solutions. These solutions, in turn, enable these financial institutions to offer their customers better and more secure services, while also reducing costs significantly.

- Funding of B2B fintechs is expected to shift from angel funding to later-stage backing. This shift (as observed since 2017) is one of the signs that the space is maturing (KPMG, 2018).

In recent years, fintechs have increasingly moved towards working together with banks through partnerships that provide innovative solutions to the banking industry. According to a survey of the top 100 banks by McKinsey (2016a), 52 per cent of the top 100 banks are in active partnerships with fintechs. One of the major drivers of growth in banks and fintech companies' partnerships is customer referrals. Another survey of 600 fintechs showed that the share of B2B fintechs had increased from 34 per cent in 2011 to 47 per cent in 2015 (McKinsey, 2016b).

The role of fintechs in retail banking is offering an ecosystem of services that cover all sectors including digital supply chain, virtual marketplace, and B2B cloud services. Fintechs can provide these services to the retail banking industry via a B2B platform that uses deep intelligence and a fully personalized and accessible omnichannel that is embedded into everyday life.

The interesting thing is that B2C fintechs are attracting lots of focus in China, even though B2B dominates the fintech funding and 89 per cent of the $10.2 billion investments in fintechs in China went into the B2B space (Pham, 2017). This could be a result of the vast amounts of untapped opportunities in the Chinese B2C space and the high capital and advanced technology expertise required in B2B ventures. The delay in Chinese fintechs pivoting from B2B to B2C markets is also because the fintech revolution in China started a few years after the fintech revolution in the Western countries.

The characteristics of B2B fintech

B2B fintechs are more focused on providing solutions to other businesses than offering these solutions directly to the end consumers. B2B fintechs solve problems that businesses face in operations and service delivery, so ultimately the end consumer benefits from B2B fintechs through improved services. Currently, B2B fintechs are filling the gap created by the banks' withdrawal from areas such as SME lending and utilizing big data analytics to improve the creditworthiness assessment process. B2B fintech firms complement traditional financial institutions with solutions that make back-office processes more efficient and effective with a business model that is easily sustainable and scalable.

WHAT ARE SOME OF THE MAJOR B2B FINTECH CATEGORIES?

- Trade finance.
- B2B payments.
- Banking-as-a-service.
- Cash management.
- SME financing.
- Tax and accounting tech.
- Trading.
- RegTech.
- B2B robo-advisory.
- B2B insurtech.
- LegalTech.
- E-invoicing.

Use cases of collaboration

According to SG Analytics (2016), there are over 5,000 start-ups operating in B2B fintech globally. The vast majority of B2B start-ups are today providing solutions to banks to reduce costs, improve process or operational efficiency, or use technology to automate repetitive tasks and actions.

Since 2014, banks have changed their attitudes towards fintechs and started seeing them as partners rather than competitors. There have been many collaborations between fintechs and banks to support this new narrative of the fintech industry, where disruption is jointly driven by the start-up and bank by focusing on specific use cases. Some examples of significant bank–fintech collaborations include:

Bocom International and FDT-AI. Bocom International is the investment arm of the Bank of Communications in China. They have partnered with FDT-AI, a Hong Kong-based fintech, to develop personalized and intelligent investment research using clients' past transactions. This partnership aims at providing each of the bank's clients with tailor-made investment advice that will work for them.

ICICI Bank and Paytm. ICICI Bank is the largest private bank in India, while Paytm is the largest digital payment platform in the country. These two giants have partnered and launched a joint digital credit account called Paytm-ICICI Bank Postpaid on the Paytm app. Paytm-ICICI Bank Postpaid offers customers instant micro-credit and uses an algorithm from ICICI to determine a client's creditworthiness in seconds using the client's digital and financial behaviour. Whether it is money for bills or movie tickets, ICICI Bank customers can now get instant small loans for everyday expenses, thanks to this bank–fintech partnership.

ING Group and Scalable Capital. ING Group is a multinational financial service and banking corporation which has partnered with Scalable Capital, a leading European online robo-advice and wealth management firm, to create digital investment solutions for ING customers. This service, however, is only available for ING's retail customers in Germany for now, with hopes of expansion later on. Customers can do a quick, paperless registration in less than 15 minutes and invest a minimum of €10,000 to get started. Both Scalable Capital and ING mobile apps enable customers to easily track their portfolios from their mobile phones while online portals allow for easy portfolio monitoring on a computer.

Kabbage and Scotiabank, MasterCard and Santander Bank. Kabbage is an online lender based in the United States. It has partnered with large players such as Scotiabank, MasterCard and Santander Bank to streamline various aspects of their core function of lending. The partnership with Scotiabank is aimed at streamlining online lending. Scotiabank customers can apply for loans within minutes for amounts of up to $100,000. The partnership enables automatic onboarding, servicing, underwriting and monitoring of the loan throughout the loan period. Kabbage's partnership with Master-Card provides a simplified loan alternative to small and medium-sized businesses (SMBs) through MasterCard's network of acquirers. This partnership provides SMBs with a convenient and flexible way to access working capital loans.

JPMorgan Chase and Digital Asset Holdings. JPMorgan Chase has teamed up with Digital Asset Holdings on a trial blockchain initiative that aims to make the trading process more efficient and cost-effective. New York-based Digital Asset seeks to use private or permissioned blockchain technology to streamline syndicated loans, US Treasury repo, foreign exchange, securities settlement and derivatives.

Other examples of bank-start-up partnerships include:

TD Bank + nCino – to digitalize the entire consumer lending process from start to finish.

DBS Bank + MoolahSense – for peer-to-peer lending capabilities, and to better serve small businesses.

Citi + CF2O – to offer an end-to-end trade finance solution that includes dynamic discounting, amongst a suite of payables solutions.

KeyBank + AvidXchange – to provide a software-as-a-service solution as part of KeyBank's treasury management platform and replace paper-based invoicing.

It is evident that banks are increasingly looking to fintechs for solutions around innovation, be it new products or faster digitalization. Fintechs allow banks to leverage on APIs to create personalized solutions and rapid service delivery for their customers. Fintechs have also allowed banks to eradicate lengthy paperwork and expedite processes such as loan approval and client onboarding through digital KYC (know your customer) processes. Looking at the benefits that banks draw from partnering with fintechs, it is easy to see that this trend is rapidly picking up speed and banks that have struggled to innovate as fast as fintech start-ups are looking at collaboration as the fundamental means to compete, and ultimately, survive.

It's not just banks and start-ups who are partnering to solve use cases, but several banking consortiums have come about as well – focused on finding joint solutions to common cross-border problems. There are several examples involving blockchain technology, where multiple banks have come together for payments and lending:

Westpac and ANZ. ANZ has been using blockchain technology to digitize the bank guarantee process used for commercial property leasing. In July 2017, ANZ teamed up with Westpac, IBM and the Australian owner of Westfield shopping malls, Scentre Group, to use this technology to do away with paper-based bank guarantee documents (Fintech Australia Newsroom, 2017).

JPMorgan Chase, ANZ and Royal Bank of Canada. JP Morgan Chase launched a new payment processing network in October 2017 that uses blockchain technology, in partnership with Royal Bank of Canada and ANZ from Australia. The Interbank Information Network allows payments to reach beneficiaries faster, with fewer steps and better security.

BBVA and Indra. BBVA has successfully completed the first global corporate loan transaction using blockchain technology from the negotiation of the deal to its signing. The pilot enabled the closing of a €75 million loan using a solution developed by BBVA.

The negotiation process and completion of conditions between BBVA and Indra (a Spanish telco) were developed on an internal solution built on private blockchain technology (Hyperledger). Once the contract was agreed, Ethereum's public blockchain (testnet) was used to register the hash or unique identifier related to the transaction's documentation.

RegTech

RegTech, or regulatory technology, is one of the largest sub-segments within the B2B fintech segment. Even though RegTech was called 'the new buzzword within fintech' by several firms in 2015, it has existed as a separate, focused space since as far back as 2010. Some of the earliest RegTech start-ups launched are now in the process of obtaining late-stage VC rounds or going through acquisitions. The space has clearly matured over the last couple of years and attracted a lot of attention from banks, vendors, service firms and regulators.

The RegTech segment includes four types of offerings, mainly targeted at retail and corporate banks, investment banks, insurance firms and wealth management firms:

1 regulatory compliance;

2 risk management;

3 financial crime;

4 KYC and onboarding.

Regulatory compliance offerings help financial institutions with all aspects of compliance and reporting, typically focused on reducing costs. They offer regulatory intelligence, improve reporting capabilities and handle policies and governance.

Risk management offerings from RegTech firms focus on helping financial institutions identify market risks, conduct risks and cyber risks/cyber-security threats. They use external data (from the market) and internal data (from within the company) to identify potential threats and protect the company from any penalties or malignant issues.

Financial crime start-ups work in real time to help institutions identify fraud, money laundering, market abuse, terrorist financing and other criminal activities.

KYC, identity and onboarding technologies have come a long way and integrate closely with all the offerings listed above. These start-ups use technologies around biometrics and facial recognition to offer quicker and better KYC, or improve the efficiency of onboarding through faster processes and quicker AML (anti-money laundering) screening.

Between 2009 and 2014, banking reforms saw regulators publish more than 50,000 documents, which is five times the number published in the previous five-year period. This was just the start of a long list of regulations that financial institutions would need to comply with to stay in business and avoid hefty fines. According to Thomson Reuters, there was a 492 per cent increase in regulatory volume between 2008 and 2015 (Nonninger, 2017). According to McKinsey, regulatory fines in 20 major US and EU banks also increased 45 times between 2010 and 2014 which led to a 10–15 per cent increase in the workforce dedicated to governance, compliance and risk management (Mindtree, 2018). Increased government and regulator scrutiny did not make matters any better for financial institutions, and created a desperate need for a solution that would help ensure compliance in banks and financial institutions. RegTechs have become an integral part of the financial industry in the light of the evolving and increasing regulations. Before RegTech, compliance had become a costly affair, especially for large banks, with some of them spending millions of dollars annually to remain fully compliant. Non-compliance was equally expensive, with hefty penalties imposed on financial institutions that did not adhere to all the regulations.

Some RegTech start-ups can verify customer details and credit using big data without breaking any privacy regulations. They can also monitor customer behaviour and flag anything suspicious that would otherwise take longer or even go unnoticed without the technology. RegTechs can also detect irregularities such as money laundering and insider trading transactions by keeping track of employee communications and monitoring customer behaviour for any anomalies. This helps financial institutions stay clean and avoid penalties, especially since regulators are very keen on eradicating money laundering and other financial crimes.

Apart from helping banks keep track of regulations and remain compliant, RegTech solutions also help in cyber-security. There has been a steady increase in cyber-crimes in the last couple of years, with financial institutions and cryptocurrency exchange platforms as the top targets. According to the FCA, cyber-attacks against financial institutions went up 80 per cent in 2017 compared to 2016, making it essential for financial institutions to protect themselves and their customers from the ever-looming threat (Ismail, 2018). RegTech solutions provide cutting-edge cyber-security technology that operates within the bounds of compliance while keeping financial institutions in the loop on any emerging regulations.

Increased collaboration between financial institutions and fintechs has created a conducive atmosphere for RegTech start-ups to expand operations by onboarding more financial institutions. Government recognition and acceptance of RegTechs has also increased in the last few years. A good example is the New South Wales government's recent backing of the country's RegTech industry with a sponsorship programme in early 2018. The UK's regulatory body, the FCA, has also spent a lot of resources on RegTech, conducting programmes, running sandboxes and working directly with RegTech start-ups to improve regulatory efficiencies.

There are currently over 550 start-ups focused on the RegTech space (Burnmark, 2018). Regulatory compliance start-ups form the bulk of these, followed by Identity Management (KYC) and Risk Management start-ups. However, the largest growth in the number of start-ups is expected to be from a small group today within RegTech that includes start-ups focused on compliance support and peripheral services around compliance and regulatory reporting.

Figures 8.1a and 8.1b show the results of a survey targeted at RegTech firms, inviting responses on their target segment and proposed business benefits.

FIGURE 8.1a What segment do you play in?

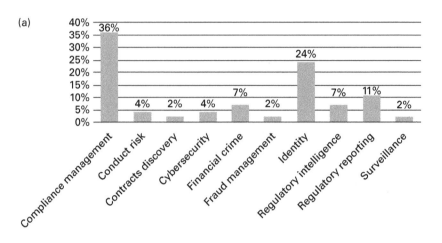

FIGURE 8.1b What business benefits do you primarily offer to banks?

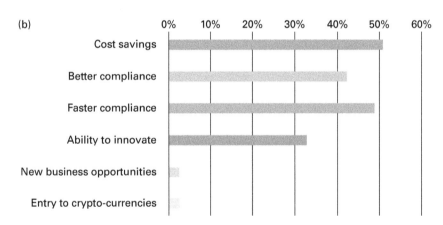

SOURCE Burnmark (2018)

'RegTech 2.0'

During the first phase of RegTech, from 2010 to 2016, start-ups focused more on the technology to drive compliance use cases and were less conversant with the nuances of the regulations in a holistic manner. This lack of understanding of regulatory complexities by RegTech start-ups proved a significant challenge for banks wanting to work with them. In the second phase of RegTech, which I like to call RegTech 2.0, RegTech start-ups are expected to collaborate more, with banks, regulators and domain experts, to demonstrate use cases, rather than technological cases.

These start-ups also handled data in a way never seen before. Data collection, monitoring, analysing and reporting in the space evolved into an entirely new industry. This was primarily driven by developments in big data technologies and the wider fintech ecosystem.

The market of regulators and central banks around the world is also struggling with the data deluge and supervision of new entrants in the banking industry. The entire lifecycle of policy making, enforcement and supervision is ripe for disruption with the use of advanced technology. Start-ups need to be patient in handling the bureaucracy of state-run organizations and even longer sales cycles, as well as improving their knowledge of regulators' underlying objectives and demonstrating unambiguously how their solutions can help the regulators do a better job than the status quo.

Equipped with past learnings and strong support from regulators and governments across the world, RegTech 2.0 is at an inflection point for a new era of efficient and effective compliance powered by technology.

Technologies used in RegTech

RegTechs merge disruptive technology with the regulations to create effective and efficient ways for financial institutions to be compliant. RegTechs use technology to automate some manual processes while eliminating the redundant ones. They use different technologies, but for a solution to be effective, it must ensure that the technology in use is cloud-based. Some of the technologies mostly used by RegTechs today include machine learning, artificial intelligence and blockchain. The most popular underlying technology used is data analytics – the larger the data set, and the more accurate and human-like the analysis, the better the quality of results from technology-based regulatory and compliance use cases. This is the case for all segments of RegTech, from KYC or onboarding to fraud and crime and compliance

FIGURE 8.2 Underlying technology for RegTech solutions

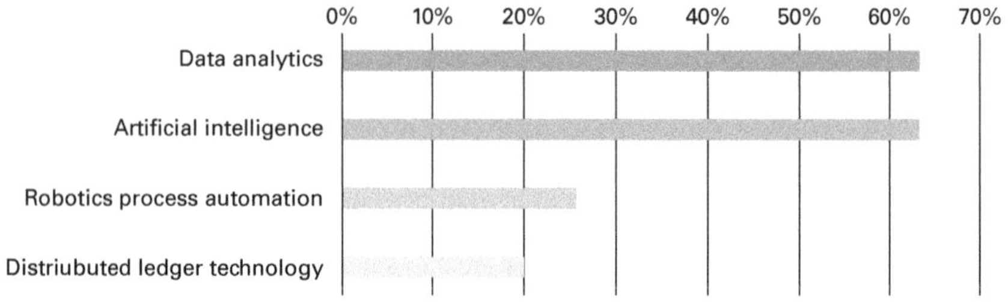

	0%	10%	20%	30%	40%	50%	60%	70%
Data analytics								
Artificial intelligence								
Robotics process automation								
Distriubuted ledger technology								

SOURCE Burnmark (2018)

reporting. There is also wide adoption of technologies supporting AI (machine learning, NLP) within the RegTech firms to mimic human behaviour in aspects of compliance, for example automating NDAs or checking legal terminology.

Distributed ledger technologies (DLT), like blockchain, were far less involved in their solutions, but this is expected to be a huge area of interest. For the firms offering DLT solutions, the most popular use cases are around digital identity and compliance solutions. According to the 2018 Burnmark report, 20 per cent of firms with an underlying DLT technology offered cybersecurity solutions (Goldfinch, 2018). Figure 8.2 shows the percentage of RegTech firms using certain technologies, as responded in a survey by Burnmark.

Regulatory sandboxes are one of the most common initiatives from regulators around the fintech space, and have helped them successfully observe and understand the boundaries of fintech solutions. This has also been one way of encouraging and supporting innovation in the industry, making data and banking/regulatory APIs readily available for interested fintechs – mostly those interested in getting regulated.

RegTech has not been a popular entrant into the sandboxes as they tend to work directly with banks rather than through regulatory channels. The first RegTech firm to get into a sandbox (FCA UK) was Tradle, a DLT-based identity firm. There are more entrants into FCA's 2017 programme, like nViso and Saffe, as well as in 2017 programmes of regulators across Asia. In fact, the largest number of supervisory sandboxes have been launched from Asia – 80 per cent of all sandboxes have been launched in Asia in countries like Singapore, UAE, Indonesia, Malaysia and Bahrain.

SupTech is another sub-segment of interest within RegTech – it has emerged as an important area of innovation during RegTech 2.0, with regulators, especially in the regions with fintech hubs, becoming clients and significant users of RegTech solutions themselves (unlike in Phase 1.0 where direct involvement with RegTechs was minimal except via accelerators and sandboxes) to keep up with the supervision challenges. SupTech, the emerging segment of RegTech, can enable regulators to take a data-driven approach to supervisory process and shift from a retrospective to a forward-looking supervisory approach (Burnmark, 2018). The technologies of RegTech deployed by the regulators (SupTech) will enable them to take data-driven and predictive approaches to supervision and potentially facilitate a shift from retrospective review to more forward-looking supervisory approaches.

Examples of promising RegTech firms

Regulatory reporting

ABIDE FINANCIAL

Abide Financial is a UK RegTech start-up that started in 2013. It offers a single solution for data processing and distribution of regulatory reports to the relevant bodies. Abide Financial's target industry is the financial industry.

BEARINGPOINT

Based in the Netherlands, BearingPoint offers solutions specific to insurers, banks and financial service providers. The company was started in 2002 with the financial industry as its target industry.

FUNDSQUARE

Founded in 2013, this Luxembourg-based RegTech company provides order management and information service solutions specific to the financial industry.

Risk management

AYASDI

Ayasdi is an American RegTech company that helps financial institutions to use topical data analysis and machine learning for regulatory compliance. The company was started in 2008.

FEATURESPACE

Featurespace is a UK-based fintech company that was started in 2008. The company uses machine learning for real-time data monitoring and detection of fraud and risk.

FINTELLIX

Founded in 2006, this Indian RegTech company focuses on providing the financial industry with risk and compliance services and products.

FINANSTRA

Finanstra is a fairly new RegTech company that provides a software solution to manage profitability, liquidity and risk. We say it is fairly new because it was started in 2017 but it has seen some impressive growth levels. The company is based in the UK.

Identity management and control

ACTIMIZE

Founded in 1999, Actimize is an American RegTech company that provides compliance and risk solutions, as well as anti-financial crime solutions.

JUMIO

Jumio is a US-based RegTech company that was started in 2010. Their main focus is security and identification using biometric facial recognition, document verification, and ID verification.

ENCOMPASS

Encompass is a UK firm that deals with KYC software for financial institutions and accountants. The company was founded in 2012.

Compliance

COMPLIANCE SOLUTIONS STRATEGIES

Compliance Solutions Strategies is an American company started in 2016 to offer solutions covering compliance disciplines such as regulatory data management, regulatory reporting, analytics, and compliance.

CUBE

CUBE is a UK-based RegTech company that provides risk assessment solutions and conducts regulatory compliance watch. It was started in 2012.

DARKTRACE

Darktrace is an enterprise security system that uses machine learning and artificial intelligence to detect previously unidentified threats and respond to them. It was started in 2013 and is based in the UK.

Transaction monitoring

IDENTITYMIND GLOBAL

This is a US-based risk management solutions company that helps track all parties involved in every transaction. It was founded in 2011 and its primary focus is the payments and money transfer industry.

NEUROWARE

Neuroware is a Malaysian RegTech firm that deals with distributed ledger and blockchain solutions. It was founded in 2014.

References

Burnmark (2018) RegTech 2.0 [online] https://www.burnmark.com/uploads/reports/Burnmark_Report_Jan18_RegTech.pdf (archived at https://perma.cc/5PFN-DU6W)

Fintech Australia Newsroom (2017) Australia's fintech industry median revenue up 200 per cent from 2016, major research report finds, 3 November [online] https://fintechaustralia.org.au/australias-fintech-industry-median-revenue-up-

200-per-cent-from-2016-major-research-report-finds/ (archived at https://perma.
cc/YMK5-LCTC)

Goldfinch, K (2018) RegTech 2.0: a new era of RegTech, 15 March, *The Fintech Times* [online] https://thefintechtimes.com/regtech-2-0-a-new-era-of-regtech/ (archived at https://perma.cc/69RY-4S4E)

Innovate Finance (2017) State Of European fintech: current trends & prediction 2017, 21 September [online] https://www.innovatefinance.com/reports/european-fintech/ (archived at https://perma.cc/E6BG-EBEU)

Ismail, N (2018) Rise in cyber attacks against financial services firms, *Information Age,* 31 January [online] https://www.information-age.com/rise-cyber-attacks-financial-services-firms-123470588/ (archived at https://perma.cc/33ZA-JTT5)

KPMG (2018) The Pulse of Fintech Q4 2017 [online] https://home.kpmg/xx/en/home/insights/2017/10/the-pulse-of-fintech-q3-2017.html (archived at https://perma.cc/XW5F-XJSA)

McKinsey & Company (2016a) Impact of fintech on retail banking [online] https://www.financialforum.be/sites/financialforum.be/files/media/1695-3-marc-niederkorn.pdf (archived at https://perma.cc/EW8T-TLVP)

McKinsey & Company (2016b) Fintechs can help incumbents, not just disrupt them [online] https://www.mckinsey.com/industries/financial-services/our-insights/fintechs-can-help-incumbents-not-just-disrupt-them (archived at https://perma.cc/4J54-6EA3)

Mindtree (2018) Reg Tech – the next wave to disrupt the financial regulatory landscape, 25 May [online] https://www.mindtree.com/blog/reg-tech-next-wave-disrupt-financial-regulatory-landscape (archived at https://perma.cc/N5QR-EPWE)

Nonninger, L (2017) Thomson Reuters launches a regtech solution, *Business Insider*, 3 May [online] https://www.businessinsider.com/ibm-thomson-reuters-launch-ai-regtech-solution-2019-5?r=US&IR=T (archived at https://perma.cc/QJC6-GNL8)

Pham, J (2017) Citi Report: continue to watch China & FinTech in 2017, *CrowdFund Insider* 22 January [online] https://www.crowdfundinsider.com/2017/01/95271-citi-report-continue-watch-china-fintech-2017/ (archived at https://perma.cc/ZX4B-BDKH)

SG Analytics (2016) The future of fintech, 14 December [online] https://www.sganalytics.com/blog/fintech-future-opportunity-banking/ (archived at https://perma.cc/2D94-DASY)

09

Collaboration models within fintech

As fintech is increasingly ridding itself of tall highs and deep lows and maturing into a strong, stable industry with the support of a strong, stable ecosystem, the extent and nature of collaboration have become key drivers. Collaboration was primarily between banks and fintechs in the early days, but no longer. The number of parties involved in identifying and deploying fintech use cases has increased significantly in the past few years.

Bank–fintech

This is one of the most obvious areas of collaboration in the fintech industry, with the existing financial architecture keen to get on board with this hugely profitable niche. An ever-increasing number of traditional banks are now collaborating with fintech firms, and we can expect to see this expand further still in the years to come.

Indeed, a report from CapGemini (2018) indicated that 91 per cent of bank executives would like to work with fintech companies in some capacity. The high regard that traditional financial institutions have for fintechs is reflected in the fact that the same report suggested that 86 per cent of bank executives believe that a lack of collaboration with fintechs will hurt their overall business. While there is an increased understanding that collaboration is valuable, the type and nature of this collaboration will ultimately define its effectiveness. Collaboration in fintech must be designed to meet the specific needs of all stakeholders, aligned with strategic business objectives and the financial goals of each participant.

The collaboration is not just a 'pull' based on demands from the banks, but also a 'push' due to several regulatory factors. New regulations, such as Europe's Revised Payment Service Directive (PSD2) and open banking standards in the UK, are encouraging partnerships between banks and fintechs by sharing data between all parties of the bank–fintech ecosystem. Considering that nearly half of bank executives also believe that working with fintech can help reduce their operating costs, it's clear that there is a raft of incentives for these partnerships.

Another challenge for banks has been the implications from platformification (Finastra, 2018). This model, in which both providers and consumers connect with platforms, interact, create and exchange value, can be seen as a much more reciprocal relationship than has been the case traditionally. While platformification is an exciting prospect for both banks and customers, it also raises significant challenges. Curating an ecosystem that can deliver innovations as quickly as possible certainly poses logistical issues. Monetizing and keeping track of partnered offerings can prove to be tricky and contentious. But the benefits for both banks and fintechs are becoming increasingly clear, especially in light of new regulations and standards.

Some of the most popular ways of bank–fintech collaboration are acquisitions, seed investments, accelerator programmes, hackathons and business partnerships.

Banking accelerator programmes for fintech

One of the earliest modes of engagement between banks and fintechs was through banks' own accelerator programmes. Banks would select 10 to 20 start-ups every year, which they thought were the most innovative in the industry, to observe, learn and possibly integrate them in. Sometimes a small seed investment would be provided.

I have observed over the last few years that there are some segments of fintech that are more popular than others for these programmes. Lending, big data and analytics, payments/remittance and cash management are some of these segments that seem to be in most of the accelerator programmes. The key to selection seems to be the level of innovation, and not necessarily the ability to be integrated into the bank as a product or channel. Thus there are B2B as well as B2C firms aplenty in each of these programmes.

Banks' acquisitions of fintechs

Banks' outright acquisitions of fintech start-ups are not as common as accelerator programmes and seed investments, but there are some great examples of innovation integration in these acquisitions. Research by CB Insights (2018) found that while the top 10 US banks have acquired 18 fintech start-ups, eight of these acquisitions took place in 2017; more than in any of the previous years.

One of the most important acquisitions (at least from my view-point!) has been that of Simple by BBVA in 2014. The news of this acquisition completely changed my career path in the fintech world – from being an early observer of a highly niche and disruptive industry that almost no one in the banking world took notice of, I was suddenly writing about a major threat to the financial services world and a global bank having the courage and know-how to significantly invest in it. It certainly made most banks sit up and take notice of the 'little' fintech world of the time.

Other acquisitions of fintechs by banks:

Ally Bank – TradeKing, 2016.

BBVA – Holvi, 2016.

BBVA – Openpay, 2016.

BNP Paribas – Compte-Nickel, 2017.

BPCE – Fidor Bank, 2016.

Capital One – Level Money, 2015.

Credit Suisse – Tradeplus24, 2017.

Deutsche Bank – Quantiguous, 2018.

Goldman Sachs – Honest Dollar, 2016.

Goldman Sachs – Financeit, 2017.

ING Group – Lendico, 2018.

Société Générale – Lumo, 2018.

Banks partnering with fintechs for go-to-market

Another area of collaboration between traditional banks and fintechs is with go-to-market partnerships through joint products or services. Banks recognize that fintechs are far more efficient with R&D and quicker in launching new products in the market, so use them as a means of testing out a new digital product or acquiring a new set of customers. Banks gain from their relationships with fintechs by gaining access to a knowledge base that would otherwise be outside of their capabilities, along with innovative new technologies, insightful use of data and analysis, and an awareness of disruptive technologies that will help enliven their existing business models.

Fintechs are also keen to form these partnerships in order to draw on the banks' centuries or decades of experience with processes, security guidelines, knowledge of regulations and levels of scale in the financial markets.

An interesting case study of a go-to-market partnership involves the Citizens Bank, a US-based bank, and Fundation, a start-up that helped the bank build digital loan capabilities. The partnership was established as a way of improving the customer experience for Citizens Bank's existing customers and to improve efficiency of credit delivery. Customers have the option of linking their online banking information to the application, providing convenience and instant access for clients. Information can also be fed back to customers, as it is collected by the Fundation platform from a variety of third-party sources. Fundation's platform is also able to perform credit checks and enact other related policies. This is expected to evolve into an omnichannel optimized experience, delivering what the customer needs, when they need it, through multiple touchpoints.

Another interesting example of collaboration in the space involves Commerzbank and IDnow. Commerzbank came to the fintech with a problem related to EU regulations. European Union laws currently require bank customers to verify their identities to banks in person, effectively making it impossible to sign up outside branches, at least for the majority of banks. Addressing this, IDnow produced a solution for Commerzbank, which enabled the institution to verify customer identity via video. This system could then be used with computers and mobile devices in order to confirm identity without requiring customers to come into branches. Clearly, this offers massive convenience for customers, and this was reflected in a 50 per cent upward surge in conversion for Commerzbank customers.

A third interesting case study involves the partnership between Bankia and Eurobits. Bankia is one of Spain's major banks, formed by the consolidation of seven banks in 2010. Responsible for managing the accounts of 33,000 SMEs, Bankia had faced huge difficulties with invoicing and billing costs, often resulting in payments to suppliers being delayed. In an attempt to address this issue, Eurobits provided an invoicing platform which enables the creation of supplier portals to operate with the bank, and which also has the capability to integrate with other enterprise resource planners. Having implemented this new approach, Bankia was able to go virtually paperless and move all invoicing to its new electronic system. As a result of this, nearly all invoicing takes place in the electronic realm, which has created massive savings for the company. Bankia has noted that the new system has resulted in a saving of €2.50 per invoice sent, which equates to millions of euros when projected across thousands of accounts. Furthermore, Bankia has been able to reduce the payment period associated with invoices to 10 days, ensuring that the payment process is smoother for everyone involved.

Numerous other prominent bank and fintech partnerships are emerging. For example, HSBC believes its collaboration with Tradeshift will represent a massive financial opportunity, due to the $46 trillion tied up in accounts receivable worldwide.

The Dutch development bank FMO and African fintech above & beyond collaboration FinForward offers innovation while aiming to foster financial inclusion in some of Africa's poorest nations. In July 2017, a joint report from the Center for Financial Inclusion at Accion and the Institute of International Finance examined how financial institutions and fintechs are partnering for inclusion. The report concluded that 'if financial institutions can continue to learn from fintechs, and if the relationships can continue to be mutually beneficial, we see a bright future for partnerships enabling financial inclusion' (IIF, 2017).

API portals

A final mode of collaboration between fintechs and banks will be the utilization of portals for developer application programming interfaces (APIs). Several banks are already involved with developing these one-stop portals including all developer APIs, with the hope of better research around their clients and the customer journey, while also providing an enhanced user interface for bank customers.

API portals will support the interconnection of third-party applications with bank systems, thus providing new and improved experiences for customers. The ability to deliver distinct B2B, B2C and B2E experiences will be valuable for banks and their clients alike. This fintech approach will ultimately deliver user experiences that are driven by autonomy, mutual gains and self-service, helping to transform the entire banking industry, particularly at the retail and customer level.

This new ecosystem of applications with multiple capabilities and its implications for the banking sphere led Goldman Sachs CEO Lloyd Blankfein to describe the bank as a 'technology company' (Brooker, 2015). This is indicative of the general direction of several banks in the wake of the fintech revolution.

Fintech–fintech

The second area of collaboration in the fintech space will involve fintechs partnering up with other fintech firms for market access or product enhancement.

While B2B fintechs will always likely compete with one another for a slice of the banking pie, there is also huge potential for them to collaborate in order to enhance one another's effectiveness and competitiveness. By engaging in well-founded collaboration and sharing skillsets and knowledge, fintechs will be better placed to go to market and achieve scale, produce superior products with a wide range of features, tap into global marketplaces, develop API partnerships and enhance the overall operational and commercial viability.

There are several examples of such collaborations in the banking-as-a-service space, where BaaS players facilitate go-to-market options for start-ups through pre-created products and licences. For fintechs looking to bring new products and services to consumers, there are several API-based banking options available that allow them to ramp up their service suite by 'borrowing' products from a white label BaaS provider. This mode of delivery is usually faster, easier, cost-effective (being on-demand) and comprehensive. This would mean that the fintech has no need of the underlying support and infrastructure offered by a traditional bank. Solaris Bank in Germany, Starling Bank in the UK, Green Dot and Cross River Bank in the United States are examples of providers of BaaS offerings working closely with fintech and non-fintech players to offer banking services to the mass market.

Other exciting players in this niche include financial data aggregation solutions such as the partnership between Salt Edge and Yolt. This smart money app and API combo enables consumers to connect to more than 3,000 banks worldwide. There are also some interesting B2B marketplace solutions emerging. Mambu is a prominent example of this, offering a variety of both localized and globalized solutions that can be integrated with an SaaS engine.

CurrencyCloud is another start-up that has achieved substantial market penetration in its young life, also entering into partnerships with several online banks. Its collaboration with FidorBank (Currencycloud, 2015) resulted in a huge reduction in forex costs for customers, while FidorBank was able to increase its client base by nearly 60 per cent. The mobile-only bank Monese also partnered with CurrencyCloud, achieving a tenfold decrease in forex costs and a massive reduction in payment fees. CurrencyCloud also teamed up with Revolut, attracting 160,000 new customers to the app, thanks to the ability to save around €40 per foreign transaction (Currencycloud, 2015). This is a great case study of how a wider fintech ecosystem has emerged with a full product portfolio, through successful partnerships.

Another field for fintech–fintech collaboration is digital identity, with one such example being the work of Avoka and Trulioo. This partnership has delivered a digital identity verification solution that enables the bank to meet compliance requirements in a more agile and flexible way.

As the fintech field develops, government bodies will increasingly invest in the technology, for example with industry clusters, which were fostered by investment from Finance Innovation France in 2007. This initiative is intended to help develop innovation in the French financial sector and encompasses over 140 corporates and banks, 300+ fintechs and SMEs, along with 30 academic institutions (Finance Innovation, 2016). This has resulted in over 2,000 innovative projects being launched in France over an 11-year period, with 600 of these being fintech certified. Between 2005 and 2016, 1,681 collaborative R&D projects received public financing of €6.8 billion. This sort of partnership is helping fintech reach its potential in a complex and fast-moving world.

Other regions have adopted different approaches. In Scandinavia, Nets fosters fintech alliances in the region, providing financial infrastructure for developments in the industry. Nets represents a major network of 240 major Nordic banks, 300,000 Nordic merchants and e-commerce merchants, and 240,000 private and public-sector companies (GlobeNewsWire, 2016). Nets' support for fintech start-ups has enabled widespread collaboration, resulting in a wide range of strategic partnerships. The organization has also built alliances with other similar initiatives across the Nordic region, resulting in partnerships with Copenhagen Fintech, IT-Branchen, IKT Norge and Fintech Factory.

And such partnerships are not limited to developed economies. In Africa, fintech collaboration is being used to help facilitate cross-border payments in a part of the world in which the financial infrastructure is still relatively embryonic.

One such example is Finserve Africa – a wholly owned subsidiary of Kenya's biggest lender. Finserve Africa has already signed up the Chinese third-party payment platform Alipay, along with WeChat, a social media and mobile payments app by Tencent Holdings. Having closed these deals, Fintech Africa then set up the acquired technology on a merchant aggregation platform, which has been providing valuable functionality to this region.

Hubs such as these have played a massive role in helping fintech–fintech collaboration develop, and are also supporting fintechs with skills and know-how, helping further widen the fintech ecosystem.

Regulator–fintech

As regulators are beginning to understand and work with the fintech industry, the level of collaboration has increased beyond what I would have envisaged in the early 2010s. In the early days of fintech, the conversations were very much around how fintechs will be regulated and how licenses will be issued by the regulators for challenger banks. However, there has been an increasing trend of regulators and supervisors working closely with fintechs on challenges faced by the wider financial market to come up with solutions to reduce market risk and improve reporting.

The FCA was one of the first regulators to provide a 'sandbox', intended to provide fintech firms with the ability to test new products and services in a controlled environment. This has enabled the UK to lead the world in terms of fintech regulatory initiatives, with 95 firms having already participated in the four sandbox experiments. Of these firms, 90 per cent have already progressed towards a wider market launch, while over 40 per cent received investment funding during the sandbox process, illustrating the success of this policy (CrowdFund Insider, 2019).

Also, the FCA is beginning to export its sandbox model to overseas territories, announcing a major partnership with 11 foreign financial regulators (Peyton, 2018), forming the Global Financial Innovation Network (GFIN).

The GFIN members are:

Abu Dhabi Global Market (ADGM)

Australian Securities & Investments Commission (ASIC)

Autorité des marchés financiers (AMF, Quebec)

Bureau of Consumer Financial Protection (BCFP, USA)

Central Bank of Bahrain (CBB)

Consultative Group to Assist the Poor (CGAP)

Dubai Financial Services Authority (DFSA)

Financial Conduct Authority (FCA, UK)

Guernsey Financial Services Commission (GFSC)

Hong Kong Monetary Authority (HKMA)

Monetary Authority of Singapore (MAS)

Ontario Securities Commission (OSC, Canada)

In launching the GFIN, the FCA has said it hopes to:

1 act as a network of regulators to collaborate and share the experience of innovation in respective markets, including emerging technologies and business models;

2 provide a forum for joint policy work and discussions;

3 provide firms with an environment in which to trial cross-border solutions.

The FCA has arguably been the most active of the regulatory bodies, having several projects currently under operation. It is also implementing the integration of search and tagging features in its regulatory handbook, building an AI-based intelligent front-end advisor intended to handhold applicants through its manual via automated guidance, and ensuring programmability of regulations to enable financial institutions to map their regulatory requirements directly to the data they hold. This will create the potential for automated and straight-forward processing of statutory returns.

With Arizona having become the first US state to adopt a regulatory sandbox, in August 2018, this concept is moving forward to the Americas, which have lagged behind Europe and Asia.

Private–public sandboxes are also emerging in Europe. Fidor Solutions recently signed an agreement with AFIN, in a consortium with Virtusa and Percipient. This will create an API-based marketplace and sandbox environment, open to both banks and fintechs, to create a collaborative ecosystem, fast-tracking the delivery of innovation and empowering new technology developments.

Aside from the sandbox environment, regulators are also beginning to work directly with fintechs. This has led to the term SupTech being coined, which refers to supervisory technology in the fintech space. Such solutions are intended to help tackle problems faced by regulatory agencies and to automate and streamline administrative and operational procedures.

SupTech involves the application of digital technology and enables the scope of financial supervision to be widened. Implementing such technology makes it easier for regulators to capture, process, store, manage, analyse, distribute and act to meet their risk and conduct goals. SupTech is currently involved primarily with data collection and analytics and enables financial regulators to transform supervisory data rapidly.

Singapore has been a pioneer in this area, with the executives at the Monetary Authority of Singapore having spoken widely about the 'active integration of technology into the supervisory process dramatically enhancing supervisory effectiveness'. They expect that:

- data analytics will finally solve the long-standing challenge that banks have had in aggregating credit and market exposures across various businesses and geographies;

- this will enable banks to derive a consolidated risk profile in real time;

- the integration of RegTech and SupTech will allow data from financial institutions to flow directly into regulators' databases in machine-readable formats through APIs.

Any fear that the traditional financial organizations have a vested interest in maintaining the status quo, and see fintech as something of a veiled threat to this hegemony, is clearly no longer valid thanks to the attitude of the supervisors. Fintech will thus become more and more seamlessly integrated in the world economic and financial system in the next decade.

There are several examples of SupTech solutions being implemented around the world. The National Bank of Rwanda has partnered with Sunoida Solutions to develop an electronic data warehouse that will pull together data from 600 supervised financial institutions. The Central Bank of the Republic of Austria has instigated a new data-input approach to regulatory reporting, partnering with the Austrian Reporting Services GmbH (AuRep). This reporting platform is helping to bridge the gap between the IT systems of supervised entities, and the supervisory agency. AuRep is co-owned by seven of the largest Austrian banking groups, and this is helping to lend efficiency and scale to this process. As European authorities adopt similar regulation mechanisms, it is expected that high-quality and more timely granular bank data will be produced.

Efforts are not limited to Europe either, with the Australian Securities and Investments Commission (ASIC) having unveiled the Market Analysis and Intelligence (MAI) system. MAI is a SupTech platform that enables all equities and equity derivatives products and transactions to be monitored in real time. With big data and machine-learning tie-ins, this is deemed to be a highly effective system which will have a big impact on identifying trading anomalies in Australia.

EXAMPLES OF SUPTECH USE CASES

- Consumer complaint oversight.
- Reporting utilities.
- Feedback on policy effectiveness.
- Market manipulation monitoring.
- Insider trading supervision.
- Policy harmonization.
- Financial centre development.
- Real-time compliance supervision.

It is clear that SupTech solutions will help regulators become more forward looking with policies thanks to the underlying data and predictive capabilities of the SupTech start-ups.

Regulator–regulator

One final area of collaboration in the fintech space relates to regulator–regulator or government-government partnerships.

In 2016, the FCA and ASIC signed an agreement to support fintech start-ups (Adams, 2016). As a result of this agreement, the two regulators will essentially refer to each other innovative companies seeking to enter one another's markets. The two bodies will also share information, as they oversee a fintech industry that has grown to be worth around $12.5bn (£6.6bn) and $1.3bn (£0.7bn) in the UK and Australia respectively.

Another influential development has been around 'fintech bridges' – the collaborative programmes between two nations that facilitate the entry of start-ups into regulatory sandboxes or the wider market in the two nations. Fintech bridges are also intended to enable document processing to take place more rapidly, with regard to licensing businesses that have previously been authorized in the other jurisdiction.

Again, the FCA has been particularly active in this area, having established the first-ever fintech bridges between the UK and Singapore in early 2016. Since then, the UK has fostered further bridges with Canada, China, Hong Kong, Japan, South Korea and Australia.

There are currently expected to be 63 bilateral co-operation agreements (KAE, 2019) signed between various countries.

Some of the most prominent of these include:

- the February 2018 agreement between the FCA and the US Commodity Futures Trading Commission (FCA, 2018) which formalizes a relationship between the two regulatory agencies to support the innovation initiatives LabCFTC and FCA Innovate;

- the June 2018 agreement between India's Department of Economic Affairs (DEA) and MAS for expanding their existing partnership model in fintech;

- the September 2018 partnership between the FCA and MAS which would enable them to work closely together on a variety of fintech solutions, including around supervisory tech, cybersecurity and cryptocurrencies.

So why are regulators so keen to enter into fintech-related partnerships? Well, firstly, by doing so they help circumnavigate any risk related to regulatory standards suffering. This could conceivably occur as different jurisdictions compete for business. Policy harmonization across borders will help banks as well as fintechs launch products (be they regional or cross-border), expand and operate smoothly.

The second reason is to help ensure that fintechs can be scaled adequately. In particular, fintech companies face challenges with expansion into new locations, while also scaling operations suitably. Each country presents different market conditions for fintechs, while the regulatory environment from nation to nation also varies quite significantly. This can actually pose major financial problems for fintech firms.

And there are several advantages of collaboration fundamentally related to the cooperation itself. Sharing experience in respected markets is certainly helpful, while creating a mechanism to aid discussion on various hot topics is also undoubtedly useful. And the ability for those regulating the fintech industry to coordinate their efforts in the implementation of proposed measures will certainly benefit from such cross-border arrangements.

Beyond these obvious collaboration models, the ever-widening fintech ecosystem is also bringing in partners like universities, training service providers, traditional software providers, domain experts, content producers and consulting firms into the mix. As the fintech sphere develops, various forms of collaboration are continuously developing. These partnerships are sprouting up among different geographical regions, and also among different stakeholders in the industry. The nature of these arrangements is still evolving as the fintech industry finds its feet in the global financial architecture, but it can be anticipated that the roots that have been planted are only the beginning of this ongoing trend.

References

Adams, D (2016) FCA and ASIC sign FinTech agreement, *FS Tech*, 23 March [online] https://www.fstech.co.uk/fst/FCA_ASIC_Regulators_FinTech_Agreement.php (archived at https://perma.cc/H7PG-SH99)

Brooker, K (2015) Goldman in Ventureland, *Bloomberg*, 28 July [online] https://www.bloomberg.com/news/features/2015-07-28/how-goldman-sachs-became-a-tech-investing-powerhouse (archived at https://perma.cc/LE9M-9NV4)

CapGemini (2018) Top-10 trends in retail banking: 2018, 29 November [online] https://www.capgemini.com/resources/top-10-technology-trends-in-retail-banking-2018/ (archived at https://perma.cc/H4MY-ZW52)

CB Insights (2018) Banks are finally going after fintech start-ups, 13 February [online] https://www.cbinsights.com/research/top-us-banks-fintech-acquisitions/ (archived at https://perma.cc/YF9H-D839)

CrowdFund Insider (2019) Delaware in a fintech future [online] https://cdn. crowdfundinsider.com/wp-content/uploads/2019/06/Delaware-Fintech-Future-060519-web.pdf (archived at https://perma.cc/7M78-9BCU)

Currencycloud (2015) Making multi-currency eWallets possible with Fidor Bank [online] https://www.currencycloud.com/company/case-study/making-multi-currency-ewallets-possible-fidor-bank/ (archived at https://perma.cc/TD7F-RFF7)

Currencycloud (2016) Building a global money app with Revolut [online] https://www.currencycloud.com/company/case-study/building-a-global-money-app-with-revolut/ (archived at https://perma.cc/9VVG-YY8E)

FCA (2018) US CFTC and UK FCA Sign Arrangement to Collaborate on FinTech Innovation [online] https://www.fca.org.uk/news/press-releases/fca-and-us-cftc-sign-arrangement-collaborate-fintech-innovation (archived at https://perma.cc/7UAS-WRUN)

Finance Innovation (2016) Key figures [online] https://finance-innovation.org/en/ (archived at https://perma.cc/XC9E-KHZF)

Finastra (2018) Platformification: how banks can transform their innovation efforts, 25 May https://www.finastra.com/viewpoints/market-insights/platformification-how-banks-can-transform-their-innovation-efforts (archived at https://perma.cc/RLA5-NYGZ)

GlobeNewsWire (2016) Company announcement No. 1/2016 [online] http://inpublic.globenewswire.com/2016/09/01/Nets+A+S+Nets+announces+intention+to+launch+an+Initial+Public+Offering+HUG2038966.html (archived at https://perma.cc/ZK2R-WED4)

IIF (2017) Partnerships Report [online] https://www.iif.com/Publications/ID/709/How-Financial-Institutions-and-Fintechs-Are-Partnering-for-Inclusion (archived at https://perma.cc/7SXE-QTFF)

KAE (2019) Fintech bridges across the globe [online] https://kae.com/infographic/Fintech-Bridges-Across-The-Globe/ (archived at https://perma.cc/4UH4-URV4)

Peyton, A (2018) Regulator syndicate unleashes Global Financial Innovation Network, *Fintech Futures,* 7 August [online] https://www.fintechfutures.com/2018/08/regulator-syndicate-unleashes-global-financial-innovation-network/ (archived at https://perma.cc/A7PJ-M5T7)

10

Challenger banking

A challenger bank, or more accurately, a bank challenger, is a digital bank that offers a product, service or delivery mechanism that challenges the traditional modes of banking. Most of these challenger banks have come up in the past 10 years and have gone on to disrupt traditional banking through a high degree of focus on customer experience as well as digital products and customer service that do not need bricks and mortar (or phone lines!) to work. They are usually website- or app-based banks with no branches. Some of the challengers need not even have full banking licences – describing all of them as a 'bank' is thus inaccurate, but we continue to do so as an industry-accepted term.

This is the topic I am most asked to speak or write about, the main reason being that the UK is a hotbed of challenger banks, thanks to the early licences given out by the FCA. There were 53 challenger banks launched or being launched in the UK in 2019 and several of them are now valued at over $1 billion, making them a popular category of unicorns. They are also the coolest cousins of fintech, with intuitive features on the apps and advertisements on the London underground.

The term 'challenger bank' originated in the UK, and the vast majority of challengers are still in the UK thanks to a friendly regulatory environment and the traditionally strong fintech and entrepreneurial ecosystem. However, the number of challenger banks globally is now almost on par with the UK, and our definition of 'challenger banking' has expanded to include any primarily digital bank that challenges existing products or processes in a traditional bank.

Types of challenger banks

There are mainly three types of challenger banks (Burnmark, 2016). The umbrella of 'challenger banks' includes multiple personalities of apps, websites, branches and a combination of these:

- **Embryonic challengers**: fintech innovators on the banking value chain who operate only through mobile apps in partnership with traditional banks or other challenger banks. Examples are Pockit and Loot.

- **Real challengers**: previously non-existent banks that have obtained a banking licence on their own or are in the process of procuring a banking licence AND have digital as the only or predominant channel for engaging with customers. Examples are Atom Bank, Starling Bank, Monzo.

- **Pseudo challengers**: the digital subsidiaries, digital partners (neo banks) and digital start-ups of existing banks which engage with customers through both branch and digital channels. Examples are Moven, Simple, Hello Bank.

Reasons for the emergence of challenger banks

Changes in technology, together with customer behaviour and the economy are bringing about disruptive and disintermediating changes to financial institutions. There are multiple reasons for emergence of challenger banks, and they also depend on the regions they belong to, given the region-specific problems that they are trying to solve. The reasons why challenger banks have become such an effective disruptor to the traditional banking industry can be summed up as follows.

Demographic change and demand from a new generation

According to the US Census Bureau (2016), those born between 1982 and 2000 are an entirely different 'generation' – the millennials. This generation has seen the collapse of several traditional financial institutions, and are increasingly concerned about financial stability due to their early years being spent in a drawn-out financial crisis. The millennials are digital natives, highly tech savvy and socially hyperconnected. They have grown up using simplified experiences like Google and Facebook, and are more comfortable with on-demand services like AirBnB and Uber. They tend to be always on the go and care about experiences rather than traditional banking. They do not like to queue in branches but want banking done on the go, using their smartphones.

This is a fast-growing market, containing approximately 2.5 billion of the world's population according to Pew Research (2018), and its own super set of customer experience needs and desires from every product or service they are looking to acquire. The fundamental shift in demographics along with economic drivers like low interest rates and the desire for a simplified, intuitive, on-demand and mostly free customer service is leading this group to explore options beyond traditional banking. The first line of challenger banks seems to have understood this market well, and they have been able to capture a large chunk of the market, acquiring millions of customers.

Smartphone penetration

Most of the developed economies across the world have very high smartphone penetration, with South Korea at 95 per cent, the Netherlands at 87 per cent and Germany at 78 per cent. The emerging economies are also showcasing high smartphone penetration, in some cases almost on a par with the developed countries – with South Africa at 60 per cent, Brazil 60 per cent, the Philippines 55 per cent, Tunisia 45 per cent, and Israel 88 per cent (Wiggers, 2019).

Countries with high smartphone penetration are fertile grounds for challenger banks to grow in. Challengers collaborate with traditional banks in developed markets with high smartphone and retail banking penetration to restore customer trust in banking. They do this by improving customer experience and by extending the benefits of lower operating costs directly to customers. Developing countries with high smartphone penetration and low banking reach are also seeing the challenger banks leading financial inclusion initiatives.

Deteriorating customer confidence in banking

In the developed market, especially Western Europe and the United States, the trust of customers has taken a beating since the financial crisis, and bankers are the least trusted professionals, ranking below even real estate agents. Most of the countries show low and very low confidence in the traditional banking industry with the UK at 3 per cent, France 33 per cent, Germany 40 per cent, Italy 24 per cent and the United States at 37 per cent.

In such a scenario, challenger banks are seen as customer-centric financial institutions that are worthy of trying in place of the traditional banks.

Meeting unsatisfied needs

Challenger banks meet the needs of a niche segment that was poorly served by traditional retail or corporate banks. This segment includes students, SMEs, refugees and those with poor credit or a lack of address history. Larger banks tend to overlook these smaller groups of people and have offered lending and accounts services traditionally to market segments such as large corporates or salaried individuals. Challenger banks fill up this void and make banking and lending services easily available to niche segments. They use innovative methods of KYC (know your customer) and new data-based credit scoring to offer these services with minimal risk.

Emerging markets

Emerging markets are looking at challengers as a means to accelerate banking innovation as well as financial inclusion. There are countries in Asia and Africa that have previously not had a strong traditional banking network but are increasingly shifting towards the widespread use of mobile phones. As mobile penetration is increasing in the emerging markets, banks utilizing digital channels to onboard, engage or serve customers are evolving to become an important medium for financial inclusion initiatives.

Differences between challenger banks and traditional banks

From size to provision of services, there are numerous differences between challenger banks and traditional banks.

Efficiency

Challenger banks are, by nature, smaller than traditional banks and can operate more efficiently due to their size and use of underlying data-based technologies. They do not have the high costs of running branches and call centres and rely heavily on onboarding through digital channels. Thus the costs of KYC and customer service are significantly lower than those of traditional banks.

Focus

Although the purpose of banking is to serve the population and government by storing money and providing mortgages or loans, the services are not that customer-centric. Banking resolved many problems by offering its services, but still many are yet to be solved. Challenger banks aim to address these existing problems by constructing a banking model that is fully concentrated on customer service.

Services

Traditional brick-and-mortar banks and challenger banks provide a varying array of services, typically under a single umbrella brand. While conventional banks offer services that require you to visit the bank, challenger banks have successfully contained services that can be acquired online. Challenger banks have all these services, from opening an account to withdrawing or transferring money, that can be done through online transactions. However, challenger banks tend to focus more on the customer experience rather than on individual products, which means that sometimes the products themselves are not visible or sold as such. The product portfolio may seem narrow, but the servicing and digital experience are usually what set challengers apart from traditional banking.

Premises

A high street bank is often seen as a busy, crowded branch with several tellers. Challenger banks may just as well spin that around. As all of the transactions done in challenger banks occur online, there is technically no need of a physical branch. There are only a handful of challenger banks that offer servicing via phones or call centres, while all the others rely on email or chatbot support and offer products exclusively via websites and apps.

Transactions, customer complaints, money transfers, everything from A–Z can be done online using just a mobile phone. Even employees and employers do not necessarily base themselves out of a corporate office.

The idea of fewer premises adds a whole new perspective to banking, as big banks traditionally spread their reign by creating new premises and acquiring valuable real estate. This is closely tied to efficiency, as fewer premises means lower costs and higher productivity, offering challengers much more flexibility in managing costs, handling downturns and focusing on innovation.

Services provided by challenger banks

Despite their small size and structure, when it comes to services, challenger banks give as good as, if not better than, the rest. The main services offered by challenger banks include: digital banking (including mobile banking and merchant accounts); generic banking (including savings and checking accounts); savings (fixed savings, savings bonds, retirement savings account, quick savings, easy savings, certificates of deposit, investment accounts, etc); credit cards; consumer lending; mortgages; and cryptocurrency trading, buying and selling. Any typical bank provides all these services, but with challenger banks they are all now available digitally. Your smartphone is enough to create these accounts and enjoy these services.

NICHE TARGET SEGMENTS WITHIN CHALLENGER BANK CONSUMER LENDING

Some of the largest and most untapped markets by traditional banks are student lending, SME lending and mortgage lending. This gap provides to niche challenger banks a fertile area in which they can grow quickly and a tremendous opportunity to do so with relatively low customer acquisition costs. These niches are witnessing a huge amount of attention from innovative marketplace lenders, P2P lenders as well as challenger banks.

STUDENT LENDING

Student debt is spiralling out of control in the UK and the US, rising from $200 billion to $1.4 trillion in just over a decade from 2003 to 2016. The average annual tuition fees for a four-year undergraduate degree in the United States is close to $9,100 at public institutes and $31,200 at private institutes (Burnmark, 2016). In such a scenario, where many students have no option but to take out loans to complete their degrees, a tremendous opportunity opens for challenger banks.

SME LENDING

SME lending is a segment largely neglected by traditional banks even though there were a record 5.4 million private-sector businesses at the start of 2015. On average, credit bureaus in the EU only have credit information on 67 per cent of SMEs, reducing SME loans. SME lending has also declined by 20 per cent since the EU implemented Basel regulations.

In the United States, of all the loan applications from SMEs in January 2015, only 21.3 per cent were approved by the largest banks, while alternative lenders approved 61.6 per cent (Biz2Credit, 2015).

MORTGAGE LENDING

In 2016 in the UK, mortgages worth £13.4 billion were approved and mortgage originations jumped to a two-year high, according to the Bank of England. In March 2016, the average interest on a standard variable rate mortgage fell by 10 basis points to 4.57 per cent. Rates on new two-year fixed-rate mortgages fell by six points to 1.87 per cent, while five-year mortgages dropped by seven points to 2.71 per cent. The buy-to-let market in the UK is a significant contributor towards the overall profitability of the sector, accounting for approximately 15 per cent of challenger balance sheets.

In the United States, mortgage balances shown on consumer credit reports stood at $8.37 trillion, a $120 billion increase from the fourth quarter of 2015.

Facts about challenger bank use

The following facts taken from Burnmark's Challenger Banking Report (2016) offer a glimpse into the mindset of people and their opinions and reasons for using or not using the services offered by challenger banks.

25- to 34-year-old males: the largest group of challenger bank users

Fifty-six per cent of challenger bank users were aged between 25 and 34, and 61 per cent were male. The so-called largest target demographic of challenger banks, the 18–25 age group, constituted 17 per cent, which was less than the 35–44 age group. The report found that customers across age groups embraced challenger banking – it was clearly not a millennial-only phenomenon.

However, the report also found that a deep desire to have an app or digital channel to access a bank account was the highest for 18–25-year-olds, the primary demographic target, with the desire mostly decreasing with age.

Most users take challenger bank accounts to 'try them out'

An interesting find by the Burnmark report was that more than 74 per cent of the total respondents claimed that the primary reason for their opening a challenger bank account was to try it out. Features such as ease of use when travelling, better rates or specific offers (mostly for students), easier sign-up process, and recommendations from friends or colleagues were also significant reasons that swayed users towards challenger banks.

These numbers make sense in the early days of challenger banks; the primary reason is expected to be existing banking users trying the new apps to see what they're missing out on.

Lack of physical branches: a reason for some people refusing to even try a challenger bank

Among non-users of challenger banks, 60 per cent of respondents had never heard of challenger banks (not just the term, but the individual bank brands like Atom or Revolut as well). A third of the survey respondents still wanted 'the option' to use a branch. These people were not necessarily regular branch users, but they still liked to know that the option was there in case they ever had an issue and needed to talk to someone or share documents. Trust and a limited choice of products and services are other major reasons for not using the challenger banks.

On the other hand, 63 per cent of non-users of challenger banks were likely to consider switching if the process of moving accounts were made easier. Fifty per cent wanted irresistible offers and 15 per cent wanted the bank to be in existence for at least five years before they would switch.

New channels of digital customer service, including chatbots and social media payments, are accepted across all demographics

Contrary to popular belief, 82 per cent of the respondents did not care if they talked to a chatbot or a human being for customer service. They were also happy to pay their friends and family over social media such as Twitter and Facebook. All the respondents liked using apps, with far fewer people enjoying using branches, websites and phones for customer service.

Threats to traditional banks

Many have argued that challenger banks bring about certain challenges for traditional banks. Reports suggest that very recently, many banks have been opening wings for online or mobile banking in fear of challenging banks slowly taking over.

With the simultaneous offerings from both traditional and challenger banks, they are head to head in competition in terms of providing services. However, challenger banks do pose some unique new threats to existing banking institutions and in many areas transcend them.

Challenger banks provide a higher level of customer convenience. The whole idea of challenger banks was to provide customers with easier means of transactions and create a customer-centric business model suiting their needs. This will bring about some challenges for traditional walk-in banks because they do not focus as highly on customers. Instead, their focus lies on making higher profits through interest, spreading globally, creating MNCs, and bringing in more clients.

The ultimate target for traditional banks is growing the business, but challenger banks create goals on the basis of customer problems. With time, they will be rapidly solving all the issues customers face and giving them exactly what they want. This is quite a significant threat to traditional banks.

Another key threat from challenger banks is their significant online presence; apart from customer convenience, this provides several benefits. Firstly, their presence being solely online makes it easier, simpler and more cost-effective for them to grow. They can spread rapidly and attract more customers. As challenger banks are not yet widely established, providing optimum services and getting more customers can give them many advantages similar to those of first movers.

Having an online presence cuts down many costs and enables the bank to function efficiently. Fewer premises are required, fewer employees are needed, and rent, electricity, and furniture costs are minimized. Employees can work remotely and in this way, a minimum but efficient number of employees can be hired, avoiding the need for additional personnel to clean and maintain premises.

Another way of being more efficient is by cutting down on paperwork and making the banking system less bureaucratic. Less paperwork means savings in terms of both money and space. As transactions are done online, no physical forms are required. Having an online presence and establishing this now will bring benefits for years to come.

Challenger banks can capture a large group of growing and lasting customers. By getting a grasp on them early, the most dominant challenger banks can be in a very prominent position within a few years. Just as the system of banking was originally introduced, the challengers may be able to revolutionize and alter the way we all view banking.

If this is done successfully, then in no time the brick-and-mortar banks will become obsolete. People can trust this new system of banking because challenger banks require a licence to operate. Where neo banks need to work in partnership and cannot acquire their own licence, challenger banks can, and this makes them more credible.

Challenger banks have a higher return on equity compared to traditional banks as they cut down on heavy expenditure. Furthermore, they have the scope to provide higher interest rates to customers and offer more flexibility. This, in turn, will attract more customers to the online banking scene.

All these benefits, along with the best use of financial technology, pose a serious threat to traditional brick-and-mortar banks. If this continues, then challenger banks will be the future of banking.

Challenger banks in the UK

While many claim that the UK is the birthplace of challenger banks, it is certainly true that the UK has a higher concentration of challenger banks than anywhere else. Many well-established challenger banks originated in the UK, such as N26, Revolut, Atom and Starling Bank. But why does the UK have so many challenger banks, and what effect will these have?

Sifting back through history, you may recall the 2008 financial crisis. Soon after that, the Bank of England started a new process that eventually led to this unique new method of banking – a simplified two-step process with lower capital requirements for setting up new banks. Soon, during 2009, the world saw its first challenger bank, the Metro Bank, originating in the UK. With a new outlook on the world of banking, and utilizing the best of financial technology, it was granted a licence in 2010.

Challenger banks were, in fact, a solution to the consumer's problems. After the financial crisis, people were frustrated, and their trust in the banking system started to falter. Challenger banks provided faster, more efficient and digitized services to their customers. They targeted a younger, tech-savvy customer base, who liked to conduct banking rapidly and were always on the go.

All their operations are conducted online, and they are heavily reliant on technology and research. Since 2015, about 60 physical banks have closed in the UK every month (BBC, 2018), owing to the thriving sector of banking by means of financial technology. The UK being the fourth-largest banking industry in the world, the fintech industry alone generates about £20 billion in revenue annually (Warner, 2018).

Another reason for the UK being the hotspot for challenger banks is that it was an early adopter of digital banking, which can be traced back to the late 1990s and early 2000s. The UK has always held its head high while operating in this area, and it is proudly one of the global leaders due to a thriving fintech sector. Furthermore, the FCA is launching new licence models to help create challenger banks in the UK, also in an attempt to increase competition levels.

The high concentration of challenger banks in the UK can also be attributed to the concentration of start-ups and SMEs in that area. Challenger banks focus on serving the needs of individual consumers and SMEs – often underserved by traditional banks – rather than large business organizations.

Although the individual businesses may be small, together they make up more than 90 per cent of the UK market. This accounts for a large customer base and, with time, more and more people will prefer to use services from challenger banks.

The emergence of challenger banks poses certain challenges for the existing banks in the UK. Although the big four in the UK, namely Barclays, HSBC, Lloyds Banking Group and the Royal Bank of Scotland Group, retain 70 per cent of the current account shares, the amount of loans given out by them has shot down while the lending of challenger banks has gone up (*The Economist*, 2018).

With the majority of UK businesses being SMEs, that is the customer group that challenger banks target. With such a large customer base, the big four may face troubles in the near future. Surveys suggest that many people, if not the majority, are in favour of online-only banks and the figures are on the rise (Finance Derivative, 2019). With time, these challenger banks may actually give the big four of the UK a run for their money.

Prominent challenger banks

As of 2019, there are approximately 220 banking challengers operating around the world. The UK is clearly emerging as the capital of challenger banking, followed by France, Germany, the United States and India, in terms of the number of challengers.

Table 10.1 summarizes the top challenger banks in the most prominent countries.

TABLE 10.1 Top challenger banks

Country	Bank	Proposition
United Kingdom	Atom Bank	A digital bank founded in 2014 that opened for business in October 2016. It created a hefty technology set-up in its run-up to the launch. Later it acquired a local digital design agency called Grasp.
United Kingdom	Monzo	Monzo (formerly known as Mondo) was granted a full banking licence in early April 2017. Monzo claims to be a 'mobile first' bank, offering a current account with a contactless debit card and a mobile banking app. The mobile app's standout features include smart notifications, instant balance updates and financial management. Furthermore, it has partnered with Thames Card Technology for debit card production and personalization.
United Kingdom	N26	N26 conducts business across 17 European countries, including Spain, Italy, Greece, Ireland and Slovakia, and plans to enter the United States. N26 is actually a German-based mobile challenger bank, which entered the UK market in 2018. UK customers receive a GBP current account with an individual N26 account number, sort code and Mastercard. N26 works with TransferWise on cross-border money transfers and is in partnership with Raisin.
United Kingdom	Revolut	Revolut is a payments and fintech start-up launched in mid-2015 and is based in a financial tech incubator in London. It offers a mobile money app that includes a prepaid Mastercard debit card, currency exchange and P2P payments. A free current account (with an IBAN) is also available in the UK. The majority of its services are free of charge.
United Kingdom	Tandem	This digital banking start-up was issued a licence in November 2015. Tandem focuses on helping people manage their money rather than on direct product sales. Its plans offer current accounts, credit cards, plus savings and loans. In addition to the digital delivery channels, Tandem will have a brick-and-mortar call centre to deal with customer queries and more complex transactions.

(continued)

TABLE 10.1 (Continued)

Country	Bank	Proposition
Germany	Consors Bank	Consors is the German sister bank of Hello bank! It is a digital direct bank and is part of BNP Paribas. It was launched in Germany in 2013 and offers online products, such as credit cards, loans, savings and insurance. CortalConsors, a European broker in consumer investing and online trading and owned by BNP Paribas, was rebranded in 2013–2014. After that, it was merged into Consors Bank.
Germany	Fidor	This bank is fully digital and was founded in 2009, based in Munich. It holds a full banking licence and uses its own in-house developed technology, which it also licenses to other financial institutions (such as Penta Bank). Fidor Bank operates its own technology firm called Fidor Solutions.
Germany	Penta	Penta is a digital bank account for high-tech start-ups and SMEs in Germany, founded in 2016 and based in Berlin. In early 2018, it raised a €2.2 million seed round. In April, 2019, Penta was acquired by European fintech ecosystem Finleap.
Spain	2Gether Global	This is a collaborative banking platform based in Spain, and is essentially an app. It launched its open beta in January 2019 and does not define itself as a bank, rather a platform. The basis of the model is a 2GT token, which can be acquired through the app. Users need to hold a minimum of €10 worth of 2GT to access the services, and they are rewarded for their contributions.
Spain	Bunq	This digital bank from the Netherlands launched in its home country in 2015 and announced its expansion into Spain and Italy in 2018. In September 2014, Bunq obtained its official banking permit with the Dutch Central Bank and in November 2015, the app became available to the public.
Spain	Denizen	Denizen is based in San Francisco and claims to offer the first truly global borderless account for expats. This allows customers to receive money in one country and pay it out in another. Solely for mobile banking, this bank does not charge international transfer fees or currency exchange fees. It comes with a debit card and a mobile app.

(continued)

TABLE 10.1 (Continued)

Country	Bank	Proposition
Spain	imaginBank	One of the biggest banks in Spain, CaixaBank came up with this innovative banking idea and launched imaginBank in early 2016. This is a pure form of challenger bank and is mobile only. It uses social media platforms such as Facebook to connect to its customers. The imaginBank current account is commission-free and allows customers to manage personal finances, make transfers and P2P payments. It also allows free money transfers to any account in Spain, no matter which bank the money is held at.
United States	Alpha Bank	Based in Washington DC, this is a start-up bank that specializes in offering services to SMEs. It has differentiated services by gaining its own charter and FDIC insurance to provide full-stack services to its members.
United States	Azlo	Azlo is an online business banking service that is fee-free. It was originally founded in 2017 in San Francisco and specializes in serving freelancers and entrepreneurs. Azlo's account provides domestic and cross-border banking services that require no fees or minimum monthly deposits. Its key services include unlimited domestic and international payments, bill payment, mobile cheque deposit and digital invoicing. Azlo is supported by BBVA Compass.
United States	Envel	Based in Massachusetts and founded in 2016, Envel is a start-up targeting millennials as their prime customers through its digital offering. It strives to be a differentiated and ethical challenger bank in the US and focuses on improving customers' finances. Envel is the world's first AI-powered bank.
United States	Joust	Founded in 2017 and based in Denver, Joust became a challenger bank in early 2019 by introducing its financial app targeted towards freelancers, entrepreneurs and independent contractors. The Joust app was developed in partnership with financial services toolkit Cambr. This enables users to open a free, Federal Deposit Insurance Corporation (FDIC) insured deposit account backed by a community bank. It also offers a merchant account to process credit and debit card payments for their products and services.

CASE STUDY
Revolut

There are many challenger banks available worldwide. Some are good, some have gone out of business and others are great. Revolut, a UK-based bank, is one such bank that has taken Europe by storm, and is referred to as Europe's fastest-growing unicorn.

Revolut's core product is a payment card that charges minimal fees when spending abroad. Beyond that, the company has additional financial services such as insurance, cryptocurrency trading and current accounts. Its mobile app supports spending and ATM withdrawals in 120 currencies and spending in 29 currencies directly from the app.

In October 2017, CEO Nikolay Storonsky raised $71 million at a valuation of $350 million. In 2019, that value has quintupled to $1.7 billion, following a record $250 million funding round led by Hong Kong's DST Global (Kharpal, 2018). The new valuation makes Revolut worth more than TransferWise, and it can proudly boast to being one of Europe's most valuable fintech unicorns. When the CEO was asked the secret to such heights of success in such a short period, he replied it was just by 'working super hard' (Bernard, 2018). It operates as a freemium business model, providing free services initially but including a paid option for additional features.

After its funding in 2017, Revolut nearly doubled its user base to 2 million cardholders across Europe, and is a direct competitor with the likes of N26 and Monzo. 'Already we are growing four or five times faster compared to them; we are a global banking alternative whereas they are local', Storonsky said in an interview (Smith, 2018). Revolut has an overall rating of 4.3 out of 5 and aims to achieve a target of 100 million customers by the year 2023.

As of February 2019, the company claimed to have over 4 million users. They aim to be present in as many countries as possible, providing financial services such as business lending, retail lending, trading, investments and wealth management.

In December 2018, Revolut secured a specialized bank license from the European Central Bank, facilitated by the Bank of Lithuania (Bloomberg, 2018). This means Revolut is authorized to accept deposits and offer consumer credits and is authorized to provide investment services.

CASE STUDY
Atom Bank

Nowadays, more and more people prefer to manage their finances in a fast and easy way. Atom is a challenger bank based in Durham, UK, which obtained its banking licence from the Prudential Regulatory Authority in June 2015. In March 2017, it had a capital of £219 million from institutional investors including Spanish lender BBVA, fund manager Neil Woodford and Toscafund (Dunkley, 2017). Atom is the first UK bank that is built exclusively for smartphones, which means it can only be accessed via its app, available in Apple Store or Google Play.

Atom Bank is also known for its personal experience as customers are allowed to design their own logo for their personal banking and give it a name of their choosing. They can log in to the Atom app using passcodes, fingerprint, face recognition or voice recognition. By utilizing people's biometric data to verify their identities, the fintech not only brings convenience for financial consumers but also improves security levels.

Customers of Atom can get instant help from its support teams by making a call or using the chatbot. Its service line includes providing loans to small businesses and mortgages to first-time homebuyers through its brokers. Atom has attracted a lot of attention from the public; during its pilot operation phase in 2016, there were over 40,000 potential users showing their interest (Dunkley, 2016).

CASE STUDY
Aldermore and Shawbrook

Aldermore Bank describes itself as 'an SME-focused bank that operates with modern, scalable and legacy-free infrastructure'. The bank, founded in 2009, has been growing rapidly and is now one of the leading alternative lenders in the UK. In 2016 alone, it grossed pre-tax profits of £133 million, which was 34 per cent higher than in 2015 (Lu, 2017).

Aldermore launched an initial public offering (IPO) in March 2015 and, through sales of new shares to investors, raised £75 million. It is listed on the London Stock Exchange, is a constituent of the FTSE 250 and has around 220,000 customers in the UK.

Accurate customer focus and low-cost operating strategy are the two prime factors in Aldermore's rapid success. Its main task is to provide commercial finance, mortgage and saving services for British SMEs, homebuyers and savers. It attracts deposits from savers and then extends loans in four specialized areas: asset finance, invoice finance, SME commercial mortgage and residential mortgage. Aldermore offers most services online, by phone or face to face in its regional offices, as a true challenger bank.

The superior and friendly service and more availability of credit for smaller businesses are two strong selling points. Moreover, Aldermore claims that it conducts customer-focused innovation. To prove this, it allows customers to post comments about its products and services online without any interference by the bank.

Like Aldermore, Shawbrook bank strives to serve the financial needs of the UK's SMEs and individuals, offering a variety of lending and saving products. Its lending division consists of five parts: commercial mortgages, asset finance, business credit, secured lending and commercial lending.

Shawbrook's investors have bought several other financial companies over the years, such as Commercial First, Link Loans, Singers Asset Finance and Centric Commercial Finance, incorporating them into the banking business of Shawbrook. In April 2015, Shawbrook raised £90 million in its IPO with admission to the London Stock Exchange, and was later admitted to the FTSE 250 Index (Wighton, 2015). It has made loans to more than 60,000 SMEs across the UK, making it a leading bank for SME financing (Roland and Armstrong, 2015).

Challenges that challengers face

Like all businesses, challenger banks have their own sets of challenges too, the first being trust and acceptance. As this is a new concept, and people are accustomed to the way banking has always been done, this can be quite an obstacle. However, the methods of transactions have been changing over the years, from notes to going cashless via cards, so this latest change can be embraced. Besides, the target consumers of challenger banks already seem to get along with the idea.

Another obstacle that must be overcome is competition. There are many existing brick-and-mortar banks, and every country in the world has an established bank that people use most. However, some users are happy to use both these and challengers if necessary. Many claim that challenger banks have the capability to give the big banks a run for their money, but although challenger banks pose a threat, they still have a long way to go.

Many people feel safe with the idea of being able to walk into a bank and discuss their queries or open an account for the first time. The concept of mobile banking may sometimes feel too far-fetched for them, and the idea of conducting bank transactions using an app may seem less trustworthy than using a traditional, established bank that generations have used before (Burnmark Research, 2016).

Of course, many challenger banks have premises that they operate solely for the benefit of customers, where they can go occasionally. After all, that is the entire point of challenger banks; to give customers a better experience.

Current trends and the future of the industry

It's an interesting time to be a challenger bank, with mixed fortunes in an industry that's grown and matured. Consolidation is undoubtedly the key to future success.

The challenger banking world has seen some tremendous ups and downs in the past few years. The industry has been staying very positive, with several new players obtaining banking licences, and more showing or announcing the desire to enter the fray, as well as several announcements of new funds coming into the industry. Up to 2016, more than $850 million in funds had gone into the challenger banking industry.

Then, inevitably, small issues started to show; early challenger banks were taking far too long to see profits. Metro Bank expected its first year of profits only after being in operation for a good three-quarters of a decade. There was also the failure of challenger banks in meeting the lofty expectations placed on them.

The industry had also seen issues that seemed to threaten the very existence and future of the challenger banks. For instance, some of them had to ask their customers to close their accounts when they withdrew too much cash, while others lost their licences when their funding didn't come through as planned. These failures might have almost been inevitable when one operated for years without seeing any profit.

The space has also seen another shift in direction – the entry of new players – in the last few years. Several fintech firms, whose previous focus was on niche fintech segments such as payments or lending, announced their plans to become challengers. The Swedish fintech firm Klarna became the largest European fintech firm to enter into the fray after it received its banking licence in 2017. Meanwhile, applying for a banking licence were some well-known fintech firms, such as SoFi, who had captured the lucrative student lending market in the United States, and the lending firm Zopa in the UK. TransferWise announced its plans to start offering borderless accounts on its existing licence; Revolut, BABB and FairFX also either joined or announced their interest in the challenger banking space.

This interest is clearly a sign that the industry has grown and matured, and has definitely come a long way since its conception. The need for consolidation as well as further segmentation has become increasingly important in this crowded space.

There has also been the emergence of a B2B challenger banking segment with significant global appeal. These include challengers that provide banking-as-a-platform services to traditional or other challenger banks. The amount of collaboration between challenger banks has also been a positive sign, with partnerships already announced between Starling Bank and TransferWise, TD Bank and Moven, and WSFS Bank and ZenBanx (which was later acquired by SoFi).

The industry has also seen highly niche segments emerging, with some banks clearly targeting heavily underserved segments such as small and medium businesses, freelancers, immigrants, refugees and students. These are usually segments that traditional banks have never given much attention to, or found profitability with.

Conclusion

The banking sector has thrived for years by providing and enhancing its services. It will be tough for a new breed of challenger banks to completely dominate the industry. However, the diminishing trust in traditional banking and agents will need to be addressed quickly by the conventional banks; if not, more and more customers may change over to challenger banking. Rapid changes are not expected but over time, millennials may go ahead with this idea in a full-fledged way.

For now, seeing traditional banks with a mobile app is common, and making both options available to customers seems to be a way to benefit both parties. Traditional and challenger banks can go hand in hand for now, but only time will reveal how long this lasts.

References

BBC News (2018) Banks close 2,900 branches in three years, says Which?, 15 June [online] https://www.bbc.co.uk/news/business-44483304 (archived at https://perma.cc/D4GP-EZ3D)

Bernard, Z (2018) The CEO of a banking start-up reveals how hard work and long hours spurred his company to a $1.7 billion valuation in less than 3 years, *Business Insider,* 26 April [online] https://www.businessinsider.com/revolut-ceo-nikolay-storonsky-hard-work-long-hours-led-to-billion-valuation-3-years-2018-4?r=US&IR=T (archived at https://perma.cc/W5PV-Y9G6)

Biz2Credit (2015) Small Business Lending Index, January 2015 [online] https://www.biz2credit.com/small-business-lending-index/january-2015 (archived at https://perma.cc/7HCY-K7ZD)

Bloomberg (2018) UK Fintech Revolut gets European banking license [online] https://www.bloomberg.com/news/articles/2018-12-13/u-k-fintech-revolut-gets-european-banking-license-via-lithuania (archived at https://perma.cc/T8HA-3HKH)

Burnmark (2016) Challenger Banking Report [online] https://www.burnmark.com/research/7 (archived at https://perma.cc/V7UX-4BLV)

Dunkley, E (2016) Atom Bank attracts early interest from mobile customers, *FT.com*, 14 September [online] https://www.ft.com/content/f86fbaac-7a73-11e6-b837-eb4b4333ee43 (archived at https://perma.cc/Y8W2-EC2Z)

Dunkley, E (2017) Atom Bank raises £83m from shareholders as it eyes expansion, *FT.com*, 3 March [online] https://www.ft.com/content/c075542e-fc09-3c27-bb98-7fe5f7d3df34 (archived at https://perma.cc/V3Z7-UKV8)

Finance Derivative (2019) 1 in 4 millennials and gen-zs are using challenger banks with monzo the most popular, 2 January [online] https://www.financederivative.

com/1-in-4-millennials-and-gen-zs-are-using-challenger-banks-with-monzo-the-most-popular/ (archived at https://perma.cc/3A3Q-WHQ7)

Kharpal, A (2018) Revolut becomes latest fintech unicorn after $250 million funding gives it a $1.7 billion valuation, *CNBC*, 26 April [online] https://www.cnbc.com/2018/04/26/revolut-raises-250-million-in-funding-at-1-point-7-billion-valuation.html (archived at https://perma.cc/7D3V-LJFN)

Lu, L (2017) Financial technology and challenger banks in the UK: gap fillers or real challengers?, *Journal of International Banking Law and Regulation*, **32** (7) pp 273–82

Pew Research (2018) World population growth is projected to nearly stop growing by the end of the century [online] https://www.pewresearch.org/fact-tank/2019/06/17/worlds-population-is-projected-to-nearly-stop-growing-by-the-end-of-the-century/ (archived at https://perma.cc/NA6T-7C2E)

Roland, D and Armstrong, A (2015) Challenger bank Shawbrook fetches £725m valuation on IPO, *Telegraph*, 1 April [online] https://www.telegraph.co.uk/finance/newsbysector/banksandfinance/11508186/Challenger-bank-Shawbrook-fetches-725m-valuation-on-IPO.html (archived at https://perma.cc/7EP6-X7U4)

Smith, O (2018) How Nikolay Storonsky took Revolut from $350m to a $1.7bn valuation in just six months, *Forbes*, 26 April [online] https://www.forbes.com/sites/oliversmith/2018/04/26/how-nikolay-storonsky-took-revolut-from-350m-to-a-1-7bn-valuation-in-just-six-months/#34abe2b36aa3 (archived at https://perma.cc/C8VT-WN38)

The Economist (2018) The digital upstarts taking on Britain's dominant few banks, 15 February [online] https://www.economist.com/finance-and-economics/2018/02/15/the-digital-upstarts-taking-on-britains-dominant-few-banks (archived at https://perma.cc/9SB6-JG38)

US Census Bureau (2016) Millennials outnumber baby boomers and are far more diverse [online] https://www.census.gov/newsroom/press-releases/2015/cb15-113.html (archived at https://perma.cc/4SD6-RAPK)

Warner, J (2018) UK fintech companies continue to lead the way, *IG.com* 21 September https://www.ig.com/uk/news-and-trade-ideas/shares-news/uk-fintech-companies-continue-to-lead-the-way-180921 (archived at https://perma.cc/SCT6-4A6W)

Wiggers, K (2019) Pew: Smartphone penetration ranges from 24% in India to 95% in South Korea, *Venture Beat*, 5 February [online] https://venturebeat.com/2019/02/05/pew-south-korea-has-the-worlds-highest-smartphone-ownership-rate/ (archived at https://perma.cc/X6ES-YBLP)

Wighton, D (2015) U.K. bank Shawbrook plans IPO, *Wall Street Journal*, 12 March https://www.wsj.com/articles/u-k-bank-shawbrook-plans-ipo-1426148798 (archived at https://perma.cc/E6ZX-FD77)

11

Data and analytics

Big data and analytics have carried the tag of being potentially game-changing technology from the beginning. Some experts have gone as far as calling it the 'new oil' (Adesina, 2018). Between 2010 and 2018, since the tech revolution, we have seen some of this potential being realized in sectors such as retail and location-based services. However, we are still a fair distance away from full adoption, let alone saturation point in any of the industries where analytics has found use. As companies continue to integrate data analytics into their operations, we can expect to see more of the transformative potential of big data.

Many factors are facilitating the move towards big data. For instance, the cost of storing data has decreased considerably in recent years, making it affordable for companies to keep data they would otherwise discard. Another important factor is that we now have the computing capabilities to handle large quantities of data. Companies excelling at big data analytics have given it a central position in their strategy; they have the expertise to take their deep-learning capabilities to the next level.

While much is said about the promise of big data and analytics, adaptors of the technology are still finding it challenging to take full advantage of the collected data. Computers may be capable of handling more data, but it is not always easy for the people operating them to perform sophisticated analysis and gain maximum benefits from it.

Moreover, the competitive advantage of using analytics is decreasing as more and more companies in the corporate sector use it for their research (Ransbotham, Kiron and Kirk Prentice, 2016). One of the leading reasons for difficulties in gaining competitive advantage is that companies have just started to use big data technologies and simply need more experience. Generally, companies are very good at capturing data but not so efficient at integrating data using insights to guide strategy and disseminating data insights.

Market trends

In the shift towards big data and analytics, open source machine learning platforms like Tensorflow and Apache Spark are leading the way. Forty-four per cent of management professionals expect to have Apache's Hadoop in production within the next 12 months, and 14 per cent within the next 24 months (Beall, 2016). The main uses of Hadoop within companies are for data exploration and data warehouse extensions. The software is also used for data staging, archiving non-traditional data, such as web and sensor data, and as a sandbox for advanced analytics. Other leading platforms include scikit-learn, H2O, Mahout, Rhipe, etc.

The use of in-memory technology is also a popular development, as it is faster than hard drive or solid-state drive-based storage. Another emerging trend is the development of big data intelligent apps. Companies are using machine learning and artificial intelligence (AI) to create apps for different functions, such as marketing and security. Big data analytics has also increased the use of edge computing. If the data analysis is happening close to the IoT devices instead of the cloud, the system performs the analysis faster and the computing costs are less.

The adoption of data and analytics varies from industry to industry. Industries leading adoption include financial services, telecommunications, advertising and healthcare, but the technology has yet to gain the same popularity in the education and manufacturing sectors. Within companies, R&D and business intelligence departments are leading the use of big data (Henke *et al*, 2016).

The main uses of big data also vary between industries. The financial services sector, for instance, mainly uses it for fraud detection, clickstream analytics and customer analysis. The insurance sector is using it for forecasting, fraud detection and supply chain. The advertising sector is using it for data warehousing and clickstream analytics. Similarly, the choice of platforms also varies from industry to industry. For example, scikit-learn is popular in the financial services industry, Apache in the insurance industry, and Rhipe in the government sector (Henke *et al*, 2016).

Disruptive qualities of big data analytics

In terms of an asset, data offers the same set of benefits as knowledge, for example because the same data can be used by multiple users at the same time. As the market for data increases, more companies are looking for specific information that will help them get an edge over their competition.

The disruptive qualities of big data have already started to come to the fore with technologies such as hyperscale real-time matching in the transportation industry. Services such as Uber and Lyft are expected to lead to fewer car purchases, fuel savings and a reduction in pollution from parking, according to reports. The use of mobility services will help average global consumers save around $2,000 annually (Henke *et al*, 2016).

Another area where big data can cause major disruptions is the personalization of information. For instance, the highly personalized information in the healthcare sector could help reduce healthcare costs by $600 per person per year, equating to 2.2 per cent of the GDP (Henke *et al*, 2016).

The retail banking sector also has tremendous potential for using big data. Data-driven transformation can have an economic impact of $400 billion to $600 billion. Banks can achieve this landmark by cross-selling and upselling products, improved risk assessment and underwriting, optimizing service capacity, automatic support functions, etc (Henke *et al*, 2016).

Machine learning

Machine learning allows systems to learn directly from examples and experience in the form of data. From IBM's Watson beating two human competitors in Jeopardy in 2011, to Google's AlphaGo beating the world champion at Go in 2016, recent developments in machine learning and AI give us a glimpse into the future.

Machine learning can be divided into four categories: supervised learning, unsupervised learning, semi-supervised learning, and reinforcement learning. Supervised learning has different use cases across a broad spectrum of machine learning applications, including speech recognition. Unsupervised learning is used for market research, clustering, etc. Semi-supervised learning is a combination of supervised and unsupervised learning and it is generally used for self-training. Reinforcement learning is used in finance for making investment decisions and inventory management.

A particularly exciting aspect of machine learning is its potential when combined with other types of analytics. Combining learning networks with compression analytics, for instance, allows for the discovery of new trends in data. Similarly, training conventional neural networks with merging techniques enables the hyper-personalization of data.

Application of machine learning

There are numerous examples of companies using machine learning to understand and potentially improve performance, one example being in marketing. Brands like Sky are using Adobe's Sensai platform, which estimates the probability of customer response and optimizes send time. The technology allows Sky to provide its customers with recommendations based on their individual preferences (Gilliland, 2019).

Another example is that of GlaxoSmithKline's (GSK) use of language and text analytics to learn about the concerns parents have about vaccinations. Using the information gained from the research, GSK created informational content to explain the importance of early childhood vaccinations (Fagella, 2017).

Other examples include Trendyol, a Turkish e-commerce platform competing in the sportswear market with big brands. Trendyol uses the services of Liveclicker for personalizing their campaigns, increasing their click-through rates and conversion rates (Gilliland, 2019). Like big data analytics, social media engagement has also gained a lot of importance in recent years. To gain insight into their customer data, popular CRM platform Zendesk used MarianaIQ's social media management platform (Fagella, 2017).

In the finance sector, several machine-learning technologies are currently in use. For example, online accounting software provider Arrow announced in May 2018 that it has made over 1 billion recommendations to customers. This includes 750 million invoice and bill code recommendations and 250 million bank reconciliation recommendations. The software learns how the business codes items and auto fills based on what it has learnt. It's capable of coding 80 per cent of transactions after just four examples (ACCA, 2019).

Risk assessment and fraud detection is another area where machine learning has great applications. Algorithms identify characteristics that justify a deeper investigation. CAG is an independent authority that audits receipts and expenditure of organizations financed by the Indian government. They conducted a study in which they trained machine algorithms to predict the risk that a given firm is fraudulent. The best-performing algorithms were able to identify suspicious firms with an accuracy of 93 per cent (ACCA, 2019).

Another example is that of the large UK Bank NatWest, which was able to prevent £7 million in false payments by using machine learning with the help of Vocalink's analytics tool for corporate fraud. The software analyses behavioural signatures left behind when a business pays and compares the signatures to historical frauds. This helps it in identifying and flagging suspected incidents (Fixter, 2018).

Along with the unmatched potential of data analytics, there are some limitations to consider as well. There is still the challenge of developing systems that have a contextual understanding of problems. Therefore, there is still need for human intervention. If a contextually inappropriate system is applied to an environment that requires human intervention, the algorithm may cause serious damage. Another challenge is, of course, the time and resources required to process quantities of data.

Another method of fraud detection and security is biometric user authentication. Companies such as ZOLOZ offer machine learning-based optical recognition technology that secures operations with biometric identification. The software identifies users by veins in the white section of their eye, for instance (RubyGarage, 2018).

Many established banks have already incorporated AI into their environment. JPMorgan Chase has introduced its Contract Intelligence (COiN) platform, which analyses legal documents to note data points and clauses. The company is also set to offer a virtual assistant that integrates a natural language interface, targeted towards employee tech service requests (JPMorgan Chase, 2016).

Bank of America has already launched its intelligent virtual assistant, called Erica. The chatbot uses 'predictive analytics and cognitive messaging' to assist the bank's large customer base (Taylor, 2016).

Public opinion about machine learning

One of the most interesting studies conducted on machine learning amongst the public was by the Centre of Governance of AI (2019) in the United States on 2,000 American adults in June 2018. The survey found that 41 per cent of people somewhat support or strongly support the development of AI, while 22 per cent somewhat or strongly oppose. Demographics also influenced the survey outcomes. For instance, 59 per cent of participants with an annual household income of over $100,000 support, while 33 per cent earning less than $30,000 annually don't.

Education and a connection with computer science or programming were also of significance. Among college graduates, 57 per cent supported the development of AI. From those with computer science or programming experience, 58 per cent were in favour. The most overwhelming results were for robotics and AI management, with 82 per cent saying that the technologies should be carefully managed. In terms of gender distribution, 47 per cent of men and 35 per cent of women were supportive of developing AI.

Data privacy is a much-talked-about social concern when it comes to machine learning. One of the concerns with current data labels is that they may not be accurate anymore due to machine learning. For example, data that isn't considered to be private may be used to indirectly reveal private information about a user. Research has revealed that publicly available information such as a person's Facebook likes can be used to predict that person's ethnicity, religious views, sexual orientation, etc (The Royal Society, 2017). Another concern is that algorithms can start to profile people by using attributes that are not accepted by society in general. Machine learning is also expected to have an impact on employment. The extent to which machine learning will impact remains debatable. Some sectors may see full automation taking place, while most may see some of the tasks within a job being automated.

Natural language processing (NLP)

When designing implementation requirements for enterprises and start-ups, strategizing how to get the most out of your big data is a key factor for success. There are many different approaches to big data analytics, but following successful technological advancements in Artificial Intelligence over recent years, Natural Language Processing has become an important tool to help enterprises manage the challenges that come with big data.

The growth of internet- and cloud-associated business practices yields a constant flood of data. Many companies do collect and store this data, in vast data repositories or in segregated and antiquated data silos; however, how can an enterprise sort and create value from it? The application of an AI platform to this high volume and high variety of data can add value to a company's strategy.

Unfortunately, this constant data input entails high-variety and high-volume big data sets. Additionally, certain kinds of big data – those related to customer feedback and social media in the healthcare or consumer goods industries, for example – arrive in text aka 'natural language' form, ie in the type of language we use to communicate with each other in real life.

Applying analytics to this sort of big data in the past has been subject to the limitations of technological processing capabilities, but now things look much more exciting, with new trends in NLP – a text analytics tool that is the solution to mining natural language big data in a way that will grant insight into new trends and new opportunities.

Creating value from this type of text data requires complex processes that can understand and create language on a deep level. The NLP model must not only understand what is being said in the data, it must be able to answer back.

The algorithms built into NLP are designed to automatically analyse and create language indistinguishable from real human speech. This allows NLP platforms to be utilized for such deep-thinking purposes as translation, query answering, paraphrasing, inference and dialogue generation.

NLP has also proven useful in deciphering trends and patterns in text-based big data, which has ramifications beyond query answering, especially in the healthcare sector.

NLP is not new, but early problems have been outpaced as neural-based models have been brought online, NLPs used in real-life business data analytics have also begun to yield results. Consequently, NLP and machine learning methodologies are now being increasingly utilized by companies in co-operation with big data associates.

NLP examines the semantics and linguistic markers in the data, and through a combination of statistics and machine learning enables a company to winnow information down into usable and significant data. Unlike previous analytics that relied on strings of words and keywords, NLP can closely decipher the intent of the text.

Trends in NLP

New trends in NLP have seen once clumsy and slow models become increasingly impressive as recurrent or convolutional neural networks have improved both performance and subtlety of interpretation. As NLPs continue to progress, it is likely their language modelling will keep pace, and soon complex human behaviours will not be beyond them.

In business sectors that deal with large-scale inputs – customer feedback, archived information on sales and sports, etc – using NLP can provide effective predictive, real-time or historical data that will be impactful in decision making at all levels of company management and strategizing.

In addition, NLP's ability to sort data into digestible chunks can create insights and improve data processing. Trends can be more accurately identified by NLP than by human evaluation. Of course, companies with a strong foundation in analytics and data application will find that their progress in adapting these NLPs is quite fast. But without that experience in analytics, AI implementation can be hit or miss.

NLP provides value in areas that require flexible function and engaging interactions such as online banking, automatic translation and retail self-service. When memory is coupled with the NLP network, answering mechanisms become richer and more realistic.

B2C interactions managed by NLP mean customer care calls can now be answered by artificial intelligence implementation. NLP can also determine the feelings and attitudes of certain demographics or locations.

NLP can replace keyword searches that slow down social media analysis and can rapidly and accurately assess queries on topics to make clear the trends that are key to successful social media management.

Future of NLP

This technology has continued to develop and new breakthroughs in NLP have shown incredible promise. Yet the technology is not at the level where ease of use is greater than the cost and time needed for localization.

Word embedding remains key in the classification of common text by an NPL but it has limitations. Some NLP models have difficulty being trained to understand word embeds with much subtlety and continue to require training in large data sets. The largest problem with NLP and other AIs is the time needed to train them to function, and then to show them how to process specific domain-related words.

Recurrent neural networks show great promise in speeding the processing of data when time and order are of first importance. Word-embedding capability can increase and the number of vectors per word grows. This is crucial for tailoring the NLP to specific domain data – training time can be shortened, and implementation quickened.

Transformer architecture use in NLP is one of the most exciting developments in recent years, as it makes it possible for the network to learn longer sequences of text and increase training speed with its parallel input system. This looks set to improve in 2019 and will increase the flexibility of NLP significantly. It will also increase the type of data that the NLP can use.

Upcoming trends also focus around new approaches to model training as well as the ability to increase the data input, leading eventually to a sort of plug-and-play version of NLP, making switching between models easy for any enterprise.

If a company can acquire an already trained model quickly and then only train it to their use, it will generate faster implementation and cost savings.

Additionally, new trends in applications focus on broader learning capabilities (BERT) that free the model from old linear approaches. One result of this is that chatbots will be able to function at near-human levels. It will be possible to fine-tune them with smaller amounts of data, reducing training time by companies and increasing usefulness.

'Zero shot learning' is another exciting direction that will allow companies to train new and more powerful models by providing them with the wide range of experience that will enable them to solve unrelated tasks. Essentially, the more data a model receives, the more tasks it can undertake without needing to be trained specifically for it.

This will allow for increasingly varied applications of these models. This deep thinking has ramifications for autonomous machine learning and will improve your NLP performance across the board.

One caveat to remember, despite the exciting growth in this field, is that potential negative impacts can be missed, especially ethical issues of AI self-awareness and fraud avoidance. Privacy and regulatory laws will also impact the use of this data and must not be forgotten, even if processing speed and applicability continue to soar.

Machine learning and the blockchain

Currently, systems are based mostly on the computing power of CPU-based computers. With an increase in the demand for AI as well as the sheer quantity of data, companies will need an alternative to CPU-based systems. One such alternative is GPU-based computing.

GPU-based systems have more storage capacity and they can also run more threads of command. Blockchain technology can connect machine learning systems to GPU computers with surplus power. Currently, researchers are working on projects that will connect people willing to share their computational resources with purchasers of computational power. Another noteworthy aspect of blockchain-based technologies is that they provide the privacy and transparency needed for good AI implementation.

Machine learning and underwriting

Underwriting automation is currently possible for large companies with vast amounts of data to train their algorithms. With continuous reduction in storage costs and an increase in expertise in data analytics, underwriting automation may become common in companies of all sizes and budgets.

Machine learning and algorithmic trading

Machine learning is playing an important role in modern high-frequency trading. The system having a latency of nanoseconds gives traders an edge over competitors using other approaches.

Machine learning and IoT

Implementing machine learning with IoT sensors is also increasing in popularity. The Internet of Trains project from Siemens combines machine learning with IoT for predictive maintenance. The project is designed to use insights for finding faults in tracks and trains to ensure that the maintenance service can be performed in a targeted fashion.

Machine learning and robotic process automation

Robotic process automation is forecasted to be worth more than $3 billion by 2025 (Joshi, 2019). Robotic automation helps prevent human errors, but it also has some limitations due to its dependency on rules. These limitations can be removed with intelligent process automation. Machine learning allows robots to detect patterns and handle sentimental directions.

Machine learning and robo-advisory

The term robo-advisory has become commonplace in the past few years. Algorithm-based systems allow digital wealth management firms to remove trading obstacles and lower the barrier for entry.

Exchange traded funds (ETFs) are popular in the United States as well as other western countries. Moreover, clients in the US are placing more trust in digital advice than in the past. The availability of digital technology and the need for personalization prompt clients of all age groups to demand access and services that are tailored to their specific requirements.

There are several niche investor segments that are expected to shape the financial landscape of the world in the coming years. One of the main changes is the transfer of wealth from one generation to the other, with baby boomers having been the recipients of this intergenerational wealth from investors born in the 1920s and 1930s. Between 2031 and 2045, 10 per cent of the total wealth in the United States is expected to move from the boomers to the next generation (Burnmark, 2017). Women are also expected to be a greater part of the financial landscape in the coming years. The CFA Institute estimates a $5 trillion increase in income for women globally in the next five years (Burnmark, 2017). Several robo-advisors are working to facilitate women investors. For example, Singapore-based firm Miss Kaya aims to 'simplify and demystify' the management of money for women, and a digital investment platform for women called Ellevest has raised $10 million in funding (Burnmark, 2017).

Foreign immigrants in the United States also represent a large market segment; about 11.6 million immigrants have a bachelor's degree or higher. These immigrants represent $2–$3 trillion of investment. The 8 million American expats around the world represent a $500 billion to $1 trillion asset market (Burnmark, 2017). Besides the changing of hands of wealth there is also a change in spending behaviour. The emerging millennial segment along with the acceptability of digital channels among investors is helping digital advice become more common.

Sectors and growth for digital advisory

Robo-advisory firms are operating in many sectors, and in some they have the potential to outperform others and prove to be a game changer. These sectors include socially responsible investors such as Wealthsimple and Grow, tax-planning solutions such as Nutmeg and Wealthfront, white-label solutions such as Bambu and Jemstep, etc. People and sectors where robo-advisors will need to do more work are high-net-worth (HNW) individuals, who are used to traditional asset management, the retirement sector, and women. Companies operating in these sectors include Zen assets (HNW), Miss Kaya (women), and Next Capital (retirement solutions).

Growth for digital advisors

In the United States, the top 10 robo-asset managers have seen a CAGR of over 100 per cent in the last five years. In Europe, five advisors have reached the €100 million milestone. Sixty per cent of the $17.5 trillion increase in wealth in 2016 came from Asia Pacific, so emerging markets will also play an important role in driving the segment. The United States has over 200 robo-advisories, Europe has over 70, while China and India have 20 and 19 respectively (Burnmark, 2017).

Digital advisory models

Several advisory models are currently in use, including D2C (direct to consumer) advisory – online platforms that provide portfolio management services without the use of human intervention. There are B2B advisories: white-label platform solutions that allow traditional advisors to use digital solutions; and hybrid advisories, which are solutions that use traditional services, including actively managed portfolios as well as computerized solutions.

Leading robo-advisors

The most common model used in the United States is D2C. Betterment is leading here, with assets under management (AUM) of $7.3 billion, followed by Wealthfront with $5.1 billion. Hybrid advisors are led by Vanguard, with an AUM of $47 billion. The UK has 18 robo-advisors, led by D2C Nutmeg with an AUM of $0.7 billion. Companies like Horizon offer robo-advice starting at only £12.50 and require only £1,000 of initial investment. Japan has 14 robo-advisors. Bambu has a business-to-business robo-advisor in Asia and has partnered with Tigerspike, Thomson Reuters, etc. Crossbridge Capital has partnered with Bambu to launch a hybrid advisory for Singapore. Australia has eight robo-advisories, six of which are D2C, including Stockspot and Ignition Direct. Macquarie Bank and Bet Smartz have hybrid and B2B models respectively (Burnmark, 2017).

Chatbot usage in digital advisory

Chatbots are AI-based tools that help customers with general questions. Recent customer research indicates that 33 per cent of customers are unhappy with the quality and responsiveness of contact services. This research also suggests that poor quality of service has led over 70 per cent of customers accepting robo-help for their investments (Burnmark, 2017). The majority of banks have implemented chatbots for customer service. The primary concerns of customers in their interactions with their bank are speed and convenience, and a chatbot can provide quick responses to help them with their questions. Moreover, younger people prefer chatbots, particularly for standard requests. However, 64 per cent of wealth management clients also ask for non-financial advice (Burnmark, 2017) – an aspect of business that is also important and that chatbots can't offer at the moment. Currently B2B is the focus of developers, but other digital platforms, such as Poly Portfolio, have chatbots for individual investors.

Online brokers' robo-advisory services

Many online brokers have included robo-advisory in their services. TD Ameritrade, with an AUM of $28 billion, has launched a robo-advisory service called Essential Portfolios. Motif investing has launched an advisor that allows customers to make investments along certain themes. In Europe, Saxo Bank has partnered with Blackrock to launch a full-scale digital investment solution for retail investors. Large online broker E*trade has introduced an advisor called Adaptive Portfolio. Discount services, such as eToro, are enabling users to benefit from social investment features (Burnmark, 2017).

B2B ROBO-ADVISORY CASE STUDY: BLACKROCK

In the aftermath of the 2008 financial crisis, the asset management industry was faced with the test of transforming itself.[1] Digital transformation and 'value for money' were the key drivers that posed the biggest challenges for investment managers looking for profitable growth. Evolving consumer expectations and a highly competitive marketplace put new demands on wealth management firms that were managed traditionally.

Digitization across all aspects of the value chain became a trend,[2] with robo-advisors entering the market. At the investment management end, high acquisition costs that could run to about $1,000 per client,[3] and the growing opportunities of an automated platform that leveraged sophisticated algorithms, led to many registered investment advisors (RIAs) and brokers syncing their services with robo-advisor platforms.

These platforms provided easily accessible financial products at minimal costs to the users, and highly personalized, data-driven investment advice. Nearly 31 per cent of banks and asset managers acquired a fintech firm as a way to improve their digital innovation.[4]

BlackRock's business model of investing in robo-advice as part of a B2B strategy[5] is a case of financial innovation in investment management. It adopted a unique model: acquiring B2B robo-advisory firms to keep pace with advances in financial technology without having to build its own customized Robo-advisor platform.

The acquisition of two low-cost robo-advisory firms, Scalable Capital and Future Advisor, by a leading asset management company was an innovation in wealth management practices. It brought together the existing customer base of a traditional asset management firm and the technology of digital wealth advisors for addressing the challenges of complex investments and encouraging millennial and Gen Z investing.[6]

BlackRock adopted the robo-advisory model of automated financial advisory platforms. These provided across-the-board algorithm-based investment management services and digital tools. By incorporating robo-advice the company complemented rather than displaced its financial advisors.[7]

It addressed the gap in its high acquisition costs with the cost-efficient, technology-driven buyout, Scalable Capital, and leveraged its other acquisition, FutureAdvisor, as an integrated advisor. The institutional capabilities were built out by private labelling the software to banks, broker-dealers, insurance companies, and other advisory firms. With this, the company tapped the unique advantage of the FutureAdvisor system – rejecting any algorithm-generated investment recommendations that did not sync with the investment strategy.

BlackRock's adoption of a 'zoom out/zoom in' approach[8] to growth looking at both time horizons, short and long term, makes it an interesting industry practice. Business issues that could accelerate the company's digital trajectory over the next 6 to 12 months were identified. The time horizon of 10 years plus, and future industry trends and customer expectations were also considered.

The acquisition of several robo-advisors and syncing them into its systems via an open API is a strategic first for a wealth management company. What makes this case study unique is that instead of building its own robo-advisor, the wealth management company acquired B2B robo-advisors working on the hybrid model. These acquisitions were B2B fintech start-ups and did not necessarily share consumer information.

These add-ons to the corporate structure added new markets, product offerings and investment capabilities, and the net result was that valuations for deals increased.[9]

This case is an example of a wealth manager partnering with B2B hybrid robo-advisors to retain clients through an enhanced and personalized service offering. The use of the robo-advisor's protection of AUM as well as portfolio rebalancing and asset allocation, help fuel its plans of optimized advisory quality.[10]

The B2B robo-advisory model worked well for the asset management company because of the low cost of customer acquisition and issues related to trust. The partnership resulted in the robo-advisors going the extra mile in terms of customization, ultimately adding value by extending the remit of the robo into other areas.[11]

As they have the potential to link up to every part of a customer's financial situation, across mortgages, bank accounts and investments for 360-degree financial planning,[12] the company is in a win-win situation and can evolve into a differentiator in the wealth management industry. This evolution will go beyond the development of underlying products and services.[13]

NOTES

1 EY (2018) The challenge of the Asset Management industry [online] https://www. ey.com/lu/en/newsroom/pr-activities/articles/article_201804-the-challenge-of-the-asset-management-industry (archived at https://perma.cc/8RGP-8R6C)

2 Fintech News (2018) The rise of wealthtech, 5 March [online] http://fintechnews.ch/ Roboadvisor_onlinewealth/rise-wealthtech-infographic/14478/ (archived at https:// perma.cc/7C8V-V3TM)

3 EY (2018) The evolution of Robo-advisors and Advisor 2.0 model [online] https:// www.ey.com/Publication/vwLUAssets/ey-the-evolution-of-Robo-advisors-and-advisor-2-model/$FILE/ey-the-evolution-of-Robo-advisors-and-advisor-2-model.pdf (archived at https://perma.cc/E388-GXX4)

4 Simmons & Simmons (2017) One third of financial institutions to acquire a FinTech firm in next 18 months, 7 April [online] http://www.simmons-simmons.com/en/ news/2017/april/one-third-of-financial-institutions-to-acquire-a-fintech-firm-in-next-18-months (archived at https://perma.cc/QNM5-6WWN)

5 Fantato, D (2017) BlackRock claims robo-advice is B2B play, *FT Adviser*, 8 December [online] https://www.ftadviser.com/your-industry/2017/12/08/blackrock-claims-Robo-advice-is-b2b-play/ (archived at https://perma.cc/M7S6-R68Z)

6 Rosenbaum, E (2018) BlackRock, world's biggest investing company, is planning to nickel-and-dime you, *CNBC*, 9 May [online] https://www.cnbc.com/2018/05/09/ blackrock-is-developing-tools-to-spur-millennial-and-gen-z-investing.html (archived at https://perma.cc/P4U5-B7E2)

7 Burnmark (2017) Digital wealth report [online] https://www.burnmark.com/uploads/ reports/Burnmark_Report_Apr17_Digital_Wealth.pdf (archived at https://perma.cc/ H2HZ-VCY4)

8 Deloitte (2019) 2019 Investment management outlook: a mix of opportunity and challenge [online] https://www2.deloitte.com/content/dam/Deloitte/global/

Documents/Financial-Services/gx-fsi-dcfs-2019-investment-management-outlook. pdf (archived at https://perma.cc/25TT-KQDR)

9 Patterson, J (2017) The deal will develop a new management interface, leveraging Cachematrix 's open-architecture platform, *Finance Magnates*, 28 June [online] https://www.financemagnates.com/institutional-forex/execution/blackrock-acquires-cachematrix-expanding-cash-management-capabilities/ (archived at https://perma. cc/LS86-NDDR)

10 Deloitte (2016) The expansion of robo-advisory in wealth management [online] https://www2.deloitte.com/content/dam/Deloitte/de/Documents/financial-services/ Deloitte-Robo-safe.pdf (archived at https://perma.cc/F4NS-PDL5)

11 https://www.thewealthmosaic.com/vendors/twm/twm-articles/the-b2b-Robo-advisor-market-enabling-wealth-manage/

12 Napach, B (2016) BlackRock snaps up FutureAdvisor: could Wealthfront or Betterment be next? *ThinkAdvisor*, 26 August [online] https://www.thinkadvisor. com/2015/08/26/blackrock-snaps-up-futureadvisor-could-wealthfront/?slret urn=20190516044604 (archived at https://perma.cc/Q8KW-2C8X)

13 EY (2018) The evolution of Robo-advisors and Advisor 2.0 model [online] https:// www.ey.com/Publication/vwLUAssets/ey-the-evolution-of-Robo-advisors-and-advisor-2-model/$FILE/ey-the-evolution-of-Robo-advisors-and-advisor-2-model.pdf (archived at https://perma.cc/E388-GXX4)

Robo-advisory demographics example – Nutmeg

Nutmeg's customers are usually younger than 30, but their average customer age is 40, meaning that they have a substantial number of customers from other age brackets as well. Customers sign up for Nutmeg services for several reasons. Some of them are first-timers looking for a straightforward way to invest. Others are interested in using the services of experts instead of taking a DIY approach. There are also those who want a cheaper alternative.

Nutmeg's top innovation for 2017 was their product for cost-sensitive investors. They offer customers a fully managed portfolio or a fixed portfolio. Since the investment team does not have to manage the fixed portfolio, the management costs are lower.

Nutmeg sees both new and experienced investors as its core customers. The new customers are looking for a good return, which banks aren't offering at the moment, so they consider investing their savings. Experienced customers are looking for solutions that aren't over-complicated (Burnmark, 2017).

Investment platform example – Huddlestock

Huddlestock is an online platform that allows investors from all over the world to benefit from strategies devised by industry experts, companies, and robo-advisors. They don't require any minimum investment. The strategies shared on the platform are for long- and short-term investment for ETFs, CFDs, and individual shares, and investors pay a small performance fee on profits set by the vendor. Besides personal advice from investment experts, individuals are also allowed to share their strategies with other individuals and firms (Burnmark, 2017).

B2B robo-advisory example – Wealth Objects

Wealth Objects has B2B robo-advisory with customizable modules for insurance companies, investment firms, banks and wealth managers. Users can launch their own platform or improve their present platform for much less than they might otherwise pay. Options for business models include traditional models with personal advisors, hybrid models with personal and robo services, and robo-advisors. The cost factor, as well as easy integration, makes Wealth Objects' products stand out from the crowd. Besides the current modules, such as financial planning, automated investing and engagement, the company also plans on releasing machine learning and cognitive computing modules (Burnmark, 2017).

Big data governance

Big data governance is the way in which a company or organization manages its huge volumes of data as a business asset. The reason for big data governance is that corporations should be confident that they are getting value from their data throughout the organization as well as ensuring compliance with regulatory standards.

Technology is only to be used to make the process easier; at its heart, big data governance is about rules for managing this resource according to regulatory standards in conjunction with a well-trained team of professionals who will create processes to get the most value from big data.

Big data governance rests on the back of the recognition that in its natural state, big data is chaos. Unprocessed, raw data carries the potential for value, but if it cannot be sorted and deciphered then there is little value in it. This is not a simple undertaking, as companies have spent years acquiring data, only to have no idea what to do with it.

Generally, big data is categorized by its volume (the size of the data collected), variety (the way data can be manipulated and sorted according to a company's needs) and velocity (the need for data to be processed and utilized quickly).

All data should logically push across the company's data architecture; however, data dissemination is not the primary issue. Maximizing the value of the company's big data for marketing, personalization, customer service or other uses comes with the caveat that issues related to data retention, data privacy, data localization and data security must be addressed.

This is influenced by the requirements of the GDPR – the European Union's privacy regulation. Compliance requirements from other countries and states – which are constantly being expanded – will continue to strongly affect big data governance. However, although they are being created, regulatory standards are not consistent across national borders, or in some cases such as the United States, within national borders.

This issue requires corporates to ensure that data is managed through its lifecycle. Data collection is now governed by privacy issues and concerns to prevent cybercrime.

The entire lifecycle of a company's big data is subject to regulation, including data processing, decisions on retention of data, data localization and portability. Big data can be monetized for the company's benefit, but it must first be processed through rigorous standards, even though global regulatory requirements are disjointed and contradictory.

Information governance and the lifecycle of data

From data collection to data portability, information governance is present at all stages of the lifecycle of data.

At the data collection stage, financial institutions (FIs) must collect more customer information and follow data privacy laws, as per KYC/AML rules. The shift towards digital solutions, such as online banking, increases the risk of cybercrime for FIs.

With data processing, banks are moving towards the use of analytical algorithms to personalize products and services for their customers. GDPR delivers transparency and fairness, so that banks clearly explain the reasons for data processing to their customers and obtain customer consent.

The data retention and disposal process has also changed in recent years. Data protection laws require FIs to delete information when it is no longer useful or when the customer wants it to be deleted.

FIs transfer internationally to make processes more efficient and to better detect fraud and money laundering. Moving private data to places with less data protection may result in heavy fines.

There are conflicting concepts at play when it comes to data portability and data protection. Open Banking and PSD2 mandate data accessibility, while GDPR and other laws want protection for data by managing access to data and tracking third-party sharing (Burnmark, 2018).

The fragmentation of regulatory standards on a global level can increase costs and reduce operational efficiencies. For financial companies, information collected by companies falls under rules that determine how personal information can be used.

FIGURE 11.1   How data and information is typically collected, processed and shared in a large enterprise

SOURCE Burnmark (2019)

Sensitive information can be collected in the interest of providing personalized products, but such data must be protected within the corporation as well as from outside negative use. In some cases, information must be deleted when requested or when it is no longer useful.

Data transfer across borders can also cause trouble, as regulatory standards differ. Inconsistent industry standards also affect data protection – portability issues often clash with data protection laws. Trying to match best practice often contradicts regulatory compliance standards and this can be expensive.

Technological evolution also affects the way companies process their big data, as data management teams are centralizing company data in anticipation of large-scale AI implementation and training. This drive away from data silos and towards a centralized approach will help businesses get the most from their data.

There is a competitive advantage in a company that can effectively utilize its data and analytics. This effective governance will also increase data trustworthiness, which is key to big data governance.

But how do we put data governance into practice? Encourage best practice and limit risk. Set policies and follow through with managing your data. Understand what the data can tell you and determine the regulatory impact of using it.

Also, the company must remember that it is not only managing its existing data, it must also search out new data and decide which is the most relevant or necessary all within a regulatory framework that protects privacy and security.

Key necessities for big data governance

- Uphold the system's reliability and availability.
- Create and support a data catalogue.
- Find ways to explore and exploit your data.
- Make sure the data stays valid.
- Protect your sensitive data.
- Understand the regulatory environment.

Companies must be aware of these upcoming trends:

- Technological advances will increase speed of processing, but they will not solve legal and regulatory issues controlled by governments.
- Management has a key role to play in getting the best from this newly exploitable resource.
- Deep learning will go on as AI networks continue to be brought into play, and these powerful neural networks become increasingly useful business assets.
- A managerial approach is needed that ensures swifter personalized services in conjunction with risk management on a global level.

When a company has a skilled staff, they will empower decision making at the executive level as quantitative data becomes more targeted and specific. The proper team will ensure that your data visualization, artificial intelligence algorithm creation and data cleansing will function at a high level.

As data privacy concerns become a global phenomenon, the driver for big data governance will no longer be technological development; it will be exploiting the data in a legal way in the differing regulatory markets of Europe, Asia, and North and South America while controlling costs.

References

ACCA (2019) Machine learning report [online] https://www.accaglobal.com/content/dam/ACCA_Global/professional-insights/machine-learning/pi-machine-learning-report.pdf (archived at https://perma.cc/M3AW-QLEM)

Adesina, A (2018) Data is the new oil, *Medium,* 13 November [online] https://medium.com/@adeolaadesina/data-is-the-new-oil-2947ed8804f6 (archived at https://perma.cc/8JK7-L73B)

Beall, A L (2016) Hadoop survey results, *SAS* [online] https://www.sas.com/en_us/insights/articles/big-data/hadoop-survey-results.html (archived at https://perma.cc/3XZL-QCC5)

Burnmark (2017) Digital Wealth: April, 2017 [online] https://www.burnmark.com/uploads/reports/Burnmark_Report_Apr17_Digital_Wealth.pdf (archived at https://perma.cc/H2HZ-VCY4)

Burnmark (2019) RegTech for Information Governance [online] https://www.burnmark.com/research/8 (archived at https://perma.cc/3KMV-7UFN)

Center for the Governance of AI (2019) Artificial Intelligence: American attitude and trends, University of Oxford [online] https://isps.yale.edu/sites/default/files/files/Zhang_us_public_opinion_report_jan_2019.pdf (archived at https://perma.cc/64EP-L4QT)

Fagella, D (2017) Three real use cases of machine learning in business applications, *HuffPost*, 6 September [online] https://www.huffpost.com/entry/three-real-use-cases-of-machine-learning-in-business_b_593a0e91e4b014ae8c69df37 (archived at https://perma.cc/94LM-XXNG)

Fixter, E (2018) NatWest teams up with Vocalink Analytics, *Vocalink*, 3 April [online] https://connect.vocalink.com/2018/april/natwest-teams-up-with-vocalink-analytics-to-protect-corporate-customers-from-fraud/ (archived at https://perma.cc/XDJ9-A98P)

Gilliland, N (2019) Six case-studies of machine-learning powered email marketing, *Econsultancy,* 4 February [online] https://econsultancy.com/email-machine-learning-ai-case-studies/ (archived at https://perma.cc/3QH4-M5SF)

Henke, N *et al* (2016) The age of analytics: competing in a data-driven world, *McKinsey* [online] https://www.mckinsey.com/business-functions/mckinsey-analytics/our-insights/the-age-of-analytics-competing-in-a-data-driven-world (archived at https://perma.cc/ZZ3P-TF97)

Joshi, N (2019) Robotic process automation just got 'intelligent' thanks to machine learning, *Forbes*, 29 January [online] https://www.forbes.com/sites/cognitiveworld/2019/01/29/robotic-process-automation-just-got-intelligent-thanks-to-machine-learning/#5229b69852d8 (archived at https://perma.cc/HQ6P-M8PH)

JPMorgan Chase (2016) Annual Report, 2016 [online] https://www.jpmorganchase.com/corporate/investor-relations/document/2016-annualreport.pdf (archived at https://perma.cc/79PF-HG5T)

Ransbotham, S, Kiron, D and Kirk Prentice, P (2016) Beyond the hype: the hard work behind analytics success, *SAS*, 8 March [online] https://sloanreview.mit.edu/projects/the-hard-work-behind-data-analytics-strategy/ (archived at https://perma.cc/YRX6-GZS4)

Royal Society (2017) Machine learning report [online] https://royalsociety.org/topics-policy/projects/machine-learning/ (archived at https://perma.cc/WQJ6-3G83)

RubyGarage (2018) 7 exciting uses of machine learning in fintech [online] https://rubygarage.org/blog/machine-learning-in-fintech (archived at https://perma.cc/PF73-V63Q)

Taylor, H (2016) Bank of America launches AI chatbot Erica – here's what it does, *CNBC*, 24 October [online] https://www.cnbc.com/2016/10/24/bank-of-america-launches-ai-chatbot-erica--heres-what-it-does.html (archived at https://perma.cc/Y7NE-KWAU)

12

Conclusion

Summary

Fintechs first emerged as a disruptive phenomenon in the shadow of the global financial crisis. This transformative event had a massive impact on the perception of the banking and financial sectors, paving the way for fintech to establish itself as a credible alternative. The increasing prominence and popularity of the sharing economy also contributed to the early rise of fintechs, and by the beginning of the 2010s, the concept was already a familiar one, among the start-up watchers in particular.

Naturally enough, banks didn't immediately warm to the challenge that fintechs represented, which led to an initial period of conflict. But even as the traditional financial sector players eyed fintechs with suspicion, rapid growth in the sector, combined with innovative technologies, caused a disruption which could no longer be simply resisted. In time, this would lead to collaboration between banks and fintechs.

A major driver of this was the shifting expectations of customers, which partly occurred organically, and can also be attributed to fintechs themselves having an influence on the customer experience. Challenger banks and digital payment systems have been particularly crucial in fintechs establishing customer bases, and these two forms of innovation are symbolic of the convenience and agility of the fintech revolution.

Ultimately, financial sector players realized that they were not going to eliminate fintechs and that some form of collaboration would instead be necessary, and even desirable. The fact is that big banks were beginning to lose customers at the start of this decade, and they increasingly realized that the technological innovation provided by fintech would play a major role in the future of the financial and banking sector. It was no longer optional to collaborate with fintechs; it was instead essential for banks to learn from these ambitious upstarts.

And while fintechs initially spoke a language of fierce independence, it soon became evident that start-ups would benefit from the markets, resources, know-how, and, particularly, the credibility that collaboration with big, established financial sector players offered them. Ultimately, a mutually beneficial relationship developed between many banks and fintechs, and this was hugely beneficial to the development of the fintech sector.

As a result of this collaboration, bank accelerator programmes and seed funding became a common part of the landscape. Many successful fintech start-ups emerged from this culture of innovation, and now even governments are getting involved with the process. This has led to a wide variety of fintech hubs, while a maturation of the regulatory environment is currently underway. There is still some distance to go, but the commitment of governments all over the world to help facilitate the rise of fintech is now tangible.

While the fintech revolution began in the Western world, emerging markets are now also embracing the concept enthusiastically. Asia is particularly vital in fintech, with the economic powerhouses of India and China making massive contributions. It should be clear from reading this book that the future of fintech is enormous, and that the technological innovations associated with the field will have a profound impact on the future of finance, economics, and money.

The future of fintech

So what is the future of fintech? Well, there are a few trends that we believe will underpin the fintech revolution going forward, and the first of these is that data innovation, and how we collect and use data, will be the cornerstone.

Big data is already an important part of the fintech field. For example, it has become possible to augment quantitative decision making with neural networks, meaning that organizations such as lenders can analyse the financial data of borrowers in order to determine their creditworthiness. As a result of this, a raft of companies is already using a combination of big data and artificial intelligence to minimize default rates across a range of credit products.

These solutions can draw together a range of data and usage behaviour to project how well consumers will deal with a credit environment. In this climate, AI will increasingly be contributing to decision making, and big data will be invaluable.

The digitizing of access to products such as peer-to-peer loans will pave the way for billions of people who currently have no access to banking services to circumnavigate the centralized banking system. This will be particularly significant in largely unbanked countries and can be compared to the way that African consumers have bypassed landline telephones, and instead opted to go straight to mobile. Leapfrogging centralized banking and the extensive credit system has already benefited hundreds of millions of consumers in China, and this will increasingly become a feature of the financial landscape across multiple nations.

The blockchain hasn't been a particular focus of this book, but there is nonetheless no doubt that this innovation has transformative potential, and indeed is already transforming the way that people think about currency. Combining the blockchain with big data and artificial intelligence will enable even the most mundane mobile browsing data to contribute to credit scores. Over time, other digital technologies, such as immutable ledgers and smart contracts, will be massive disruptors to the old banking system, enabling consumers to build additional trust and benefit from transparency, on top of the already established peer-to-peer lending models.

Aside from the benefits to fintech innovators, it is also clear that this climate will be hugely beneficial to consumers. There has been something of a financial aristocracy dominated by the big banks for many years, and fintechs, big data and artificial intelligence have the potential to change this unenviable and exclusive situation.

Archaic systems

Observers of the existing financial system have noted that it continues to be based on institutions that were founded before the Industrial Revolution. The advent of banking at this time was intended to deal with the physical paper moving between human beings and buildings, long before the arrival of digital money and all of the payment systems and architecture that we take for granted today.

Thus, while banks have not exactly become obsolete, many of their working practices are so dated as to approach this status. There needs to be a revolution, and the revolution that we are seeing is one of platforms. Everything is becoming digitalized, and in this climate, the industrial-era entities will inevitably become increasingly irrelevant, unless they are willing to modernize. This has been the central plank in the banking industry in which banks are being challenged to keep up with technology, and increasingly making the tough decision to collaborate with some of the powerful and innovative fintechs.

Rather than the traditional banking model, the future of currency and finance will be all about the digital distribution of data via software and service, underpinned by a sophisticated global network. The big difference with this new open system will be that anyone will have the potential to launch simple plug-and-play software into this effective map of functionality, serving a massive customer base and becoming a significant part of the overarching financial architecture.

Traditionally, the back offices of financial companies have been focused on the product, with the middle office concentrating on platforms, and the front-office dealing with customer experiences. This will be reversed in the years to come, with a new digital model dictating that connecting with the customer becomes central to all office practices.

Data is central to the new digitalized processes as such a revolution cannot be achieved in a vacuum. It would be impossible for the new fintech service companies to exist without application programming interfaces, with software providing a huge amount of information to this burgeoning infrastructure. For example, a hugely successful company such as Uber can only work because Google Maps provides the business with a wide variety of services via its sophisticated software and data. This is a trend that we will see expanding across multiple global organizations in a new digitalized future.

When we have talked about challenges in the financial sector in this book, the text has often been focused on the challenges that fintechs have faced, and continue to face, in establishing themselves as credible financial platforms. While this is entirely valid, it is also important to emphasize that, in many ways, the challenges of the future will start to shift towards the established banking sector, who will find that they are facing the challenge of entering and playing in evolving markets.

As digital technology becomes more established as a central feature of the financial field, banks will increasingly have to improve their operations to deal with the changing environment. Currently, most lenders have had zero professional experience of technology in their entire working lives, meaning that it will be a Herculean task for them to introduce a digital vision and cultural change that will be necessitated by the new environment. Many observers indeed question the perception of existing banks and assert that they are poorly placed to deal with this digital revolution.

Data as oil

In this climate, data can almost be viewed as a resource akin to oil, with the future of the financial sector pivoting on who owns and controls this data. This is a critical area of concern for existing banks, as they are poorly placed to gather and generate such data, while fintechs are ideally positioned to do so. This craving for data will undoubtedly be the gold rush of the coming years in the financial sector and will be another factor in the increasing collaboration between fintechs and banks.

While personal bank accounts will not disappear, it will be increasingly common for members of the general public to utilize banking software in order to move their money around. Already there are a wide variety of start-up banks that have attracted huge numbers of customers to their platforms because they are able to enrich transactions by linking to open data and other application programming interfaces. People increasingly want more than basic services from financial applications, instead demanding 24/7 access to an overview of their accurate financial picture.

Banks such as Monzo in the UK potentially pose massive problems for traditional banks. As soon as customers utilize Monzo cards for transactions, the actual bank to which the consumer is attached has no idea what activity the customer is conducting. In this scenario, the bank has effectively lost all data, and all they are aware of is that Monzo has acquired several consumers in this area. Episodes such as this will be opportunities for collaboration in the financial sector going forward, with data, blockchain and artificial intelligence all central to this fundamental conflict.

Leveraging data in sophisticated systems involving artificial intelligence is undoubtedly challenging when unintelligent and fragmented systems are relied upon. The biggest challenge for financial institutions will be reinventing the heritage structures on which they have relied for centuries. The big banks were built for a slower, antiquated age, and they must now shift their operations to deal with a new and vibrant digital epoch.

Another challenge for established financial companies in this climate will be the possibility of large tech giants increasingly moving into the digital currency and finance space. The ability of these companies to cope with an environment in which 60 terabytes of data is uploaded to the internet every second will place them in a privileged position. Big banks have big questions to deal with in terms of their ability to cope with this data-intensive environment.

Robo-advisors and AI

Some of the fields in which data and information will be particularly important are already clear. Robo-advisors are one such area of the digital financial future and are almost entirely reliant on being fed vast quantities of data. Robo-advisors leverage sophisticated algorithms in order to deliver automated financial planning and investment services. This is fundamentally driven by technology, with algorithms handling all of the investment decisions, and minimal human intervention involved. This is evidently one field in which technology companies will have a huge advantage over existing financial sector players.

Another area in which fintechs are already making ground is risk analysis, with credit reference agencies and credit scoring companies already reliant on data science and machine learning. AI can predict the risk levels of customers, separating good borrowers from potential bad ones, and doing so more quickly and more accurately than would be possible for any human being. And similar processes are also used in fraud detection, with data science techniques utilized to identify fraud in financial transactions.

This latter area is a growing field, with the potential for fintechs to leverage big data and analytical techniques, using vast amounts of online information in order to identify fraudulent transactions. This treasure trove of information can then be used and modelled in such a way that technology operators can predict and flag fraud in future transactions. Data science and machine learning techniques such as deep neural networks will be key to this process, and this is another area in which we can expect a true fintech revolution in the years to come.

Another huge area of concern for banks where data and artificial intelligence will be crucial going forward is customer acquisition and retention. It will become increasingly feasible for banks and financial institutions to create extensive and detailed customer profiles based on available data, which can then be used to tailor customer experience and provide personalized services. Algorithms will make it possible to largely predict what additional products and services customers would like to purchase based on their historical behaviour, or what sorts of products should be promoted to various demographics.

Again, this is an area in which fintechs will have an enormous advantage over banks. Not merely in having access to the information in the first place, but perhaps even more concerning the ability to effectively analyse the data. Algorithmic analysis of data will over-take human assessment in terms of effectiveness, and indeed is already doing so, meaning that banks will need to leverage the skills, knowledge, and innovation of fintech companies in this area.

Another big user of data science is the insurance industry, which uses algorithmic intelligence to manage risk and ensure that businesses remain profitable. Claims departments in insurance companies are already using data science algorithms to separate fraudulent and legitimate transactions. And big data can also be used for other insurance-related purposes, such as credit scoring, customer acquisition, marketing, customer retention, and designing new insurance products.

Massive impact

We can see from all of this that artificial intelligence has already had a massive impact on the fintech field. But this is expected to expand quite considerably in the years to come, as the ability to analyse larger portions of data faster and more effectively becomes possible. AI can even assist with security, with the implementation of AI enabling finance firms to improve their procedures over mere anti-virus software. The ability of AI to keep learning will allow companies to fine-tune their systems, vastly improving security. This is particularly valuable in the financial sphere, in which companies must offer a tremendous amount of reassurance to customers that their systems are safe.

The unique qualities of machine learning and artificial intelligence, and their ability to analyse far more substantial volumes of security and information than has ever before been possible, offers considerable advantages to financial firms in terms of security. Fintech providers of AI services are also able to scale their products to the particular work requirement of companies, meaning that the technology can help in identifying fraudulent behaviour, suspicious transactions, and potential future attacks.

In addition to improving the security of information, artificial intelligence also has the potential to vastly decrease processing times in financial services. Processing receipts and other financial documentation has always been an extremely time-consuming task in the world of finance, also requiring the patience and perseverance of significant human resources. And, of course, as soon as you have people involved in a process, it becomes prone to human error.

By contrast, AI will enable fintechs to process information related to processing more accurately and quickly. Machine learning can recognize specific patterns, and also improve the tasks rapidly as it carries them out. Whereas human beings will plateau in the ability to conduct processing, artificial intelligence systems can process information quicker and quicker over time.

While human beings must remain in the loop with artificial intelligence, machine learning does have the potential to validate and double-check the information for duplicate expenses and other common human errors. One example of this technology is PixMettle, a start-up from Silicon Valley, which has already developed enterprise AI-based tools which will help detect fraud proactively. Testing conditions have already revealed that PixMettle is significantly superior to any conceivable human operator, while also shaving a considerable amount of time from processing.

Fintech and AI expert Kapil Dhingra, founder of PixMettle, notes that 'AI helps in flagging duplicate expenses and expenses with corporate policy violations early on, even before they get added to the system. This saves lots of headaches and back-and-forth with accounting and employees' (AITopics, 2017).

AI will make it possible to automate processes across the financial system, providing another massive advantage to the fintech revolution. Fintech start-ups will be best placed to deliver these complex and innovative systems, which have the potential to automatically generate expenditure and expense reports quickly, efficiently, and with massively reduced error counts.

Another exciting aspect of artificial intelligence is that it will empower smaller companies to compete with the established behemoths of the finance industry. AI is truly a democratizing technology that will be available to businesses of all sizes as it becomes increasingly accessible to all strata of society. This will be particularly important in emerging economies, where fintech promises to help disadvantaged consumers gain access to financial services for the first time.

We also see the influence of artificial intelligence in the chatbot field. This will become even more prevalent in the future, but chatbots are already established as a valid way for companies to communicate with customers. Many businesses already trust this technology with a variety of internal and external communications, and the potential for artificial intelligence to become more proficient over time means that this will only be extended in the future.

Big players on board

This is one area in which big corporations are already fully on board with the fintech revolution, with the likes of HSBC having already created its own AI-powered chatbot, which helps customers with a variety of tasks and queries (Olson, 2019). American Express has also developed Amexbot, which deals with customer questions regarding accounts, and a variety of personal information (American Express, 2017). This is only the beginning for this machine learning-driven field, and it will become commonplace for customers to engage in conversation with bots in the foreseeable future.

Chatbots will also make it possible to shop more seamlessly, to make orders directly from social media channels, to edit and check bank account details, to supervise the scoring of consumer credit, to inform customers of upcoming payments and offers, and to assist consumers with creating more realistic and accurate budgeting. Fintech will apparently be central to the process of developing such technology, and this is another area in which start-ups will offer a considerable amount to big banks and financial institutions while attracting their fair share of customers organically as well.

While some established financial sector players have been unwilling to embrace AI technology, the youthful, agile and innovative nature of fintechs means that they are already fully on board with the AI revolution. Numerous fintech companies are already employing artificial intelligence to solve customer issues at a wide variety of financial institutions, with a multitude of different applications possible.

Deep learning is making the jump to the mainstream in the world of technology, and the potential of this innovation should definitely not be underestimated. Increasingly, we will see that fintech innovation and machine learning will go hand in hand, as the companies that thrive in this field begin to challenge the big financial players.

Massive though the future is for artificial intelligence, and vital though it will be in the rise of fintech, it is important to briefly note that human involvement and stringent testing will always be requisite. It won't be possible to implement AI without keeping a very close eye on the processes involved, if the technology is to be integrated effectively.

Because AI is such sophisticated technology, the software involved is as prone to bugs as any other, perhaps more so in some cases. There are undoubtedly testing challenges present in relation to fintech platforms, and any AI software that may be incorporated, and these must be taken extremely seriously. When any fintech platform is undergoing a QA or user acceptance testing process, particular attention should be paid to any AI software and machine learning initiatives included. And they should generally be conducted in-house, as any third-party validation will compromise the decision-making process.

Naturally enough, the primary goal of any online mobile banking platform is to be secure without compromising user experience. It is therefore essential to test and authenticate platforms rigorously, and also include a wide variety of devices in the process. Users should also be sought who are entirely independent of any aspect of the development process. Once this accurate and unbiased test information has been delivered, AI can then be implemented. And once it is implemented effectively, AI technology will likely become a dominant aspect of the fintech sphere, particularly as data becomes ever more critical.

Emerging markets demographics

Another crucial trend in fintech is the importance of emerging markets. China and India, in particular, will play a significant role in this process, due to the scale and level of innovation inherent in these societies.

China will undoubtedly become the largest economy and the most important market in the world in the coming years. The International Monetary Fund had predicted that the Chinese economy would surpass that of the United States in 2016 (Weisbrot, 2011), and while this hasn't quite occurred, it is inevitable. *Market Watch* (Arends, 2011) noted: 'Naturally, all forecasts are fallible. Time and chance happen to them all. The actual date when China surpasses the US might come even earlier than the IMF predicts, or somewhat later. If the great Chinese juggernaut blows a tire, as a growing number fear it might, it could even delay things by several years. But the outcome is scarcely in doubt.'

The magazine *Foreign Policy* (Fogel, 2010) predicted that by 2040, the Chinese economy would be worth $123 trillion. This would represent three times the entire economic output of the world in the year 2000. China's per capita income will hit $85,000; more than double the forecast for the European Union, and also much higher than that of India and Japan. To make a rather rudimentary observation, this means that the average Chinese person will potentially be twice as wealthy as the average European.

China has also been confirmed to be the world's leading purveyor of higher education, awarding more university degrees than the United States and India combined. In 1996, China produced only 5,000 PhD students per year. By the end of 2007, it had awarded 240,000 doctorate degrees, and just two years ago it was confirmed that the country has double the graduates of the United States (Maslen, 2013). Meanwhile, India has now become the country with the third-highest number of people in higher education, and India's enrolment in higher education has increased by 1,800 per cent since it was granted independence in 1947. With a particular emphasis in these countries being placed on technology and information, there is a rich source of labour for innovative fintechs to benefit from.

Emerging economies still face challenges. But the BRIC (a loose union between Brazil, Russia, India and China) nations, with over 40 per cent of the world's population, over 15 per cent of the world's GDP (Global Sherpa, 2016), rapidly growing economies and economic structures that are well placed to facilitate the likely industrial pattern of the 21st century, small amounts of government debt, and particularly in the case of China, huge amounts of credit, considerable access to valuable resources and commodities, and populations that are being rapidly educated, will provide a fertile environment that will particularly help the growth of fintechs.

We can exploit innovation to be inherent in the fintech experience emerging from developing economies, for two reasons in particular. Firstly, the number of technology graduates and enthusiasts in these countries means that a culture of innovation has already been established; indeed, it is embedded in the commercial fabric of these nations. And secondly, there is a less established financial and economic hierarchy in many of these countries, which means that businesses and governments are more open to the prospect of experimentation, while there are fewer powerful players opposed to this process. The likes of China and India are happy to embrace innovation, whereas this process can be viewed with something approaching suspicion in Western counties, particularly by those with established and vested interests.

Don't believe the hype!

While there is no doubt that fintech is already having a transformative effect, and that this will expand further in the future, impacting on people's lives all over the world, it's important not to believe the hype. This text has strongly promoted the idea that there is a fintech revolution underway, and it is challenging to deflect or handwave this concept when one is presented with the raw data.

However, revolutions don't always run smoothly, and the proponents of revolutions are prone to exaggerating their scale. There have been false starts in the fintech field, and it is essential to emphasize that the existing financial architecture will remain significant for many years, and indeed decades, to come. We are not going to see an instantaneous undermining of everything that we have experienced, and become accustomed to, in the financial sphere. The fintech revolution will be inexorable but also a steady process.

Furthermore, it is essential to note that the level of academic research into fintech has been quite limited. That is why, in this book, we have tried to present some of the most cutting-edge and important research available on the fintech sphere. Yet, as recently as three years ago, there was almost no academic research included in the top journals in finance, even though vast amounts of venture capital were flowing into this field. Clearly, this was a situation that needed to change.

Top-quality research is vital in any financial niche, as it is here that the rigorous testing and analysis takes place that is required for the economic community to understand a particular field. Thus, recently, the *Review of Financial Studies* received 156 proposals from 409 authors representing 183 universities and 22 research organizations or government agencies, spread across 20 countries.

This research examined a wide variety of different areas, finding, for example, that robo-advisors do deliver excellent results. In their sample of investors in India, 'most of them become better diversified and reduce portfolio volatility once they adopt robo-advising. Importantly, robo-advisory demonstrates a clear benefit in mitigating the most prominent behavioural biases, such as the disposition effect and momentum chasing', according to the editorial summary.

Yet the same researchers will doubtless uncover areas where fintech still has work to do to live up to the proclamations of its most enthusiastic promoters, so all of us would benefit at this time from cooling our jets, taking a backward step, and approaching the whole question of fintech with a healthy dose of scepticism.

This is a field with massive potential, which is already achieving incredible things, but not everything claimed by fintechs or fintech proponents is happening, or will happen. There will be hype. There will be bluster. There will be several PR and advertising campaigns pushed at consumers. It is incumbent upon the shrewd fintech investor and proponents to see through this.

Bank–fintech collaboration will increase

However, despite the importance of scepticism, one prediction that we can make with overwhelming certainty is that collaboration between banks and fintechs will continue to increase. All forms of collaboration in the fintech field face challenges, as the upstarts and the established order continue to become accustomed to one another.

With data and digitalization becoming ever more important, it will almost become incumbent on the established financial players to seek collaboration with the fintech industry, to deliver the digital products that will come to define the industry. The advent of banking as a service, and plug-and-play software, to build financial products is becoming increasingly common since different parts of the financial system have been dropped into new software by thousands of companies. Technology innovators have the ability to deliver a wide range of financial products with aplomb, and this is something that will become an increasing feature of the financial system going forward.

The success of fintechs in attracting investment was already becoming clear five years ago, when the amount poured into ventures globally tripled to $12.21 billion in 2014 (Accenture, 2015). This has led to a climate in which collaboration is at the heart of the fintech niche, and something that many big banking players already view as an inevitability, and an inevitability to which they are increasingly receptive, rather than hostile.

This is partly because banks recognize that they will need to look outside of their traditional industry partners in order to generate value in the future, and partly because fintechs are offering something unusual and valuable. And banks that are quick to get on board with the fintech revolution will benefit from disrupting their own business models, rather than passively sitting on the sidelines and watching the financial industry leave them behind. In this context, there is no room for prejudice or institutional complacency.

Indeed, most banks now recognize that some form of collaboration and partnership with fintechs is necessary for their prosperity, in a future in which complimentary alliances between diverse players will become an increasingly prominent feature of the financial industry. This is part of the reason that collaborative engagement with start-ups, via such initiatives as innovation labs and accelerator programmes, has become so popular – banks are willing to explore multiple avenues in order to broaden their portfolio of products and services, effectively hedging their bets while the market continues to mature.

The big challenge for established players in the financial sector will be their ability to tweak their organizational culture. Accepting this new collaborative approach will go against the grain to some extent, even though the majority of banks already accept that they must collaborate extensively with fintechs – not to mention other industries – if they are to thrive in the challenging global financial markets of the future. Yet despite this reality, research has indicated that most banks already recognize that their working and organizational culture will be their biggest barrier to achieving successful collaboration with fintechs.

Nonetheless, even as banks continue to realign their operations in order to cope with the fintech reality, one thing that has become crystal clear from preparing this text. Banks are already enthusiastically collaborating with fintechs, and there are clear advantages for both 'sides' if this is extended in the future. This has been seen clearly in the field of big data, where the strong collaboration between traditional banks and fintech companies has led to new forms of big data usage, such as personalized finance and advanced analytics.

With governments getting involved in the process as well, the foundation for fintechs to become an ever more significant part of the economic climate is definitively cemented. The increasing prominence of fintech in the financial system, and indeed in all of our lives, is now absolutely inevitable.

References

Accenture (2015) The future of fintech and banking: digitally disrupted or reimagined? [online] https://www.accenture.com/gb-en/insight-future-fintech-banking (archived at https://perma.cc/HMG7-FAJW)

AITopics (2017) How AI is changing Fintech, 27 November [online] https://aitopics.org/doc/news:5F7258FC/ (archived at https://perma.cc/PDL8-ABQZ)

American Express (2017) American Express previews new Amex bot for Messenger feature at Facebook's F8 [online] https://about.americanexpress.com/press-release/american-express-previews-new-amex-bot-messenger-feature-facebooks-f8 (archived at https://perma.cc/ZC9F-QYHA)

Arends, B (2011) IMF bombshell: Age of America nears end, *Market Watch*, 25 April [online] https://www.marketwatch.com/story/imf-bombshell-age-of-america-about-to-end-2011-04-25 (archived at https://perma.cc/S4XE-ZD2S)

Fogel, R (2010) $123,000,000,000,000 China's estimated economy by the year 2040. Be warned, *Foreign Policy*, 4 January [online] https://foreignpolicy.com/2010/01/04/123000000000000/ (archived at https://perma.cc/8NMB-CYN6)

Global Sherpa (2016) BRIC Countries – background, key facts, news and original articles http://globalsherpa.org/bric-countries-brics/ (archived at https://perma.cc/J4MU-FMWF)

Knowledge@Wharton (2019) Fintech: what's real, and what's hype [online] https://knowledge.wharton.upenn.edu/article/fintech/ (archived at https://perma.cc/JX6A-3QWE)

Maslen, G (2013) The changing PhD – turning out millions of doctorates, *University World News*, 3 April [online] https://www.universityworldnews.com/post.php?story=20130403121244660 (archived at https://perma.cc/2LJQ-44EJ)

Olson, P (2019) Banks are promoting 'female' chatbots to help customers, raising concerns of stereotyping, *Forbes,* 27 February [online] https://www.forbes.com/sites/parmyolson/2019/02/27/banks-are-promoting-female-chatbots-to-help-customers-raising-concerns-of-stereotyping/#c5560b15a8f0 (archived at https://perma.cc/W72S-HFLN)

Weisbrot, M (2011) 2016: when China overtakes the US, *Guardian,* 27 April [online] https://www.theguardian.com/commentisfree/cifamerica/2011/apr/27/china-imf-economy-2016 (archived at https://perma.cc/QS9E-RGQZ)

INDEX

Printed in the USA
CPSIA information can be obtained
at www.ICGtesting.com
LVHW061630180923
756757LV00055B/364